Sorry Honey, But The Critters Come First

Kelly Meister-Yetter

Copyright © 2016 Kelly Meister-Yetter
All rights reserved.

ISBN: 153759169X
ISBN 13: 9781537591698

FOR TJS
Your friendship is missed.

Not all those who wander are lost.

- J.R.R. Tolkien

Acknowledgments

Special thanks to Whoville Animal Control Officer Dave for being willing to work together time and again for the sake of animals in need. Much gratitude to fellow critter author Bob Tarte, for his patience and knowledge. A big shout out to Gary Bendig of Kohne Camera and Photo for his awesome work on the cover picture. Thank you to all my Facebook fans who have been so supportive of my books. Love and thanks to Duddy, for tagging along on all my critter adventures – I couldn't have gotten this far without you!

And, as always, thank you Jean Cook. Without whom.

Table of Contents

Acknowledgments......vii
Preface......xiii
Introduction......xv

Then......1
In The Beginning......3
Kidnapped......5
Sickly......7
Conversations......11
The Vet Ladies......15
Troublemaker......21
Food Fight......25
Fame......27
Spoiled Rotten......29
Hero?......33
Death & Dying – 101......37
Disaster......41

Table of Contents

Death & Dying – Advanced Course......47
After......51
A Few Final Words......55
In Between......61

Now......63
Screaming Like a Girl......65
Barn Urchins......71
Whatever Happened To All Those Ducks?......79
The One I Couldn't Save......83
Chasing Chickens......85
The Thing in the Road......93
Stuff......97
A Matter of Taste......103
More Stuff......107
What If It Happened To You?......111
Boyfriend Duck......117
Russell's Rabbits......125
This Means War!......129
The Kill Zone......133
They Have an App for That!......139
What Does a Dying Walrus Sound Like?......143
Back to Basics......145
Ethel......151
Skunky......157
The Open House......163
Gotcha!......173
Going Solo......181
Rocky III......187
Best. Trail Ride. Ever.......189
A Barn Christmas......193
Making Do......199
A Change of Mind......205

Groundwork......209
Almost Like The Old Days......213
My Favorite Doctor......217
To The Rescue!......221
The Horsemobile......227
Big Blue......233
A Visit With Mandy......237
Cats!......241
Rats!......247
The Good Dog......249
Introducing Ducky and Gimpy......255
Equine Affaire!......259
Munster Man......273
Ducky the Dickhead......281
Again With The Rabbits!......287
The First Horse......289
A Very Close Call......297
Another Dickhead Duck......303
Blue Ribbons......307
The End of Things......311
Nothing Works Like An Apple......323
The Right Thing To Do......327

Epilogue......333

Preface

If you've read either of my first two books, *Crazy Critter Lady* (CCL), or *No Better Medicine* (NBM), then you'll know all about my dedication to caring for animals in need. But neither book mentioned what got me started down the rescue road. It's a story I've kept to myself for almost two decades. After considerable thought, though, I decided it was time to tell that story.

I first wrote about that rescue experience a year after it happened. Then I put the manuscript on a shelf and more or less forgot about it. Thinking about that time in my life was simply too painful. But while I was in the process of trying to decide whether to use it in this book or not, I pulled that manuscript off the shelf and read it for the first time in fifteen years. The story – and my feelings about what I went through during that year of caring for a desperately ill cat – still seemed relevant; relevant enough, anyway, to share with you now.

So I've divided this book into two sections: **Then**, which tells that rescue story from long ago, and **Now**, which picks up where *No Better Medicine* left off, with fun new tales about many of the same critter characters you met in my previous books. I hope you'll enjoy reading about them as much as I enjoyed caring for them.

Kelly Meister-Yetter
Whoville, Ohio

Introduction

While I had a number of pets, through the years – hamsters in my youth, stray cats in adolescence, and the ubiquitous parade of toy poodles that my grandparents owned – the one who started me on the roller coaster ride of animal rescue was a deaf white cat named Macavity.

Macavity originally belonged to someone else, a man so firmly entrenched in drug addiction that he scarcely merited a minute of my time, much less the seven years I devoted to trying to clean him up. Suffice to say that I learned the hard way that the only kind of "help" I was giving him was an entirely unhealthy co-dependence with the dubious benefit that it allowed me to defer dealing with my own nightmarish problems for a very long time. The relationship lasted much longer than it should have. In the end, I rescued his cat, and myself. "Then" is our story.

Then

In The Beginning

I'd known he was sick when I kidnapped him. I'd known that his liver wasn't working right. I had also known that he required daily "treatments": sub-cutaneous infusions of saline solution, in order to help his diseased liver flush out the toxic cooties that his body could no longer eliminate on its own.

For Macavity, I would overcome a lifelong aversion to needles.

For Macavity, I would incur a veterinary bill in the thousands of dollars.

For Macavity, I would put my life on hold.

For Macavity, I would do anything.

Kidnapped

The break-up with boyfriend Terry had been ugly, and long overdue. I'd spent too many years of my life trying to clean up a drug addict who didn't particularly want to be clean, and it was time to call it quits. I had seen it coming for some time, and was relieved when it was over, but for one thing: Macavity. He was Terry's cat, and he would be leaving when Terry did. Many times, I had whispered in his ear, "You're the one I'm going to miss," and, indeed, losing Macavity was the worst blow of all.

Terry had raised him from a kitten. Mom-cat had been escorting her brood across the street when along came Terry's car. Macavity lingered for a look and never heard mom calling him: he'd been born deaf. Mom and the rest of the brood ran off, leaving Macavity to be adopted on the spot.

I didn't meet Macavity until he was eight – approaching middle age in human years. I used to sing him that song about having been a beautiful baby as he was, in my estimation, an absolutely stunning adult. He was pure white, but for the peach of his nose and ears. He had a handsome face, a regal bearing, and a charming personality to boot.

He had not been happy about my intrusion in his life. I was the interloper, the strange person taking up his space in the bed, and diverting the attentions of his master. For me, there were growls and hisses; for Terry, there were bites and clawings. After many months, though, it finally occurred to him that two people meant twice the handouts, twice the attention, twice the spoiling. Macavity was no fool.

We spent the next six years becoming friends. Terry spent those years living the nightmare of drug addiction, and was frequently unavailable: days on end at the crack house, stints in jail. I became the substitute, in Macavity's eyes. I was the consistent one, always there for a large part of every day, always ready with a treat, or attention. The thread of our eventual life together began in fending for ourselves, and each other.

When the break-up came, Macavity had already spent a year living with the effects of a liver infection. He was tired most of the time. He had lost weight. He could only digest certain foods. And he was getting worse. Terry and I began those saline treatments mere days before we parted ways. When, only a week after he left, Terry called and said that Macavity needed more care than Terry could provide at the moment, and would I be willing to look after him temporarily, I jumped at the chance.

I didn't realize that Terry's request came with ulterior motives. My caring for Macavity gave him a ready-made excuse to see me on a regular basis. In no time, given the madness of addiction, his visits turned into stalking. After several months of insanity, I had him arrested and sent to jail for seven months. During that time, Macavity and I picked up stakes and moved across town, leaving no forwarding address.

Kidnapped!

Sickly

I had known little else but that Macavity was sick. I did not know that his life would be significantly shortened. I did not know how much sicker he would get. I *did* ask the vet, Dr. Morris, if he cared to give me a ballpark figure as to how much longer Macavity had, but he declined. It was just as well: had I known that Macavity was only expected to live a couple of months, things might've been different. I might not have agreed to take him. I might not have done any of the things I ended up doing. I might've put him to sleep.

The saline treatments, or "Go Juice," as I called it, had been my idea. Macavity had had to be hospitalized several times, when he started looking really sick. During those hospital visits, he received an I.V. cocktail of saline solution, various antibiotics, and nutrients. At a hundred bucks a day. Clearly, hospitalization every other week or so was not an affordable option. I inquired about alternatives, and was told that I could do the saline solution treatments at home. Those treatments would be considerably cheaper, and had the added benefit of super-charging Macavity anytime he needed it. There was one drawback, though: my life-long phobia of needles.

Needles were a factor to be considered whenever I had to visit a healthcare professional. At the dentist, my first question was always, "How many shots will that require?" I frequently made health-related decisions based on whether or not a needle would be involved. I *hated* needles, and here I was being told that in order to save myself several thousand dollars – not to mention the stress Macavity endured every time he went to the vet's – I would have to set that phobia aside.

After watching Dr. Morris demonstrate the procedure on Macavity, though, it was clear that he didn't suffer nearly as much as I did when faced with a needle. In fact, the only real discomfort involved was in the Go Juice itself: unless you warm it up first, that bag of saline is rather chilly. Imagine getting 100cc's of chilly liquid under your skin. Unfortunately, Dr. Morris neglected to tell me that, and it was only months later, when the Vet Ladies clued me in, that I understood what Macavity's fussing was all about.

The accoutrements that I came to be intimately familiar with were these: the bags of Go Juice, the hoses that attached to the bag, which were supposed to be replaced every three bags or so, and eighteen-gauge needles – long, hollow, mean-looking brutes. Later, as Macavity's illness progressed, there would be added to the list a nutritional paste, an iron supplement, antibiotics, syringes for getting all of those items down his throat, and prescription (read "expensive") food.

In the early days following the kidnapping, Macavity required 100cc's of Go Juice a day. He was not fond of the treatments, and it would be months before I felt determined and confident enough to try to administer them by myself. Until I mastered the technique of kneeling on the floor with Macavity pinned between my legs, I had to rely on whoever was available to help hold him steady.

It took me some time to realize that gravity played a part in the treatments: the higher up the bag, the faster the Go Juice went into Macavity, the sooner the ordeal was over with. Eventually, I nailed a picture hook into the wall, and that was where the bags of saline solution resided for the duration.

Doing those treatments every day, I got to be pretty fair at trouble-shooting. I learned what to do if the Go Juice wasn't flowing (check the hose for crimps), how many times I could use a needle before it got too dull (three, tops), and how to handle leaks from the injection site.

I learned that old skin – and by this time, Macavity was fourteen, a geezer – loses some of its elasticity, and doesn't close up right away. In anticipation of this, I got into the habit of pinching his skin after I had withdrawn the needle, and rolling it between my fingers for a few seconds. He wouldn't have leaked a substantial amount of Go Juice, but to me, it was the principle of the thing. I wanted him to receive the benefit of all 100cc's.

I learned that just above the shoulder blades is the best place to insert the needles. I learned that Go Juice tends to float to whatever area of the body has room to spare, which, in Macavity's case, turned out to be just above his breastbone, earning him the nickname, "Goiter Boy."

I learned that Macavity's illness would not remain static for long, and that the best policy was to expect the unexpected, at any hour of the day or night. I learned to watch for the tiniest changes in his appearance or habits, because many of them meant impending doom if they weren't addressed immediately. And, most importantly, I learned that Macavity did not hold grudges against people who put needles in the scruff of his neck on a daily basis.

He seemed to understand my explanation that, "It's Go Juice, it helps you go." After I had withdrawn the needle,

I would spend a few minutes fussing over him, smothering him with kisses. He would wander off then, various body parts bulging with saline, the incident apparently forgotten.

The rate at which those bulges were absorbed was a telling indication of the state of his liver: the faster those bulges disappeared, the more his body was struggling, that particular day, with demands with which it could not keep up. Amazingly, he remained cheerful throughout it all.

It was that cheerfulness, that desire on his part to keep going, that kept *me* going. I decided, early on, to let Macavity set the pace. When he was ready to throw in the towel, I would respect his wishes. But Macavity – whom the vet and his staff believed would not live more than a couple of months – would not be ready to quit until more than a year had passed.

Conversations

It was during those times when Terry was unavailable that Macavity and I started talking. I enjoyed those conversations, and I felt sure that he did, too. We talked about many things, but our one recurring topic was London.

He sat watching me pack, preparing for my first trip to England's capital. He asked where I was going, and why. I told him that I was going to have tea with the Queen. Immediately, Macavity hopped into my suitcase and announced, "I want to go, too!" I explained to him that the Queen was really more of a dog person, and that she would be horrified at his shedding all over Buckingham Palace. His last word on the subject was a promise not to shed.

It was a beginning. *Our* beginning. Until then, Macavity was someone else's cat, with an identity I had been unfamiliar with. Through those talks about London, I created a new identity for Macavity, that of an aristocrat with Royal connections. He certainly *looked* the part, with his regal bearing and imperious manner. In my imagination, Macavity would fit in quite well with England's Upper Crust, and thus, a star was born. I promised Macavity that one day, he *would* go have tea with the Queen.

Occasionally, I teased him about his name – or, rather, what he *could've* been named.

"You're lucky you were found by someone with a modicum of good taste, Puddin'," I'd say, "you could've ended up being called 'Snowball'!"

Macavity would look at me funny and announce, "That's stupid, Kelly, I'm not a snowball!"

All the same, I would remind him, being a white cat invited all sorts of goofy names that would not have suited him one bit. He refused to consider the matter; as far as he was concerned, Macavity was the only possible name for him, and Macavity it was.

There were other conversations as well. Day-to-day chats about things like the state of his coat, which he had begun to neglect in his illness. He would wash the salient parts – face, rear, front paws – but ignore the rest. After some months, his once-proud coat looked matted and dull. His response to my urgings to bathe was to pull out tufts of hair. I never figured out whether this was a behavior problem, or a genuine, if feeble, attempt to maintain his coat. Either way, I repeatedly told him that pulling out tufts didn't count as bathing, but my comments fell on deaf ears.

We had talks, too, about his impending death. One-sided affairs, mostly, in which I told him that it was o.k. to go when he needed to. I told him to let me know when he'd had enough, and I would take care of the rest. Macavity never said anything in response, he would only look at me as if to gauge whether I really meant it or not. In truth, I *didn't* mean it. I wanted him to go on living indefinitely and there were days and weeks in which it seemed that he would do just that. Then some symptom or other would come along and the panicky process of whisking him to the hospital and worrying whether this time it was fixable would begin again. But I didn't want him to think he had to keep going just for me, if he wasn't up to it.

The best talks of all, though, were the ones where he didn't say a word, he just purred. I found it an interesting paradox that this particular deaf cat could meow loudly enough to wake the dead, but purr so quietly that you had to be right up against him to hear it.

Macavity had gotten into the habit, in the last year of his life, of climbing up on my shoulder for a visit each night. When I had settled into bed, he would jump up, meow for me to roll over onto my back, walk the length of my body from foot to shoulder, and settle, half on me, half on my pillow.

He would stretch out on his side, get comfortable, shove at least one paw up my nose or in my mouth, and rest his face on my cheek. I could feel his breath in my ear, and the sound of his purring was music to me.

We had not shared such intimacy in the previous seven years. He was Terry's cat, and it was Terry he snuggled up with at night. Even when Terry was spending the night elsewhere, the most Macavity ever did was curl up by my legs. His desire, in that least year, to be so physically close, was extraordinary to me. I looked forward to our nightly snuggles, and I treasured every one of them. And in spite of the lack of words, I knew exactly what Macavity was saying: "I love you!"

THE VET LADIES

The Vet Ladies were a team of exceptionally dedicated staff at Dr. Morris's office, who always had time for my frantic phone calls. They were always ready with advice, or suggestions, or helpful information. Not a week went by without a conversation, or a visit, if I had business at the office. Unfailing in their support of me, and their admiration of Macavity, they came to be trusted friends. They were wonderful!

Macavity, of course, hated all of them. In his view, they smelled bad, and Donna, in particular, had claws even longer than his! He hated Dr. Morris with a passion, and I was witness to the extent of that hatred the day he whirled around and swatted a syringe right of Dr. Morris's hand, and sent it flying across the room. From then on, Dr. Morris treated Macavity with wary regard.

It was Donna – she of the lengthy claws – who became not only a trusted friend and confidante, but also Macavity's minder, the time I took a brief vacation. I had intentionally left the instructions loose: she knew how to care for sick animals, after all. The only absolutes were daily treatments, food and water, fussings – lots of fussings, hospitalization if he needed it, and put the body on ice, if it came to that. From her notes during that time, I could see that Macavity, in spite of his hostility toward anyone who reeked of animal hospital, had worked his charms on her. She had fallen in love with him, while I was gone, and later, when it was "that time," she insisted on being there, and her tears at the loss rivaled my own.

It was Sam, the Office Manager, who knew what to get from whom, and how to get it. She was a freight train of efficiency and concern, always supportive, never willing to give up. When I made inquiries as to whether the same antibiotics that were used in his I.V. cocktail during hospitalizations would be efficacious when administered at home, it was Sam who called Dr. Morris at his house, asking what was given, and where on the premises it could be found. I don't think it occurred to either one of us – or mattered – that Dr. Morris might actually like some quiet time away from his office!

There was Dr. Amy, Dr. Morris's associate. Dr. Amy was still young and idealistic enough to take as much time as was necessary to explain a problem to the pet owner. I'm certain that the inevitably-backed-up waiting room drove Dr. Morris up the wall, but the times I dealt with Dr. Amy, I never walked away with any doubts about the illness or the medications it required. She was a gentle woman, with a genuine fondness for her charges, and even Macavity could only manage half-hearted hisses when in her care.

There were others working at the hospital. Some groomed pets, some cleaned cages. All of them came to know who Kelly and Macavity were. I confess that to this day, I still don't know all of their names, but I remember their faces, and their kindnesses, and the way that Macavity and I were always treated like their number one priority. It was among these people, and the wonderfully supportive atmosphere they provided, that Macavity and I would fight the good fight. We could not have done it without them.

I loved the Vet Ladies, and came to rely heavily on their experience and advice. It was they who taught me to warm the bag of saline solution. It was they who told me that the needles – meant to be used once and thrown away – could actually be used several times before they got too dull. It was they who told me that you could give a cat small amounts of Kaopectate for diarrhea (don't do this at home without consulting your vet first!). They who frequently gave me the accoutrements of the ordeal and waved me away with a hand. "On the house," they'd say, "you've earned it." And it was they who explained to me the two most important items on the agenda: knowing when Macavity had had enough, and the process of being euthanized. I will come back to these later.

Macavity's illness was fraught with uncertainties. I never knew what was coming, or when. There was the day I noticed that his nose and ears were a waxy white color. I placed a call to the Ladies, feeling certain that this time, they would surely laugh and call me paranoid. It turned out, though, that the white nose and ears were a symptom of anemia, and it was Sam who brought me up to speed on this latest in a long list of liver-related problems. It was also Sam who told me that the iron supplement would be waiting for me when I stopped by, as she knew I would.

There was an after-hours emergency service available across town. They were open all night, and you paid through the nose for that convenience. Aside from the financial considerations – and I *did* have to consider the finances from time to time – there was little they could do for Macavity, and I learned not to think of them as my first line of after-hours defense. My first line of after-hours defense came to be me.

I would never bother to add up all the hours of sleep I lost in that year – and it wouldn't matter in any case. I did what I did for love, not for ego or accolades. But I *did* lose many a night's sleep maintaining a vigil, watching Macavity for signs of further deterioration. I became something of an expert at being able to judge what could wait until first thing in the morning, when Dr. Morris's office opened, and what absolutely had to be dealt with right away. I didn't mind the long hours. As I told Macavity, "I worry about you. It's my job, it's what I do." And I meant it.

Toward the end of his life, Macavity's bowels started passing something that was a sinister shade of bile green. In fact, it *was* bile, expelled from a body that was almost surely at its end. When I phoned the Ladies, I was told that Macavity's poop would, in all likelihood, remain that color; it was yet another indication of a failing liver. But like many other predictions, this one, too, surprised everyone by going away after a few days. No would could offer an explanation.

After a while, the Ladies gave up trying to explain such phenomena. Macavity was a piece of work unto himself, and had defied so many of the Ladies predictions that eventually, they just shook their heads in wonder and pronounced him "amazing." And indeed, he was.

Occasionally, the Ladies would call me a hero. I always thought that was a bit much. I was only doing what needed to be done, after all. But they insisted that very few of their other clients went to such pains for a pet. Apparently, the customary choice was to put that pet down. But death was not an option, as far as I was concerned, and never had been.

I could see in their eyes that the Ladies were impressed by my attention to detail, the fact that I noticed all the weird things that went on, like a white nose, or green diarrhea, and was concerned enough to mention it to them. But I wasn't trying to impress them, I was trying to figure out what the hell was going on. I had no previous experience to fall back on, and was frequently confounded by Macavity's symptoms.

Never once, during this time, were the Ladies too busy to take my phone calls. Never once did they consider the doctors too busy to answer a question. Never once did they let on that they thought Macavity was not long for this world. I had no idea. But they did. And so did Dr. Morris.

Dr. Morris was a skilled and dedicated veterinary surgeon with a lousy cat-side manner. It was Dr. Morris who voiced his opinion, more than once, that perhaps it was getting to be "that time." Meaning that he thought he knew better than Macavity when Macavity should give up. I took Dr. Morris's technical advice on matters of medication, and symptoms related to liver disease, and chucked the rest. *Macavity* would decide when it was "that time."

But the Ladies were in a league of their own, truly a team who cared, and when it eventually came to be "that time," there was not a dry eye in the house. I could not have found better back-up in this endeavor, nor would I ever feel that I had thanked them enough for all their encouragement, advice, and support. *They* were the true heroes.

Troublemaker

In his prime, he was King Puss, ruler of all he surveyed. Which generally included kitchen counters, and the most comfortable spot on any piece of furniture. He was also fond of kitchen sinks, and I have several pictures that show him sitting in a sink attacking the stream of water that's issuing from the faucet.

While he liked catnip, Macavity rejected most catnip-filled toys in favor of a stuffed replica of a mouse. We've all seen them in the pet stores, sitting in front of a sign reading "real mouse hair" or some such. Macavity loved this kind of mouse with a passion unmatched by anything but his love of pork chops. Macavity particularly loved them at 5:30 in the morning.

There was an apartment – our first, Terry and I – with all the grandeur of the Victorian age. Graceful arches divided the rooms, radiators provided the heat, hardwood covered the floors. Those floors held a certain fascination for Macavity. He liked to get a running start in the sun room, build speed through the living room, slalom at maximum warp around the corner into the hallway, and gleefully skate the length of that hallway until he hit the bedroom. He liked doing all of this at 5:30 in the morning.

He particularly liked to do it with one of those toy mice in his mouth, which would not have bothered me but for the ungodly yowl that emanated from him as he skidded through the straightaway. He couldn't manage a normal meow with the mouse in his mouth, hence the noise that sounded like nothing so much as someone in the agonizing throes of death.

This wildly thrilling game would continue until I intervened. Working a night job as I did, I simply couldn't muster a full appreciation for it, and so, with a glare for the offending cat, I would snatch up the mouse and hide it where it would take Macavity at least several hours of diligent hunting to find.

Unfortunately, one morning, he elected to look for it on the mantle, an area I had adorned with a collection of Terry's cookbooks, held up on either side by a set of ceramic unicorn head bookends that I had made myself, a few years earlier, and happened to be rather fond of. The tell-tale crash that morning told me all I needed to know. Even before crawling out of bed to investigate, I knew that from that moment on, I would be the proud owner of a unicorn head book*end*. Macavity looked completely unconcerned about the whole affair, and went off to search for his mouse elsewhere.

Regardless of the mischief he got into, over the years, it was hard to stay mad at him for long. Hell, it was hard to keep a straight face through most of it. He had a way of smiling at me – not a mocking smile, but an innocent one, as if to ask, "What did I do that was so bad?" And I couldn't answer him. If I had been a cat, toppling the waste basket in order to fetch out the remains of last night's pork chop dinner would seem perfectly reasonable to me. And if my claws needed some work, I would probably choose to work them on a nice scratchy couch. But I was not a cat, and in my exasperation, I developed Sign Language for Deaf Cats.

There were two main signs: the repeated crooking of the index finger, which meant, "come here," and the shaking of the index finger (accompanied by a fierce frown), which meant, "You are *so* busted!" Macavity came to learn what both of these signs meant, and usually responded accordingly by coming, as directed, or running like hell in the opposite direction.

Because Macavity had been allowed so much leeway, before I came along, he possessed a certain presumption that everything which was mine was also his. It would take him a few years to learn the rules, and I probably didn't help matters when, as I tried to discipline him, I stood over him shaking that index finger and laughing at the same time. Eventually, he got the message, but it never stopped him from trying: it was only in getting caught that he expressed any concern; the deed itself was always fair game.

His favorite mission involved jumping up on the stove in the evening, to see what sumptuous goodies had been left behind in the pan. Perhaps a little pork chop grease? Maybe a bit of fat that had stuck to the pan when the steaks were pulled off? And in spite of previous experience, you'd think that I would've caught on to this, but no. Only when I heard the telltale licks, moving the pan around on the stove, would I realize what was going on.

I'd sneak up on him from behind – one of *my* favorite tricks – and tap him on the rump. After a few years, I didn't even need to shake my finger at him; he knew who was doing the tapping, and he knew enough to at least *attempt* to look embarrassed as he jumped down and took off running.

Still, as I'd settle back onto the couch and glance in his direction, I could see that mischievous smile playing around his whiskers, and I knew he was plotting his next mission.

Food Fight

As I said before, Macavity's presumptuousness knew no bounds. After a few years around me, though, he knew who enforced the rules and who didn't. At mealtimes, in particular, I was not nearly as inclined as Terry to toss treats from my plate. I did do it, but not all through dinner, and certainly not every time Macavity meowed.

When his pleas went unanswered for too long, though, Macavity would get bold: standing on his hind legs, his forepaws on the coffee table, he would reach out and take a swipe as your fork traveled from your plate to your mouth. If you weren't paying attention, he would actually bag himself some food.

At other times, if you got up to refill your glass of milk, he would simply jump up on the table and help himself to your plate. And while I learned, early on, to instruct Terry, "Watch my plate," he was not concerned about food theft. Until...

He had gone to the kitchen for more of something, leaving behind a plate with a pork chop – Macavity's favorite food. My attention was focused on the t.v., and Macavity took full advantage of the situation: he pulled the chop onto the floor with his paw, ran a few feet away, and settled down to dinner. It was only when Terry inquired, "Hey! Where'd my pork chop go?" that I turned and saw Macavity eating as fast as he could, trying to rid himself of the incriminating evidence. I laughed all the harder as Terry tried to wrestle the remains of his dinner away; Macavity was not happy about the sudden turn of events.

In Macavity's view, that what's-yours-is-mine thing applied most importantly to food. If you were sitting on the floor with your plate, he thought nothing of walking over and reaching out a paw to sample the goodies. His table manners were appalling by anyone's standards, and after reminding him several thousand times that the Queen would not go for this sort of thing, he got into the habit – with *me*, anyway – of sitting a few feet away and waiting as patiently as he could. If I took too long to notice his extraordinary patience, he would remind me with one of his specialty meows, the one that said, "I'm dying, Kelly, and I won't last much longer unless you give me some of what you have!"

Naturally, I fell for it every time.

FAME

In front of the camera, Macavity was a ham. He seemed to know exactly what was going on: the recording of his good looks for posterity. And, clearly, getting his image on paper for the masses to appreciate was a matter of some importance to him. He was a photographer's dream, never moving from his spot once he noticed the lens aimed at him. He was happy to look directly at the camera, and he was equally happy to strike a pose. In short, he was a *ham*.

It was a fine sunny day, and Macavity was enjoying himself in the garden. He never wandered too far away, and he was always under careful supervision. Ordinarily, I wouldn't let him out at all, but he loved the outdoors so much, it seemed almost cruel to refuse his requests to go out. This time, I had brought my camera with me, following his adventures, snapping pictures here and there. It was when he climbed up on an old wooden barrel and started bathing that I began shooting in earnest.

It was something about the way the sun was hitting him, and the odd collection of junk behind him, that intrigued me. When I got the developed pictures back from the lab (years before I ever considered buying a digital camera), one in particular caught my eye. The composition was perfect, Macavity had struck a fetching pose, and I knew immediately that this would be the picture that got accepted for the juried show at the Whoville Museum of Art.

They had turned me down several times before. I suspected that my photographs were a little too real for their avant-garde tastes, and I had despaired of ever producing anything funky enough to pass muster with the judges. But this would be the picture. If *this* didn't get accepted, nothing I did ever would. Imagine how pleased I felt when I received the notice that "Find Me" had been accepted.

Excitedly, I shared the news with Macavity. He had little practical knowledge of art museums, so I had to explain it to him: "You're picture is going to hang in a big building for everyone to see! You're going to be famous!" And while I didn't keep track of how many people actually looked at my photograph, I must say I was fairly bursting with pride to look across the crowded room and see my Little Bunny hanging on the wall.

It was immensely satisfying to know that I was the instrument of Macavity's fifteen minutes of fame, and I was pleased to be able to do it. Macavity, in his turn, was immensely pleased to be famous.

Spoiled Rotten

Given the vagaries of terminal liver disease, there was little I could do for Macavity beyond the daily infusions of Go Juice, and the various dietary supplements. I could not give him a liver transplant; those did not exist in the feline world. I could not make him better; there was no cure. I could only do what came naturally to aid in his comfort and quality of life, and that was to spoil him rotten.

What I was no longer able to give him in table scraps – his malfunctioning liver could no longer tolerate anything but prescription kibble – I more than made up for with love and kisses, cuddles, and grooming with the flea comb. Macavity didn't have fleas, but he loved being fussed over, and it bothered both of us that his once-lustrous coat had become so neglected and ratty. I combed him at every opportunity, and there many times, during the course of the day, that he would walk over and sit directly in front of me, waiting expectantly for some attention from me and the comb.

Towards the end, when I struggled frequently with the question of whether Macavity was still enjoying any semblance of quality of life, I would give in, against my better judgment, and slip him a snack treat. I found that very small pieces of Arby's roast beef usually stayed down, but that donuts – a curious favorite – came right back up. And so, on Arby's dinner day, I would surprise him with a few pieces of meat.

He had given up all hope of handouts, by that time. He didn't even bother to get up and beg anymore. Consequently, I felt a small measure of satisfaction at being able to dredge up a small yet enjoyable part of his previous existence. And, by then, I felt it no longer mattered if it was going to shorten his life – by then, all that mattered was that he was *having* a life.

Macavity took being spoiled rotten as his due, although he never copped an attitude about it. He merely seemed appreciative that someone thought he was as wonderful as he did. As I was fond of telling the Ladies, "When he meows, I ask 'how high?'" When he was in the mood to be fussed over, which was usually twenty or thirty times a day, he would trill at me. I loved those trills, the little half-mew that came from the back of his throat. You could hear the question mark at the end of it, as if he was asking, "Hey? Could I have some attention?"

He came to know that I would drop whatever it was I was doing – cooking, reading, whatever – and come to where he was the couch and fuss on him. When he'd had enough, he would get up and stretch, and wander off to his food bowl. The ritual would repeat itself endlessly, and I never tired of being relied on, needed, in such a way.

There was, however, one ritual that tested my patience, and Macavity would invoke this ritual very nearly on a daily basis. At some ungodly hour of the morning, six or seven – a time I am not accustomed to awakening for anything other than a quick pee – the meows would start.

Blindly, half-asleep, I would make the Sign Language For Deaf Cats sign for "come here." Macavity knew the gesture, but him coming to me was not what he wanted. I would glance at his food bowl, to ensure that he hadn't run out of kibble, then collapse into an exhausted heap. Minutes later, he would stalk my pillow, the meows going directly into my ear. I haven't yet worked out how a deaf cat would know that a meow in my ear would be effective.

Groggy, I would offer some feeble attention, petting him as he danced around on my pillow. And then I would fall asleep. When it became clear that none of his previous tactics was working, there would be the paw on my face – gently, without claws, but a firm paw nonetheless. It was an endearment I could not refuse, no matter how little sleep I had gotten the night before.

What all that song and dance had been about: he wanted not the dry food in his bowl, but a helping of what I called the "crappy wet food," the stuff you buy for a quarter at the grocery store, and that Macavity loved. He had repeatedly turned up his nose at the prescription wet food, in spite of the exciting claim on the label that it was "Highly Palatable!" Anything with the words "highly palatable" on it was anathema to Macavity, and he endeavored to prove them all wrong.

In the end, I decided that it was more important *that* he eat, rather than lose sleep over *what* he was eating. His life was ending, there was little energy left in him to enjoy the basics, like bird-watching – what did it matter if the crappy wet food wasn't terribly beneficial to him? At least he was able to keep it down, and he usually ate quite a bit, with great gusto. And *that,* to me, was an important element in having a life.

Hero?

Those times that the Ladies called me a hero, I tended to blow it off. *Well, how silly!* I thought to myself, *He's my Little Bunny, what else would I do?* But when I said as much to them, they would look at each other knowingly, as if to say, "She has no clue, does she?" It was true: I'd had no idea what I was getting myself into, no idea of how close to death Macavity had been all along.

Most of the time, the treatments of Go Juice worked fine by themselves. Periodically, he required hospitalization, when the toxins became more than 100cc's could eliminate. Eventually, I added antibiotics to the regimen, along with a high-calorie dietary supplement, which he hated: another in a long list of "highly palatable" claims.

The dietary supplement had the consistency of molasses, and I found that the only way to get it in him was with a syringe. At least once a day, we could be found: Macavity on the floor, wedged between my legs as I sat over him. I would have to pry his mouth open to get the syringe in, and then smother him with kisses to make up for the indignity. He only ever growled in protest when he was feeling exceptionally crummy.

The pills, or liquid antibiotics, or the highly palatable supplements only took a few seconds to administer. The kissing and making up took longer. So out of a twenty-four hour period, a grand total of perhaps ten minutes was actually devoted to the machinations of keeping Macavity going. The rest of the time was open to naps and snuggles, combings and fussings.

Me, a hero? I didn't think so.

But later, when I thought about up all the time I spent on the phone with the Ladies, and all the observations I shared with them –

"Hey, Sam, should I be concerned that Macavity's ears and nose are white?"

"Hey, guys, what does it mean when his diarrhea is green?"

"What's the story on the nutritional supplement – can I give him *more* that the directions say?"

– it was no wonder they held me in such high esteem.

The big question, the one they always came back to during every crisis, was, "Is he still eating?" The Ladies were of the opinion that as long as Macavity continued to eat, the rest was truly gravy. I, on the other hand, wanted results: it was not enough that he was eating if it was coming out the other end in a hideous shade of green. I realized that there was very little I could do about many of his symptoms, but if the Ladies had something short of a placebo to offer, I took it, and watched diligently for results.

One of the tricks they turned me onto was rice and tuna water. Take the water from a can of tuna (the tuna itself was too high in protein for him), mix the tuna water with some cooked rice, and it will alleviate some of the diarrhea when your cat eats it – unless, of course, your cat is Macavity, and he's willing to spend the necessary amount of time picking around the rice. Jeez!

I could never trick him into eating the rice, no matter what sumptuous flavor I mixed in with it. Eventually, I gave up on the rice, tried Kaopectate, and gave him tuna water as a special treat, to entice him when he'd stayed away from his food bowl too long to suit me.

How did I know, those times he avoided his food, that he wasn't throwing in the towel? Perhaps he was, but my instincts told me otherwise. My instincts told me that he just felt too crummy to get up and go to his bowl. In those instances, I would break out the crappy wet food, put some in a dish, and put it where he could be found on crummy days, behind the couch. Then I would move out of his line of sight and peek around: sure enough, he'd be eating! And, maybe ten minutes later, he would come out looking for more.

Me, a hero? I was just doing what needed to be done.

I *loved* Macavity. Passionately, proudly, unabashedly. He needed me, needed my help, needed the magic potions I was continually discovering with the help of the Vet Ladies. I wasn't working a job, I had nothing more important to occupy my time, and I was devoted to him. What else *would* I have done?

As time went on, and I became aware of exactly how much time, energy, and love I had invested in caring for him – the sleepless hours spent monitoring his progress; the vigilance with which I watched for changes in his symptoms; the visits during his hospitalizations; the determination that always compelled me to try *one more* type of medicine – I came to see that this thing, this caring for Macavity in his time of need, and receiving so much unconditional love in return, was the finest thing I had ever done.

Me, a hero? Maybe.

Death & Dying – 101

A friend of mine had cared for her beloved Bob in much the same manner as I with Macavity. There were daily treatments, nutritional supplements, antibiotics, and all the rest. But when dying time came for him, she could not bring herself to put him to sleep, and he ended up spending his last days in the solitary comfort of his litter box, and dying alone while she was at work.

Her story was unbearably sad, and I privately considered the selfishness involved in keeping an obviously-dying animal alive to the last, for one's own sake. I vowed I would not do that to Macavity. I had signed on for the duration, and to me, that meant taking care of dying-time, as well as living-time. Macavity would not suffer, nor would he live out his last days in a litter box.

The Vet Ladies most fervent wish for me – one they expressed on numerous occasions – was that Macavity would go in his sleep. I understood their feelings: *I* wished Macavity would go in his sleep. Peacefully, painlessly, with dignity. In the event that it didn't work out that way, though, I felt I needed to prepare myself. I had never had to euthanize a pet before, and I had no idea what to expect. I didn't want any traumatic surprises.

I spent several sessions in consultation with Dr. Amy and a few of the Ladies. I wanted to know exactly what happened, right down to the gruesome details of whether the eyes remain open. Gently, they explained to me the process of euthanasia.

They told me that the injection given was an overdose of Phenobarbital. Sam likened it to a person being anesthetized, an analogy I understood, having been put out a few times in my life. I remembered how quick it had been, "Ninety-nine, ninety-ei...," and I felt a large measure of comfort in knowing that there would be no undue pain or stress for Macavity. And, there would be no seizure-type activity, as I had unaccountably feared. In seconds, he would be "asleep," relieved of his burden.

I was also told that the eyes do remain open, and that if anything was in the bladder or bowels at the time of death, it would be released. They made it sound very quick, painless, humane, and "easy."

The Ladies neglected to tell me about the emotional side of euthanasia, though, and this I would have to find out the hard way, when it came time for the Advanced Course. To be fair to them, having seen first-hand so many animals euthanized, they may have felt it was best that I *didn't* know beforehand how awful I would feel afterward.

The emotional side of euthanasia never occurred to me. I was so busy catering to Macavity's every need that I simply could not conceive of a time when there would be no Macavity, no paw stuffed lovingly up my nose, no loudly insistent wake-up meows. It was probably just as well that the Ladies left out this worst part of the equation.

In educating myself about the details of death, I was in fact preparing myself for the toughest job I would ever do. It was my responsibility to see Macavity through to the end, not just drop him off at the vet's office and leave them to handle the procedure without me. I knew how much he hated going to the vet's, and it was unthinkable to me to put him through that final visit without my presence to comfort him.

Truth be told, I didn't want to take Macavity to the vet's at all. I wanted his passing to involve as little stress and anxiety for him as possible, and my solution was to see if I could have him put down in the comfort of his own home. I was incredibly fortunate to have in Dr. Amy a compassionate and decent young woman who understood how important this was to me, and who agreed to make that final house call. Dr. Morris would not have done it, and I didn't even ask. But I will always remember who it was that was willing to go the extra mile for my beloved cat.

Disaster

In the movie-like existence that is my life, it is the soundtrack that haunts me. Phil Collins had come out with the *Tarzan* movie music that summer, and it was his "You'll Be In My Heart" that came to stand for the struggle that Macavity and I were engaged in. The words "when destiny calls you, you must be strong/I may not be with you, but you've got to hold on"[1] took on a profoundly personal meaning as I sat, Macavity cradled in my arms, crying on the floor of Dr. Morris's hospital while disaster rained down around us.

Macavity had been displaying some particularly severe symptoms of ataxia, that Thursday. It was a condition in which the toxic cooties were too much for his meager defenses, and it was more than a couple hundred cc's of Go Juice could handle. He was rapidly losing his fine motor skills, staggering and falling as he tried to get to his food, or his litter box.

---

[1] "You'll Be In My Heart" lyrics Copyright Edgar Rice Burroughs, Inc. And Walt Disney Music Company

I put in a call to Sam, inquiring about the possibility of having Dr. Morris put in a shunt, so that I might administer I.V. fluids at home. This time, I felt sure, Macavity would not survive another hospitalization. Desperately, I quizzed Sam for alternatives, but there were none. Dr. Morris, I was told, would consider it malpractice to put in an I.V. and not have the cat there in the hospital to monitor. I was urged to bring Macavity in, and this I did, feeling certain that I would not be bringing him home again.

When we arrived, I requested a heating pad for his cage, as the hospital was air-conditioned and Macavity was very thin. I expressed my concerns to Sam, and then I went home and got virtually no sleep at all. First thing next morning, I called and asked nervously, "Is he still alive?" Indeed, he was, and I arranged to go for a visit when the doctors were at lunch.

When I pulled Macavity from the cage, I noticed that his chest and front paws were wet – sopping wet. He had been lying in his litter box, which disturbed me no end. I drew the woman on duty's – not one of the Vet Ladies – attention to the fact of his wetness, which she dismissed by way of saying that he had, after all, been lying in his litter box. It was only upon further inspection on my part that I discovered that the towel he had been given to lie on was completely soaked – which explained why he had been in his litter box – and that his hind end was completely dry. He had not been lying in his own urine after all. The woman on duty – a notoriously lazy employee named Patsy that Sam and Donna had nothing nice to say about – remained unimpressed by these observations until she saw for herself the puddle of I.V. fluid that had formed at my feet: Macavity was leaking.

After a night on the I.V., I had seen no noticeable change in him, and I had been alarmed: the I.V. cocktail *always* worked. It was my last line of defense. What the hell was going on? I had to ask Patsy for a dry towel, which she eventually produced. The heating pad was nowhere to be seen (it had been appropriated that morning for a cat fresh out of surgery), and when I asked, Patsy told me that she wasn't authorized to give me one. Or some such bullshit. Things were going from bad to worse.

Apparently feeling inadequate to handling tasks that were actually in her job description, Patsy placed a call to one of my Ladies, who was home on lunch break. I assume that the Lady on the other end of the phone had a few choice words for Patsy because suddenly, things started happening: a heating pad was produced, the soaking wet towel in the cage was removed. But nothing could be done about the leaking I.V. until Dr. Amy returned in thirty minutes time. They were the longest thirty minutes of my life.

So we sat, Macavity and I. I placed him directly on the heating pad, wrapped them both in a dry towel, hugged him close, and cried helplessly as Phil Collins, via the office radio, encouraged us to be strong. Macavity's motor skills had barely improved over the day before, and his head lolled on my arm. He looked up at me once, and I could see a vagueness in his eyes, as if he appreciated the attention, but had no idea who it was coming from. Finally, Dr. Amy arrived, and I stepped outside for a much-needed cigarette. Almost immediately, Patsy called me back in, telling me that Dr. Amy wanted to confer with me before she did anything.

Sam had told me once that starting an I.V. is a painful process, very traumatic for a cat. I was told that there had been other times, other hospitalizations, where Macavity had gotten shocky during the procedure. In essence, in his weakened condition, starting another I.V. could kill him. This is what Dr. Amy wanted to discuss. It was clear that she was reluctant to do the procedure, but the decision was mine to make, and I told her, "I can't take him home in *this* condition."

As she walked back toward the surgery, I stood nervously in the lobby, waiting for the yowling that would tell me that Macavity still had enough fight in him to protest this painful thing. In a matter of minutes, I was rewarded with a weak but definitely-came-from-Macavity howl of protest, and I smiled gratefully at no one in particular and said, "That's my boy!" When Dr. Amy finished, I went back and held him a while longer. All together, I had been there for four hours.

Before I left, I placed him gently back in the cage and issued the edict, "There will be no dying here!" Then I went home and got virtually no sleep that night, either.

I had planned for Macavity to be hospitalized for his customary two days. He ended up staying for three. He had been subjected to cold, wet, miserable conditions at the hands of the only woman in that establishment who possessed a lazy streak. I would be charged for the I.V. solution that ended up on him, his towel, and the puddle at my feed and – an enormous indignity to myself and Macavity – *two* I.V. procedures. In spite of my exhaustion, I was livid.

As I reported to Sam, who had had that awful day off, the money was not the issue. The *principle* was the issue. And the principle was that this sickly, dying cat – whom I had entrusted to these people – had been let to suffer for who knew how long, being wet and cold, and resorting to lying in his litter box, not receiving the benefits of the I.V. solution that I was paying roughly a hundred bucks a day to ensure that he got. Regretful and angry, Sam agreed that there had been no quality of care from Patsy, and promised to handle the matter.

The issue was far from over. Patsy received loud reprimands from both doctors. An angry letter from me was put in her employee file. And there was a wonderful letter of apology from Sam, assuring me that the matter was being dealt with.

After I had rattled the cages and vented my anger, though, none of it really mattered. What mattered was Macavity, and that third day in the hospital was the charmer: he had returned to normal, recognizing me as I pulled him from the cage and carried him triumphantly into the lobby to announce,

"My Little Bunny – takes a licking and keeps on ticking!" The Ladies could not have been happier at his truly miraculous recovery.

It was to be his last hospitalization. A month later, he would throw in the towel.

After Macavity died, Phil Collins and his you-must-be-strong song followed me everywhere: to the laundromat, where they had an easy-listening radio station playing; to the grocery store, and any other place I happened to drive, because I always drove with the radio on. And, invariably, the tears streamed down my face very time.

"They'll see in time, I know, we'll show them together."

And indeed, we had. We had shown them many times what love and perseverance could do. Several times, in that year, Macavity had gone into the hospital, and everyone but me was surprised when he came out again. Every time, we had proved the naysayers wrong. It was a heady feeling, and despite my own warnings to myself, I had grown cocky. Cheating death so many times will do that to you.

But in the end, all I would have to show for that cockiness would be a shoebox full of pictures, treatment accoutrements that I no longer had any use for, a much-too-quiet apartment, and Phil Collins reminding me of glory days which had, inevitably, had to end.

The loss was excruciating.

Death & Dying – Advanced Course

It had been a quiet Friday. I had spent the evening watching t.v. and answering Macavity's trills for attention. I loved the expectant look on his face, the way he unquestioningly knew that all of those trills would be answered with attention, with fussings, with combings. Would be answered with love. It was a day like any other: Macavity had eaten several times, used his litter box, napped, and trilled. He looked more tired than usual, though. Exhausted. I could see it in his eyes.

On Saturday, he went off his food. His eyes were sunken, and he looked as if he'd lived a hundred years. By Saturday noon, when Macavity had refused even his favorite forbidden treat, I knew he was throwing in the towel. I placed a call to the vet's, and Donna promised that she would bring Dr. Amy over after the office closed. I spent those few hours sitting several feet away from Macavity, respecting his desire for space, and I cried.

I was not emotionally prepared for this eventuality. Regardless of the fact that I had known for some time that he was going to die, I was not ready to do this thing. But I felt I had no choice: I was unwilling to put him through another hospitalization, and unwilling to make him drag it out to the very last, as my friend had done. Numbly, I forced myself to go through the motions. It no longer mattered what I wanted. What mattered was that Macavity had had enough, and I had made him a promise that I must now keep.

I thought out the choreography in my head, then made the preparations. Macavity would be put to sleep on the balcony he had so loved. There had been so many summer nights that he had fallen asleep on a chair out there, and, when my own bedtime approached in the wee hours of the morning, I'd go out and fetch him in. He probably would've stayed out there all night.

When the Ladies arrived, I told Dr. Amy how I wanted to do this last thing, and said I first needed a moment alone with Macavity, whom I had stayed away from all afternoon. Gently, lovingly, I picked him up and carried him out to the balcony. I held him close, whispering in his deaf ear how very proud of him I was, and how much I loved him. I told him that it was time to go have tea with the Queen, to mind his manners, and to for God's sake not claw up all the furniture at Buckingham Palace. Then I turned to Dr. Amy and nodded.

We three knelt in a circle around Macavity. Donna, having done this sort of thing many times before, gently eased him onto his side so that Dr. Amy could access his hind leg. Macavity offered no resistance, no struggle, not so much as a hiss. Dr. Amy noted all that and remarked, "Yes, it looks like it's time." Donna gave him one last kiss on the top of his head, and then Dr. Amy administered the injection.

I had put my hands on Macavity's body as a gesture of reassurance, and I felt that body relax as the narcotic coursed through his veins. He lay his head down, and then he was gone. Dr. Amy offered an apology for my loss, Donna cried, and I, in a state of shock, blindly thanked Dr. Amy for being willing to make this house call. Then I was left to mourn privately. Tenderly, I kissed him, more times than I can remember. I smoothed his white coat. I held his paws. I ran my hands over his body. I cried. I spent perhaps half an hour saying good-bye. I placed him gently on a towel in his cleaned-out litter box, a catnip mouse he used to bat around on good days beside him. Ultimately, that mouse would be cremated, too, as per my wishes.

It was as I said good-bye to Macavity that I noticed how small, how skin-and-bones, he had become. How much he had wasted away. And in the days following his death, I came to no small measure of amazement that he had determined to carry on as long as he had. What had compelled him to keep going, in spite of feeling so tired and worn-out, in spite of the year of endless diarrhea, the treatments, the supplements, and the hospitalizations? I would never know for certain, but the Vet Ladies emphatically believed that Macavity had lived so long because I had loved him so much.

I choose to believe that that they're right.

AFTER

There was a void in my heart, and in my life, where Macavity had been. A huge void, deep and black. I adopted a three-year old cat from the local Humane Society, and while she was a pleasant, agreeable, and healthy cat, she served as a daily reminder of what was no more.

There would be no more tufts of hair strewn about the apartment. I would find leftover tufts long after Macavity was gone, behind the couch, under the dining room table. The office chair that I sat on to write had been his favorite spot, and it was weeks after his death before I could bring myself to remove those piles of hair from that chair.

There would be no more "digging to China" in the litter box, and no more puddles of diarrhea. While that may seem like a blessing, the new cat's dainty litter box habits made me sad: the messes were gone because Macavity was gone, and I would no longer have to concern myself with ensuring that I had plenty of paper towels and plastic grocery bags on hand. All that diarrhea had been unpleasant, but I had loved Macavity dearly, and I was happy to do whatever was necessary to care for him; a few puddles of poop were no problem for me.

There would be no more frantic phone calls and visits to the Vet Ladies. The healthy new cat would only require yearly visits. I no longer had "reason" to maintain contact with those wonderful women.

I missed them. I missed our mission, our common cause. I missed their support and encouragement. I did stop by, on occasion, to say hello, but it wasn't the same. They were still wonderful, but Macavity, and the crushing blow that was his death, loomed large, and left us little to talk about.

There would be no more trills for attention. No more snuggling half on my shoulder, half on my pillow, purring ferociously in my ear. No more licks on my cheek, no more loudly insistent wake-up meows. The new cat would never need me as Macavity had, would never love me as he did. The finest thing I had ever done was over, and not only did I feel as though I had lost the battle, I felt like I had lost the most precious thing I had ever been given: the gift of unconditional love.

I received a sympathy card from Dr. Amy. It was Dr. Morris's hospital, and yet it had been Dr. Amy who was compassionate and thoughtful enough to send a card. It was a wonderful gesture, and her admiration for Macavity's long fight came through clearly in her words. Her card would be the only tangible recognition that Macavity had been more than just a pet, that he had been the light and love of my life, and that his passing was profoundly devastating to me. I, in turn, thanked her, and the other Ladies, by way of a gift basket filled with goodies from various shops, and catnip mice that I had made myself from my crop of homegrown.

I made the mistake of reading the last in Cleveland Amory's loving trilogy about his own white cat, Polar Bear. It never occurred to me that his cat would one day grow old, and sickly, and die, too, but that was what happened in the last chapter of *The Best Cat Ever*. Even the title saddened me, being only sightly off the mark from my own assertion that Macavity was the Best Loved Cat. When I read Amory's last chapter in his last Polar Bear book, the tears streamed down my face. In his own way, he managed to write virtually the same things I felt, and he said one thing in particular that summed up my devastating loss perfectly:

"It was not just that Polar Bear was not there – it was the awful, overpowering weight of knowing that he would never ever be there again."

A Few Final Words

There were other stories about my time with Macavity, stories that my brain forgot to tell when I initially wrote these chapters. Stories about things I had never mentioned to anyone because there was always something more important to talk about. And, after Macavity's death, I got the distinct impression that no one really wanted to hear any more: it was done, it was over with, let it go.

But it wasn't that simple for me, and even now, years after Macavity's passing, he's never far from my thoughts. I still miss him. I still choke up when "that song" comes on the radio. I still struggle to make my way in the world with what little amount of my soul Macavity left me. He took much more than just his presence with him when he died, you see.

I never told anyone about my secret trips to the litter box. Those times when Macavity became severely ataxic, he'd stagger and fall, and I had witnessed the indignity of him losing his balance and falling over sideways as he tried to do his business. I got into the habit of following him, peeking around the corner to monitor his progress. When he'd start listing to one side, I would gently reach down and right him, then return to my hiding place around the corner so that he could finish in private.

I never mentioned the plastic grocery bags. Sopping up puddles of diarrhea five times a day, I rarely had enough of them on hand. One day, a sympathetic cashier handed me a huge wad of them. Over a year after his death, I still had a large cache of reminders.

I never mentioned that the times when Macavity was hospitalized, they would shave a patch of hair off his foreleg for the I.V. That hair took forever to grow back. When internal organs are failing, hair growth is no longer a body's priority. For the longest time, he would have a patch of fuzz on that spot. I used to run my finger over it, smile at him, and announce brightly, "You got your fuzz!" "Fuzz!" Macavity would reply, not understanding that hair taking that long to grown back was not a good thing. In fact, when he died, there were two patches of fuzz that hadn't grown back yet – one on each leg from the last, disastrous hospitalization.

I never told anyone about trying to teach Macavity how to head-butt. I spent that last year showing him how it was done, explaining that all cats did this sort of thing, and that he got taken away from mom before she'd had a chance to teach him. He looked dubious.

I never forced him. I would merely put a reassuring hand on his back, slowly lean toward him, and try to give him a gentle butt. He always pulled away. Being deaf, his orientation was visual, and a human head blocking his view tended to make him nervous.

Toward the end, though, he seemed to understand that this head-butting thing was somehow important to me. And while he never actively butted back, he reached a point of indulgence in which he actually allowed me to butt his head. Such was his trust in me: he allowed me to block his view.

Every now and then, I dream of Macavity in my sleep. The details elude me upon waking, but in them, he is alive, and he is healthy. Sometimes, I even get to pet him. Once, a week or so after he died, I head him meow.

The new cat was not content to let me wallow in sorrow alone. Those times I was in need of a good cry, I took to putting sad music on the stereo and letting the tears roll. Muffin was never far behind, and before I knew it, she would curl up in my lap, purring and head-butting, and not leaving until I had finished crying. Animals always know when something is wrong.

Phil Collins earned an Academy Award for Best Original Song for "You'll Be In My Heart." As I watched him accept the award, my chest swelled with pride, and I felt, in some inexplicable way, that our struggle – Macavity's and mine – was now somehow vindicated. The world had no idea what we had done together, but the song that would forever serve as my link to my finest endeavor had been deemed worthy of high creative honor.

Macavity's ashes spent several years in my home. They belonged in London, and I spent a considerable amount of time plotting the ultimate final resting place for the Best Loved Cat. After discarding several possibilities – Buckingham Palace and the Tower of London among them - I settled on Kew Royal Botanic Gardens.

I spent an afternoon there, once. It's an enormous place, with trees and meadows and a lake, located in a quiet, leafy suburb some twenty-five minutes by Tube from central London. There would be plenty of bird-watching opportunities, and I knew that the Royal connection would please my Little Bunny no end. It was an altogether fine place to spend a few of those remaining eight lives. Several years after his death, I arranged the trip that would include bringing along a friend of mine for company, and figuring out a way to smuggle Macavity's ashes into the country.

This was no small consideration. At that time, Britain had a 6-month mandatory quarantine for any animal one wished to bring into the country: Britain had eradicated rabies, and had no intention of allowing it back in. While I assumed that cremated ashes didn't count as something that required quarantine, I took no chances. I found, at a local bath product store, a trial-sized container of scented bath salts. I bought two, dumped out the salts, and replaced them with Macavity's remains. If Customs had searched my baggage, they would've found nothing more than two small plastic bottles of what looked like bath salts. If they had opened the bottles, they would've smelled lavender. It was the perfect disguise! As it happened, I was never searched by Customs. I simply made my way through Heathrow and set about planning the trip out to Macavity's final resting place.

It was a fine, sunny afternoon the day my friend and I headed out to Kew Gardens. We said little on the train, other than the instructions I gave her on how to use my SLR camera. I wanted her to document my scattering Macavity's ashes. When we arrived, I made a beeline for the lake, circling around it until I found just the right spot.

It was an open area, devoid of trees and shrubs. There was a small island out in the lake, with willow trees bending toward the water. It was an altogether fetching spot, made more so by the gang of ducks who swam over to investigate what I was doing. As my friend snapped away with the camera, I knelt down and gently tossed handfuls of ashes onto the ground before me.

It was over in minutes, though I lingered, crying, for a while. There could be no finer resting place than the lake at Kew Gardens, and there could be no cat who deserved it more than Macavity. I've visited that spot by the lake on subsequent trips, and have always found a measure of peace there.

I didn't scatter all of his ashes. I have some at home with me. A few years ago, I commissioned a local jeweler to create a small hollow decorative tube made of gold. Inside it, he sealed a sprinkling of Macavity's leftover ashes. It's a lovely piece of jewelry that I can wear on a necklace, which beats keeping a box of ashes on a shelf somewhere.

And while my heart remained in agony for a very long time after Macavity's death, fifteen years has put it in some perspective: I no longer cry when I hear "You'll Be In My Heart," but I always pause and give some thought to what a profound experience caring for that wonderful cat was. He is the reason I do what I do today, and I look forward to seeing him again one day at the Rainbow Bridge.

In Between

Initially, Macavity's death proved so devastating to my fragile psyche that a protracted period of depression followed, in which, on one memorable occasion, I turned up at my therapist's office in my pajamas and bathrobe. At other sessions, I curled up on the floor and cried. Many days, I could do no more than that. Even when the depression began to subside, I still struggled with my lack of noble purpose. Eventually, though, life began to happen again, and I found myself at the precipice of change.

The years that followed were like a snowball rolling slowly downhill but gaining momentum as time passed. Initially, I put one toe in the waters of animal care and rescue, then my foot, then eventually, I jumped into the deep end. I did all this while battling with the aftermath of having been molested as a child. Depression and PTSD were never far away, and frequently slowed my progress to a snail's pace. Still, I kept seeing light at the end of the tunnel, and continued to move forward, even if sometimes it felt like I was crawling on all fours.

I volunteered my photography skills to the Whoville Humane Society, taking pictures of the animals up for adoption. I did similar work for Critter Fix, Whoville's low-cost spay/neuter clinic, when they needed publicity photos.

I met the flightless domestic ducks who'd been abandoned at McKinnon's pond, and began a decade's-worth of daily feedings, championing their cause, and attending to their medical needs.

I fell on the ice while attempting to skate and cracked my skull, which in turn led me to riding lessons (straw providing a much softer landing than ice), and ten years of volunteering at The Harmony Barn.

More recently, husband Duddy and I found each other, and he turned out to be the instrument by which my animal commitment became more focused. As a birthday gift, in our first year together, he began leasing my equine pal Bit for me, and we continue that lease now, several years on. In the process of training, I've learned an incredible amount about horses, and about myself, and I've found reserves of patience and perseverance that I never knew I had.

We began rescuing some of those domestic ducks from McKinnon's Pond, building them a secure pen in the back yard, and a small pond as well, and we delight in the pleasure they take in simple things like worms and mud puddles.

And there was the dog I hadn't realized that we needed in our lives until we adopted him....

Now

Screaming Like a Girl

I'd been mucking out Jem's stall uneventfully for a good ten minutes that sunny summer day. It was the last stall in the aisle, and once I finished it, I could turn my thoughts to whether or not to saddle up Bit for a ride. I still had some poop to scoop, though, when I felt the first sting of pain. It didn't register in my brain until I felt the second one. My subconscious took over, then, telling me that I needed to vacate the stall in a hurry. Without thought, I began backing out, lurching back and forth across the aisle as I went. As my feet moved, I heard the strange sounds that were emanating from my mouth.
"Huuuhhhh?"
"*Hey!*"
"Whaaaaa?"
"*Ow!* Sonofaaaa......"
"Bees! Hey, guys! *Bees!*"
In spite of the fact that I now stood ten feet away from Jem's stall, two more yellow jackets stung me for good measure. In all, I suffered seven stings, scattered in four locations

on my body. They moved so fast that I never even saw them. Indeed, the only reason I know they were yellow jackets is because once I made my way into the viewing room – intent on getting something cold from the freezer to put on the injured sites – I found one more of the little bastards clinging to my jeans, with a look on his stupid little insectile face that made it very clear that he had no intention of giving up until he'd penetrated the denim and nailed my kneecap. I knocked him to the floor and squashed him like a grape. A certain paranoia hit me as I rubbed an ice cube over one of the stings, and I called volunteer Lydia into the viewing room.

A seventeen-year old senior in high school, Lydia had been coming to the barn for enough years that she passed from annoying kid that I studiously ignored, to becoming well-respected by my curmudgeonly self, having earned her props by turning up, over the years, in even the most dreadfully severe weather, and working without complaint. What sealed her place on my short list of worthies was the fact that whenever she got on a horse, she listened to every single bit of riding advice I gave her and came back the next week clearly having memorized what I'd said. As a result, she became an adept rider fairly quickly.

As she stood before me now, I yanked my jeans off in a panic, telling her, "Look at my back and see if there are any more of those little fuckers on it."

"No," she said, looking me up and down.

"Under my arms?" I asked as I lifted them above my head.

"Huh-uh," she replied

"Check the boots!" I exclaimed as I grabbed one, turned it upside down and began to vigorously shake it. Lydia did the same with the other. No yellow jackets. I glanced down the inside of my shirt and announced, "There better *not* be any down there!" There weren't.

I will go ahead and say what you're probably thinking: no one Lydia's age wants to see a middle-aged woman in her undies, even if said undies *are* from Victoria's Secret! I felt a little sorry for her, but along with the immediacy of my situation, I also happened to be having a bad acid flashback to another yellow jacket incident that has haunted me for decades. As I shakily brushed at my jeans one last time, I told Lydia about it.

I was six years old. On vacation with my brother, my mother, and her second husband Harold, who was a complete bastard. He genuinely believed that children should be seen and not heard, and he also believed in corporal punishment. Not the kind meted out to murderers, you understand, but the kind meted out to small children and involving the kind of ass-whipping that more enlightened parents like my mother didn't do. There were frequent arguments about his use of this type of punishment, but he never listened to my mother, or perhaps she didn't argue forcefully enough. Either way, those spankings were terrifying.

In any case, we were at the seashore, somewhere in Massachusetts. There was a bluff overlooking the bay, and there were a number of historical cannons on that bluff. My brother – two years older than I – climbed atop one of the cannons, and I, always keen to imitate the fun he was having, climbed up on another. And, apparently, disturbed a nest of yellow jackets.

I remember little else except running away from the cannon as fast as I could. I had made some distance when I heard my step-father yelling. Certain that I was now in trouble for running away, I stopped running. And the yellow jackets caught up with me. Sadly, Harold had been yelling at me to keep running. But he was such a terrifying bastard that I assumed otherwise. I ended up getting stung innumerable times. Shuddering at the thought of the twin assaults, a small embarrassed laugh escaped my lips.

"Kinda screamed like a girl, didn't I?!" Lydia shrugged non-committally, no doubt thinking that it could have just as easily been her in Jem's stall. "Anyway, thanks!" I told her as we left the viewing room. It was then that Wendy rounded the corner of the aisle-way.

"You know," I remarked, "I *expect* a certain amount of risk out here, from the *horses,* not from *bees!*"

She smiled at me as she shook the can of hornet killer. "Thanks for taking one for the team!" she replied cheerfully.

"Sorry?" I asked in confusion.

"Just imagine," she said, "what would've happened if they'd stung Jem instead of you."

"What would have happened? Wouldn't his hide be thick enough to protect him?"

"No," she answered. "It would've been horrible: Jem trapped in a stall, no way to get out. You definitely took one for the horse!"

"Hmmmm!" I replied. I sure didn't *feel* like a hero! Mostly, I felt annoyed. I mean to say, I'd been in that stall for *ten minutes!* How had I not noticed any insect activity? And, regardless of that can of hornet killer, I had no intention of ever cleaning Jem's stall again!

The very next week, my old volunteering buddy and favorite nemesis, Mandy, showed up. Thoroughly immersed in the task of earning her Master's Degree in speech pathology, Mandy had to choose how to spend her free time carefully. This meant that her Saturdays at the barn were exceedingly rare. I always looked forward to those days with keen anticipation. This day, I told her all about the stinging incident as we mucked out stalls in the other aisle.

By the time we got to Jem's stall, I think she'd forgotten all about my traumatic incident. Either that or she's even more twisted than I give her credit for, because she kept insisting that I join her and Wendy in cleaning out that damnable stall. Considering that there's really not enough room in there for three people with pitchforks, I can only assume that she was challenging the validity of my story. Indeed, she kept on challenging me – right up until Wendy made a small noise and announced that she'd just been stung.

"Oh, *really?*" I remarked rather smugly as Wendy rubbed her arm. I said no more until I walked Mandy out to her car.

As we discussed the incident, she observed, "You're glad she got stung, aren't you?!"

I laughed gleefully as I replied, "Yes!" Then I thought it over for a few seconds and amended my answer. "Wait! I feel *vindicated!* Not happy, vindicated." And so I did: for even as Wendy handed me the bottle of horse remedy to put on the stings that day, I had felt nonetheless that she hadn't taken me entirely seriously. A sting of her own would certainly prove that I had suffered a horrible, life-altering trauma at her barn, or, at the very least, an annoying interlude. Privately, I was a little bit glad that she'd been stung, too. That made the possibility of uninvited barn guests a reality. Indeed, when I came out to the barn to ride a few days later, I noticed that a second can of hornet killer had taken up residence by the door of Jem's stall. Hopefully, that would teach the little fuckers to pick a better nesting site.

Barn Urchins

When I first started blogging about my experiences at The Harmony Barn, I took to referring to the younger volunteers collectively as "Barn Urchins." This had as much to do with my general dislike of children as it did anything else. A number of kids came through the Barn, over the years. Some lasted only a couple of Saturdays, while others stuck it out for a long time. Several of them earned my grudging respect while others earned a sort of quiet enmity based on either their personalities or their complete lack of work ethic. Or both.

    Allen, Lydia, and Olivia, (and Mandy, who I mentioned at length in NBM) had been coming to the barn the longest. They would bring friends from time to time, but the friends never lasted very long once they realized that the horse riding was peripheral to the stall cleaning. One of Allen and Lydia's friends, Raylene, spent far more time playing on her phone in the viewing room than she did actually working. And since all three were friends, Allen and Lydia would follow her into the viewing room when she didn't feel like working anymore.

The three would hang out in there, waiting for a chance to ride the horses. Barn owner Wendy was always much too nice to say anything directly to the kids so I took it upon myself to light a fire under their butts.

"Hey!" I'd say, walking into the viewing room. "You guys want to ride today?!" I always asked this question in an enthusiastic tone of voice so they wouldn't know what was coming next. They'd all look up at me and answer in the affirmative. *"Then get your asses out here and do some work!"* That did the trick!

Eventually, Raylene stopped coming altogether, and I doubt that anyone actually missed her.

One of the truly memorable volunteers was a young girl named Britney. Britney was a ten-year old horse-lover who played horse games on her computer. She was a troubled girl who came from a sadly troubled family; the barn was her one chance in the week to escape familial difficulties, if only for a few hours.

For the same reason that cats will glom on to the one visitor who dislikes cats, Britney would make a beeline for me and never leave my side. I might not have minded so much if she hadn't been such a talker. Whenever I heard her coming, I'd dive into a stall and hope she wouldn't find me. But she always did, and insisted on helping me muck it out. She never seemed to notice that I was studiously ignoring her, and indeed, would often keep the conversation going for both of us.

"So I was playing my horse game online, natter natter natter, and guess what?" She'd pause and wait for the indifferent grunt from me before continuing.

"And then I natter natter natter, and you know what?" At which point I would turn my back on her and roll my eyes.

I'd glance at the other stalls and see Mandy grinning from ear to ear. She knew how I felt about children, and Britney's attempts to engage me in conversation never failed to amuse her.

"*Fuck you!*" I'd mouth in her direction before turning back to Britney. When I'd finished with the stall, Britney would follow me into the next one, and the one after that, nattering cheerfully the entire time as though we were the best of friends. And while it pains me to admit it, I will allow that all that innocent cheerfulness finally got under my skin and I grew to like her. A little. Somewhat. You know how it is.

There were adult volunteers as well. I recall a fellow named Matt whose marriage had hit a rough patch and he wanted to learn more about horses to please his horse-loving wife. He worked seriously hard on the stalls, and never complained. Once, though, he brought his high school-aged, football-playing son and the son's friend along to help. About half-way through stall cleaning, I heard the son say, in that whiny voice that teenagers are famous for, "Da-aad! My back hurts!"

Inwardly, I laughed. None of the usual Barn Urchins had ever said such a thing! It was then I began to see the Urchins in a slightly different light. Sure, they were annoying children. But at the same time, they showed up no matter what the weather, they tended to the tasks at hand and performed them well, and they turned out to be genuinely likeable kids. Who knew that was possible?!

It might've been around this same time that I noticed something else. When it was too cold in the winter to ride the horses, Wendy would come up with games that we could play with them on the ground, like Keyhole. Keyhole worked like this: Wendy would get two PVC poles and set them in the arena, perpendicular to the wall. She would place them about eight feet apart, forming a three-sided square. The task began with dividing us volunteers into two teams. Both teams would have a chance to talk and discuss strategy before we started.

Once we started the task, though, we weren't allowed to talk to each other or the horse, and we weren't allowed to touch the horse, either. In all of this silence, we had to get the horse from wherever he happened to be standing in the arena into the 3-sided square. Preferably from the open side, rather than the horse walking over one of the pipes.

Think about that for a minute. No talking, no horse-touching, no bribing with treats, no *tsk tsk* noises, no nothing.

If you can't come up with a way to get the horse moving under those conditions, don't feel bad. The whole idea of the task is to challenge you to come up with other ways to communicate your wishes to the horse, to think outside the equine box. It's not easy. And while I'm no expert, I *did* once do a few sessions of a thing called Equine Assisted Psychotherapy, in which you, a horse expert, a horse, and a psychologist with horse training all get together in an arena and do tasks like Keyhole, which gave me a slight advantage when it came to playing it with the Urchins.

So I came to these Keyhole games with a few tricks up my sleeve. Not all horses behaved the same way, though, which added to the challenge. Indeed, you really needed to know something about the horses that Wendy chose to use. Blondie, for instance, wouldn't budge an inch if there was food in front of her. But if you moved the food away, she was all yours and almost always did what we wanted her to do. Baby, the skittish wild mustang, was easy to move for a different reason: she didn't want *anyone* coming near her, which made moving her ridiculously simple. All you had to do was walk in her direction, and she would go anywhere you wanted, as long as it was away from you.

Nicky Naylor, on the other hand, was old and tired and didn't give a rat's behind about kids playing games, and it was a rare day in the barn that we could budge him. But for the Urchins, getting the horses to move wasn't always the point.

As I said a few paragraphs ago, I began to notice something when we played these Keyhole games. I noticed that after Wendy appointed team captains – usually myself and any other adult who was willing to participate – all of the kids wanted to be on my team. Suddenly, I was the cool kid that the other kids wanted to hang out with, and while it was a tad embarrassing (mainly due to their heightened level of enthusiasm), it was also flattering as hell! *I was the cool kid!*

Since you may be wondering what it takes to silently move a thousand-pound animal, I'll let you in our tricks: many times, simply walking into their personal space worked. If not, we'd step it up a notch by waving our arms over our heads, clapping, maybe linking arms and looking like a giant moving human wall. We had to make sure that we didn't stand in front of them (which would prevent them from moving forward) – a thing we found ourselves doing surprisingly often – and we had to remember not to talk to each other – another thing we found ourselves doing from time to time. It was easy to forget the rules while in the midst of all that fun.

As the years went by, I didn't actually notice that, well, *years were going by!* We were all just ourselves, horse-loving volunteers, helping out The Harmony Barn every Saturday morning that we could. So it came as quite a shock the day I learned that time had, indeed, passed by while I wasn't paying attention.

It happened one day while Allen and Lydia were on bucket patrol. They had dragged the hose out to a water trough by the big arena door that let out onto the mud lot, and were standing around talking while the trough filled. For lack of anything else to do, I wandered over to where they were. I wasn't paying attention to what they were talking about; I was surveying the property and wondering whether I felt like saddling Bit up for a ride. Then the word "senior" penetrated my fog of preoccupation, and it took a few seconds to compute.

"Wait! What? Who's a senior?" I asked with some confusion.

"We are," Allen replied.

"You and Lydia?" He looked at me funny, then. I was supposed to know this already.

"Yeah!"

"*Since when?*" I inquired suspiciously.

"Umm....since this fall?"

"No, seriously! You guys are *seniors?*"

"Yeah," he said again. He looked at me like I was an idiot, and who could blame him?

"Let me get my mind around this," I said, trying earnestly to do just that. "You," I pointed at him, "and *you,*" I pointed at Lydia, "are *seniors.*"

"Yes," he said yet again.

"*In high school!*" I clarified.

"Yes!" they answered in unison.

"Are you *sure?*" I simply couldn't fathom it!

"*Yes!*" came the answer.

"You're absolutely <u>positive</u>?" I was trying to buy myself some time, then, because I had no idea how this had happened. When they started coming to the barn, they were in seventh grade, for heaven's sake! Now they were seniors in high school, set to graduate in a few months' time, and I could do no more than stand there with my mouth hanging open, wondering how much this new state of affairs was going to change things. *What if they go off to college and don't come back here anymore?* I thought. But of course, there was no immediate answer to that question. Time would tell whether they continued to volunteer as they grew up and discovered all the things life had in store for them, though our common love of horses suggested that they would still find a way to show up on Saturdays, even when other parts of their lives had moved on.

Whatever Happened To All Those Ducks?

If you've read CCL, you'll know that I spent over ten years as the self-appointed duck tender at McKinnon's Pond, looking after the abandoned ducks who lived there. These were the flightless domestic ducks that people bought at the local feed store to put in their children's Easter baskets, only to dump them at the City pond once they started getting big and noisy. These domestic ducks were no more able to survive in the wild than you or I, and without regular feeding and medical care from me, they would've died horrible starvation deaths – assuming, of course, that they weren't eaten by predators first.

If you've read NBM, you'll know that my gang of domestics – generations of whom I knew by name, on sight, loved thoroughly, and grieved deeply when they died – ultimately ended up being rescued by one of Whoville's more prominent do-gooders in the midst of a record-breaking Arctic blast of cold. And while a couple of vague invitations to help with the round-up came my way, the rescue was Aimee Van Staten's baby: she rounded up a group of helpers, she executed the plan, and she decided where the ducks would go next. Having spent so many years looking after them, it was almost impossible to process the idea that I'd never see them again. Indeed, only when I stopped by Officer Dave's holding facility to say good-bye to them did reality finally hit me: this was it; this was The End. What would life be like without them?

It was quieter, for a start. And it freed up more time in my day in which I didn't have to drive ten miles from my house to the pond and back in order to feed them. And, since I'd already brought Boyfriend and Ethel home to live in my back yard, I was still able to get my daily duck fix. But I wondered about the gang all the same, and keenly hoped that the farm sanctuary Aimee had sent them to was a good place to live happily ever after. The ducks certainly deserved it after all those years of roughing it on a pond where numerous predators lived. Unfortunately, though, their nice sanctuary life turned out to be very short-lived.

Aimee had mentioned pictures, messaging me on Facebook and promising to let me know as soon as photos of the ducks were available. Evidently, I'd be able to get a look at them in their new home at the sanctuary. And while a Facebook update was quick in coming, it wasn't at all what I expected. In the first place, the farm sanctuary had adopted them all out as a group to one person. I'd been under the impression that the ducks would be living their lives out at the sanctuary, so this news unsettled me. But there was more to come. There was the video.

The video showed a man unlocking what was effectively a utility shed – the sort of thing you'd store your lawn mower in – and shooing the ducks out. He then aimed them toward a large pond and encouraged them to go in. The video ends with the camera panning the pond, and you can see the ducks swimming in it *en masse*. The striking things about the pond were not only the large size of it, but the fact that there was no fencing around it whatsoever. Which meant that the ducks were in *the exact same situation* that they'd been in at McKinnon's Pond. There was no difference whatsoever.

Aimee posted the video on her Facebook page, and expressed enthusiasm over their new home, and how they would be safe from predators, and horrendous weather conditions. Naturally, many of her rescue friends "liked" the video. I myself said nothing. Inside, though, I was seething.

How on earth, I asked myself – and Duddy – *does she think these ducks are better off now?* What the hell had changed besides the location? How did Aimee think the man who adopted them was going to round them up every night and get them back in the shed?

There on the video I could see my old friends – Big Boy, Little Peeps, Little Nipper, and the other six, and it was clear that they had no idea what was going on, or why they'd been moved to a strange new place. Why on earth had Aimee put them through all of this if they were only going to end up as predator bait on a different pond?

I couldn't begin to fathom why she didn't see the problem. Equally, I couldn't begin to fathom how she could be so damned pleased with herself over this so-called rescue. Grabbing the ducks and taking them to a nice farm sanctuary to live out the rest of their days in peace and safety was one thing, and I was all for that. But putting the ducks through the stress and fear of catching them, only to ultimately release them into *a pond situation that was virtually identical to the one at McKinnon's Pond* was just plain cruel, in my view.

They were better off where they'd originally been, at McKinnon's Pond where they had multiple volunteers feeding them, keeping an eye on them, and letting me know any time there was a problem. Aimee's rescue plan turned out to be an epic fail. I could see the fear plain on their little duck faces in that video, and it pained me. There was Big Boy, no longer king of the hill, but just another duck whose life had been disrupted for no good reason. And the bitch of it was that I couldn't say a word.

For the rest of my life, I would have to bite my tongue any time I happened to run into Aimee. The local rescue circle was a small one, and in order to keep the peace, my lips had to remain sealed. It was a state of affairs that I with my big mouth was completely unaccustomed to, and ranting to my therapist only took the edge off; it didn't put the matter to rest.

"Look how happy they look and how connected they are to each other!" Aimee wrote as a caption to the video.

I wanted to scream at her, "They're not happy! They're terrified! That's why they're huddled together out in the pond!"

But I couldn't say a word.

Until now. I simply can't keep my mouth shut any longer.

They weren't happy, Aimee. They were terrified.

The One I Couldn't Save

The squirrel came from out of nowhere and dashed into the road. I swerved wildly to avoid him but the *thud* from under my car told me I had failed. As I slowed to a stop, I glanced in the rear-view mirror. I saw his tail twitch a couple of times and felt a small surge of hope. I turned the car around and drove back to him, but in the fifteen seconds it had taken me to do that, the squirrel had died. I knelt beside him and stroked his fur, searching for any small signs of life. There were none.

Forgoing the shovel that I kept in the trunk for just this sort of thing, I picked the squirrel up and carried him to the side of the road. It was after I laid him down that I saw my hands were covered in blood, and, indeed, so was a goodly portion of the road: in the time it had taken me to turn the car around and drive back, that squirrel had lost a hell of a lot of it. I said a prayer to the Gods, asking that they take the poor creature right up to heaven, and I drove off, subdued. I'd only ever hit one other squirrel in my life, and apart from a knock on the head which had probably given him a heck of a headache, I'd never hit – let alone killed – another animal with my car. In all the years that I'd been driving, I'd been very lucky.

Some of that luck might've come from the fact that every time I get in my car and drive somewhere, I say a prayer to the Gods, asking that they please keep the critters safe out of the road. This time, apparently, they hadn't been listening, and my heart was saddened by the loss. Hurting any animal is the last thing I ever want to do.

Chasing Chickens

It was as I made my way toward the River View Park trailhead that I noticed the two chickens. They were scratching around at the edge of the parking lot, which might've been an everyday sight except that the park was located inside the Fordway city limits, where farm animals weren't allowed. River View was a great little park with a view of the Mansing River and a 1-mile loop trail that the designers created with a couple of serious hills to maximize your cardio workout. I tried to do two laps at least three or four times a week.

River View Park was also a decent place for wildlife sightings: over the years, I'd seen a red fox, any number of chipmunks (a specie that, strangely, didn't live anywhere near the Critter Shack), squirrels, birds, and a multitude of whitetail deer. The one thing I never saw there, though, was domestic chickens. I went about my walk frowning thoughtfully. Perhaps they'd escaped from a nearby back yard. I made a mental note to check that out when I'd finished walking.

I investigated several houses on either side of the park, knocking on the occasional door and snooping just enough to determine whether there was a backyard coop of some kind, but my efforts proved fruitless and no one answered the doors I'd approached. Reluctantly, I went home, hoping that the issue would resolve itself in my absence. But of course, that rarely happens!

When I returned the next day, the chickens were still in residence. Before I headed off on the trail, I opened the bag of duck food that I'd bought a few days prior and forgotten to unload at home. I tossed a few handfuls of corn in the chickens' direction, then took my walk. When I'd finished two miles, I made my way to my car and found my phone. I called 911, explaining that mine was not an emergency but that I needed to speak to someone at the Fordway police department.

When I had the Fordway dispatcher on the line, and explained my problem, she sent an officer my way, and he arrived in a matter of minutes. Fordway didn't have an Animal Control Officer, he told me, and I already knew that Fordway was out of Officer Dave's jurisdiction. The Fordway policeman was friendly enough, though, and when I told him that I was going to arrange a rescue, he encouraged me to call him if I needed assistance. I tucked his business card into my pocket, and went about trying to figure out what I needed in order to facilitate rescuing two chickens.

The first thing I did was call Officer Dave, of course. He was more than willing to lend me a cage large enough to transport the chickens in, and he wished me good luck. The second thing I did was get in touch with step-daughter Lauren, with whom I had a lunch date the following day.

"Change of plan," I texted her, "I need your help catching some chickens!" We agreed to meet in the River View parking lot the next day at 2:00. Other than that, I just needed to formulate a plan for actually rounding up the chickens, and this I did based on my experiences catching ducks.

I assumed that the process would be fairly straightforward – straightforward, that is, until we actually got started!

As I'd done with my duck rescues, I set up Officer Dave's cage a few yards away from the chickens. The idea was to get behind the birds and walk them toward the cage. Evidently, though, frightened chickens don't huddle together *en masse* like frightened ducks do. The minute we started moving, each chicken ran off in a different direction. It soon became clear that we would need more bodies. I placed a call to the Fordway police officer I'd talked to the day before. It must've been a slow crime day because he showed up almost immediately. Happily, he was up for a critter rescue and gamely went wherever I directed him.

Although Lauren had baby Stella perched on her hip, she was still able to move about pretty quickly, and two-year old Liam also did his best to keep up, but because the chickens were so quick to out-maneuver us, we kept coming up empty-handed. The park terrain did nothing to help us, either: right next to the parking lot was a densely-wooded hill, and the chickens were able to scramble up and down it with a dexterity that I in my mid-fifties no longer possessed. In desperation, I started recruiting passersby.

"You! With the red shirt! Wanna help rescue some chickens?"

Red Shirt shrugged and said, "Sure!" I directed him where to stand. A few minutes later, two more guys walked past.

"Hey! You two! Wanna help us catch these chickens?" They willingly joined in, and I pointed to where they should stand.

By now, we had eight people, altogether, and the chickens still eluded us! We adjusted our strategy several times, fanning out along the edge of the woods while I raced back and forth among the trees, trying to shoo the birds toward the top of the hill. At that point, one of the fellows caught one of the chickens. He placed him carefully in my critter carrier, then we went back to work and caught the other bird fairly quickly. When I say "fairly quickly," though, I'm afraid it's a little misleading: it actually took us almost an hour to catch both chickens.

By the time we were done, we were all pretty sweaty, and mighty pleased with our success. The only unhappy member of the group was little Liam, who never told anyone that he needed to pee, and consequently wet his pants. Not even Lauren minded, though – he'd helped us with our noble endeavor, and that was what really mattered.

We loaded the critter carrier into my car, and the larger cage that I'd borrowed from Dave onto the back of Dud's work truck, which Lauren was driving. I thanked all our helpers profusely, and then Lauren and I made our way to the Perry County Humane Society with a view to dropping off the birds. It was when I walked into the building, crated chicken in hand, that the shit hit the fan.

"I'm dropping off some chickens that we rescued," I told the girl at the front desk.

"We don't take chickens," she replied, as if that was the end of it.

"Well, neither do I," I replied. "But they weren't going to live much longer where I rescued them from." The girl asked me where I'd found them, and I was careful to tell her that they were found inside Perry County limits. As it happened, this was not only true, but it would prevent her from telling me that they didn't accept rescues from outside County limits. Even so, she repeated the no-chickens rule.

"Well," I shrugged, "I don't know what to tell you. I can't take them home, they don't belong in the wild, and Perry County is an agrarian county. So how is it that you don't accept farm animals?" She had no answer for this, other than that it was shelter policy, so I asked to speak to her supervisor.

The Cruelty Officer was quickly apprised of the situation by the front office staff before she came out to talk to me. She also told me that the shelter policy did not include accepting chickens, and that they had no idea how to care for such animals, or what to feed them. I reiterated my stance, adding that I had duck food in my car that I was happy to donate so that they could feed the birds. At that point, tempers got heated and voices got raised.

"*Look!*" I exclaimed, my voice matching the pitch and tone of the Cruelty Officer, "I'm *not taking these chickens with me!* I rescued them, now it's your turn to deal with them!"

"Ma'am, if you leave here without them, I'll charge you with animal cruelty!" She wasn't kidding.

"Let me get this straight," I replied, "I did the right thing and rescued them, but you want to charge me with cruelty?"

"Ma'am," she said, doing what I assume was her best to maintain a level of civility, "*we don't do chickens!*"

"You're in an *agrarian* county! How can you *not* do farm animals?"

"We don't know how to care for chickens," she answered, as though this somehow made it o.k. to turn away animals in need.

"I have duck food in my car. You're welcome to it!" At this point, one of the office girls came out into the lobby and told the Cruelty Officer that the Chicken Guy – whoever he was – was willing to take the two birds. Apparently they had a source for fowl, although the C.O. had pointedly failed to mention it.

"Great!" I remarked, "can I have my cages back now?"

As they were transferring the chickens to a holding cell, the C.O. said, "Ma'am, next time, *call first!*"

"Why?" I asked angrily, "so you can turn me down over the phone?"

"Because if we get a head's-up in advance, we can help co-ordinate local Animal Control." This was a complete load of bull: as the Perry County Cruelty Officer, she already knew that Fordway didn't have an ACO, and she also knew that Fordway was outside Officer Dave's jurisdiction. She *should've* known all that, and if she didn't, then she was a pretty crappy Cruelty Officer. Chances were that she was hoping that *I* didn't know.

"There *is no* Animal Control Officer in Fordway," I said through gritted teeth. I walked out of the building without further comment, but the incident rankled. That the C.O. would even *consider* filing cruelty charges against me was deeply troubling. That I had done the right thing (and it took seven people to help me accomplish it) but had been threatened with charges by the *County Humane Society* – an entity whose sole reason for existence was to help animals in need - was beyond ludicrous. There was nothing else to be done, though, but to file the experience away for future reference.

Actually, there *was* one other thing to be done, and once I'd thought of it, I made my way to the local craft store. I was looking for a small trophy, or a blue ribbon; something to denote success. My choice was limited to some small stickers in the shape of First Place blue ribbons, and lacking any better ideas, I bought them. Several days later, when Lauren and the kids came to visit, I put the blue ribbon to use.

"Can I have everyone's attention?" I interrupted. They all looked at me expectantly.

"Liam, do you know what a hero is?" He was only two, but he was smart as a whip and picked things up very quickly. He gave me a confused look, though, so I pressed on.

"A hero is someone who helps people. Like Spiderman helps people. Does that make sense?" He nodded. He knew all about Spiderman.

"So a hero is someone who helps other people. That makes *you* a hero, Liam, because you helped us catch those chickens, remember?"

"Chickens!" he replied gleefully.

"Yes!' I agreed, "And since you're a hero, you earned this blue ribbon!" The blue ribbon had "First Place" emblazoned across the front, but Liam couldn't read so it didn't matter. I stuck the ribbon to the front of his shirt and told him, "Good job, Munchkin! Way to be a chicken hero!" Lauren and Grandpa Dud fussed over him then, as he strutted proudly around the room.

Later that night, I thought back on Hero Liam and his blue ribbon. In those quiet nighttime minutes, as I lay in bed waiting for sleep to overtake me, I allowed the success of the rescue push the Cruelty Officer's stupid threat to the back of my mind as I mused, *What better way to educate a child about kindness to animals than to have him participate in the rescue of them!*

The Thing in the Road

The thing in the middle of the road looked like a flap of rubber tire. I glanced at it as I drove by, and was horrified to find that it was actually a small grey kitten. I slammed on the brakes, engaged the hand brake, and jumped out of the car. The kitten looked up at me and meowed in fear, but it didn't get up. Initially, I could see no outward sign of injury – no blood, no nothing – so I picked the thing up and dashed back to my car.

Upon closer inspection, something appeared to be wrong with its left front leg. When I set the kitten down on the passenger seat, it immediately dragged itself to the edge, then dropped down to the floor, meowing piteously as it did so. That left front leg wasn't moving, and indeed, seemed to hinder the little cat. As I tried to get the car going – and, in my panic, couldn't understand why it wouldn't – a woman pulled abreast of me and shouted from her car, "Did you grab the kitten?"

"Yes," I answered, "I'm going to take her to my vet."

"Bless you!" she replied, "I'll say a prayer for you!"

"Say one for the cat, will you?" She nodded in affirmation.

As I looked around the inside of the car, then, I realized why it wouldn't move: the hand brake was still engaged. I released it, shifted into first gear, then drove off, trying to steer while at the same time find the vet's phone number among my contacts. Once I'd dialed the phone, I waited while the receptionist put me on a brief hold, and then asked how she could help.

"I found an injured kitten in the road. I'm about ten minutes out and headed your way."

"O.k.," she said, "we'll have a vet ready for you when you get here."

As I drove to the vet's, I thought about what would happen next. They would want to x-ray the kitten, and then there would be talk of a treatment plan. But I already had four cats at home, and husband Dud would never forgive me for spending hundreds of dollars on a cat that we wouldn't be keeping. I had one ace up my sleeve, though, and I chewed on it as I pulled into the parking lot.

Suburban Animal Care is a huge facility, with ten veterinarians on staff, all of them women. Their prices tended to be a little on the high side, but I'd never had a bad experience there, and liked every vet who had worked on my critters. When Doctor Henny walked into the exam room, I remembered her from previous visits, and I remembered liking her, as well. I knew she would take good care of this kitten.

I explained to her how I had come across the cat. She nodded and looked the little kitten over carefully. She agreed that there was something wrong with the left front leg, and said she wanted to do an x-ray. It was then that she asked the question I knew was coming: "How much work do you want me to do on this cat?" I considered the matter carefully.

"My husband will kill me if I spend a bunch of money on her," I replied. And then, throwing out the ace up my sleeve, I asked, "Is there any chance we could make her a City kitty?"

Pictures of City kitties turned up regularly in the *Whoville Journal*. Cats and kittens that Officer Dave confiscated for any reason often ended up boarding at Suburban Animal Care. The staff would clean them up and give them their shots, and then adopt them out for a small fee. It was a far better arrangement than simply euthanizing everything he caught. The pictures the *Journal* printed always showed a cheerful Dave loaded down with five or eight kittens. I was hoping that this little one might be among them. Dr. Henny shrugged and suggested that I give Dave a call.

I explained the situation when he answered his phone. He hesitated, knowing that the City wouldn't want to pay a steep vet bill. I handed the phone to Dr. Henny, and they chatted briefly. The upshot was that she would take the x-ray, see what the problem was, then go from there. The situation was out of my hands, now, and I thanked Dr. Henny as I made my way out the door. The kitten remained in my thoughts, though, and the next day, I called Suburban and asked for an update.

I was put on hold for a minute or two before a vet tech picked up. I told her who I was and why I was calling. The girl responded carefully, explaining that Suburban didn't ordinarily give out information after a surrender. I replied that I was a writer, and was hoping to follow up on the kitten's situation. That got the tech talking, although what she had to say was rather disturbing.

What she had to say was this: that due to the fact that the injury – and subsequent nerve damage – had been to the kitten's *front* leg, and given that it's very difficult for a cat to navigate with just one front leg, they had opted to euthanize the kitten. The girl then reiterated Suburban's policy of not giving out information about surrendered animals. I listened quietly but my thoughts were churning.

The thing that kept coming to mind while the vet tech talked about that front-leg difficulty was the fact of my own Gracie Ellen Tripod and her missing front leg. When I'd first found her, Gracie had been hindered by a broken leg that had healed badly. It had curled around in spiral fashion and served her not at all; the thing merely dragged along as she moved. Once it was amputated, she got around just fine with one front leg, hobbling rather than walking, but running every bit as fast as if she were doing so on four feet. I said nothing as the vet tech talked, but thanks to Gracie Ellen and her perfectly able mobility, I knew I was being fed a line of bull. I thanked the girl for her time and hung up. I started at my phone thoughtfully for some minutes afterward.

I understood Dave's position: he had to answer to the Chief of Police, and while the Chief was rumored to be a decent guy, he was in no position to sanction expensive veterinary care for every injured animal that came down the pike. I understood that, and could accept it on an intellectual level. Being fed a load of bull by a vet tech was another story, but there was nothing I could do about it: I had surrendered the kitten, making a conscious decision not to adopt it. Which meant that I gave up any right to object to the decisions made by the other people involved. Giving up the right to object, though, didn't mean giving up the need to grieve, and this I did for a time before I refocused my energies on those critters who were still in my purview.

STUFF

When I started leasing Bit the horse, almost four years ago, I didn't need any tack or horse-related items such as brushes and combs because The Harmony Barn already had them in abundance. So many people had come and gone, through the years, that the barn actually had multiples of pretty much everything. Some folks left grooming accoutrements, some left saddles, or bridles, or lunge lines. Just about everything you might need is there somewhere! Along the way, though, I've found that sometimes, you need a specific thing that the barn either doesn't have, or that belongs to someone who isn't there at the time you want to borrow it. Which is why I ended up acquiring my own complement of stuff, even though I'm only leasing.

The first thing I decided that I needed was my own grooming kit. I'll admit that the main reason I wanted it – as Dud and I were checking out the items on offer at our local western store – was because everything in the set was pink. Bit may not be a girl, but I sure am, through and through, and pink is one of my favorite colors. So Dud bought me the grooming set, complete with pink curry comb, brush, and hoof pick. Later, he bought me a plastic carry-all to put all my pink things in, and that carry-all resided in the trunk of my car for quite some time.

Because Bit can be a stinker, I found that the best way to get him to move when I said move was to use a lead rope with a chain attached to it. The chain goes through the ring in his halter, over his nose, and hooks to the ring on the other side of the halter. This tends to reinforce my commands much better than just hooking the lead rope to the ring underneath the halter. While I suspect that some people are probably a little harsh when using the chain in this way, I'm always very careful not to yank on the lead rope or do anything else that might hurt Bit. The point is *not* to injure him, or order him around through pain and fear, but to be carefully firm in backing up my verbal commands. Since Bit is the head of the herd, and therefore somewhat attitudinal about whether he is the boss of our sessions, or whether I am, this reinforcement is necessary. But again, I am *very* careful not to hurt him in the process.

In any case, the barn only had one lead rope with chain attachment; the rest were just rope. So instead of hunting all over the barn to find that one special lead rope, I went back to the western store (called, in case you're interested, Sonseeahray Western Store), and bought myself a nice lead rope with chain extension. It, too, resided in the plastic carry-all.

I should mention that Baby Jack, a small Quarter Horse rescue with neurological issues that make it challenging to put his two back feet where they need to go, accidentally stepped on my plastic carry-all a few too many times, over the years, which meant that I found myself in need of a new one. I found the perfect replacement in the tool box aisle at Nelson's, our local "Save Big Bucks," do-it-yourself store. It's much sturdier than the plastic version was, and I'd recommend it to anyone who needs a good solid carry-all for their horse-related items.

Once I started trying to train Bit, I realized that I needed for my arms to be a few feet longer. Since it was unlikely that I would be able to grow them any longer than they already were, I went once again to Sonseeahray and bought a riding crop. You might've seen old movies on t.v. where the rider used a crop to beat the horse into going faster. While I was not entirely certain what the usual use is for a riding crop, I *did* know that there would be no hitting. If I want Bit to go faster, I know how to do so without scaring or hitting him. The new crop was meant to be an extension of my arm and nothing more.

At the time that I particularly needed longer arms, I was trying to teach him that he needed to stand still next to the mounting block so I could mount him safely. I must say in hindsight that the crop didn't help the training nearly as much as bringing in riding instructor Connie, who has a degree in barn management from the University of Findlay. Connie figured out almost immediately what I needed to do to get Bit to do what I wanted, so the crop was relegated to the trunk of my car until I started bomb-proofing training a year later. With the remnant of a plastic grocery bag tied to the end, the crop was resurrected as an aid to get Bit moving when he would've preferred to stay put. Again, I did *not* strike him with the crop, I merely waved it around near his hindquarters.

After one of our rides, one of the reins that I had laid across his neck fell to the ground. Bit promptly, though inadvertently, stepped on it, jerked his head, and snapped the leather rein in two. Since the reins belonged to the barn, I felt honor-bound to replace the one that had been broken on my watch. So back to Sonseeahray I went for a new rein, and, while I was at it, a new girth that was much more comfortable for Bit than the one that was already on the saddle. I painted my name on the new girth in pink nail polish and it, too, resides in my trunk when not in use.

Golly, but that's a lot of stuff! And we're not done, yet, either!

When my original Justin barn boots wore out, I went, yet again, to Sonseeahray for a new pair. The new ones have pink leather and little bits of bling on the sides. Even though my jeans cover those pink parts, *I* still know that they're there! In addition to new barn boots, Duddy bought my wedding boots at Sonseeahray, too. They're a flashy dress pair (as opposed to the work pair that I don't mind stepping in horse poop while I'm wearing), black leather with designs cut out all around them, with hot pink leather in the designs. I wear that pair strictly for dressing up and going out to dinner; the only time they were ever in the barn was the day I got married.

One of my more recent purchases had to do with Bit's girth issues. The entire time I've leased him, every time I'd try to saddle Bit, he'd get very upset about it. Initially, he'd move around in the cross ties a lot, and paw the ground with his front hooves. This would escalate into squeals and mini bucks. Sometimes, he'd kick the wall. While I worried for my physical safety, I worried more about the *reason* for his behavior, and the idea that I might be hurting him had me mighty concerned. I consulted barn owners Ron and Wendy, and instructor Connie – who all thought that he'd probably been treated roughly by a former owner – but to no avail. No one seemed to have any idea how to fix the problem. And if you can't cinch the girth, you can't keep the saddle on the horse. The only alternatives were to not ride, or to ride bareback.

Since I had very little experience riding bareback, it seemed like an opportune time to give it a try. Happily, Bid didn't have any apparent qualms about me riding him in such a way; indeed, he stood still and patient as I climbed on and adjusted the saddle pad that I was sitting on. We rode bareback several times and while I did o.k., I also made a mental note that I needed to keep working on balancing myself and generally having a better seat. In the meantime, I discovered the existence of bareback pads and went – yet again! – to Sonseeahray to check them out.

The selection wasn't very big, and, to my surprise, the bareback pads all had stirrups and girths attached (meaning we would be back at square one again with another girth). I bought one on clearance – why buy something expensive when you're just going to putz around with it? - and put it in the trunk with all the other stuff.

Meanwhile, some years ago, when my cheap, crappy barn coat had worn out, I happened to come across a nice Schmidt insulated coat at Tractor Supply Company. The best part: it was bright pink! I promptly bought the matching insulated overalls, too, which made me the butt of innumerable jokes at the barn, given that I looked like a giant frozen bar of Pepto Bismol! The matching gloves and hat did nothing to offset the look.

The coat had a tail that came down below the waistline in the back, which proved useful for those times when I had to bend over or crouch down. But as I got older, and noticed that it was still possible to get a cold draft up the backside, I decided that a longer coat would be more useful, particularly for cold-weather riding. So I started looking around online.

Contrary to what my frugal husband thinks, I *don't* just get a bee in my bonnet and immediately want to buy something. I have a process, which involves thorough research and a fair amount of time: I want the best possible product at the best possible price. You can't just find that with a small amount of looking. And since the coat I was looking to buy was rather expensive ($200 new), and since I knew that Dud would have a cow at the idea of me buying a $200 coat, I kept looking until I found something marginally cheaper: the coat I wanted at a slightly lower price owing to the fact that it was being sold used on eBay. And, after a fair amount of explaining to Dud exactly *why* I felt the need to own a coat with butt flaps, I received his (grudging) blessing in buying it.

The reason I felt the need to own a coat with butt flaps: because it had butt flaps, of course! The new riding coat has flaps around the backside that are not only long enough to keep drafts out, but you can snap them closed if you just want to wear the coat out in the world, or unsnap the flaps so that they sort of fan out around your butt while you're sitting on your horse, keeping it well-insulated along with the rest of you. Ordinarily, a shorter coat tends to ride up when my arms are outstretched, which they are when I'm steering Bit. If I want to get more riding in during colder months, a longer coat with butt flaps is the way to go. In addition, I get a major kick out of turning my back to the Urchins, waving those flaps around and gleefully announcing, "Butt flaps!" Nothing amuses them more these days than Kelly showing off her butt flaps!

A Matter of Taste

We were gathered in The Harmony Barn's viewing room for our annual Christmas gift exchange. This mostly involved Wendy and I doling out small gifts to the Urchins, and, on occasion, an Urchin giving us something in return. Olivia, in particular, was a gifted artist, and one year, she gave me a small clay horse that she'd made as a Christmas tree ornament. It hangs from my desk even now.

The gifts we gave the kids included horse calenders from Wendy, and framed pictures that I'd taken the previous year of each Urchin with their favorite horse. Sometimes, the kids' parents made plates of cookies for us to share, and sometimes, Lydia's mom would gift me with Reese's Peanut Butter Cups because I'd given Lydia free riding lessons. All in all, it was a festive day of gifts, yummy treats, and a little poop-scooping as well.

This particular Christmas, I'd bought an apple flavored lick for Bit as my gift to him. Flavored licks are cube-shaped things that hang in a horse's stall, and are mainly intended to occupy them while they're waiting to be put out to pasture.

Salt licks, in particular, act as a supplement to help replace what they sweat out during the hot summer months.

"Check it out!" I said to the gang, "I got Bit an apple lick!" I proceeded to open the package and give the thing a cautious sniff. "Doesn't smell like apple," I remarked suspiciously. I gave it a small lick.

Allen laughed. "Only Kelly would taste-test a horse lick!"

"It doesn't *taste* like apple, either! Here," I continued, handing the apple lick to Lydia, "see what you think." Lydia gave it a small lick, too.

"Doesn't taste like apple," she said. No one else wanted to try it. They just chuckled.

In the midst of the previous summer, a heatwave of epic proportions had reared its ugly head in the form of hot, humid ninety+ degree days. Ever-mindful of Bit's welfare, and knowing that horses need to maintain their salt intake just like humans do, I texted Wendy, "Do you think Bit would like a salt lick?" "Sure," she replied. So I drove to the farm supply store and picked out one that I could hang from his stall door. I installed it the next day.

While it may seem obvious to you, I have to admit that knowing what a salt lick tastes like was not obvious to *me*. Back when Cricket the donkey (from NBM) was still alive, and I saw her licking one, I got curious and gave the thing a lick myself. Wow! Was it *salty!* The Urchins got a big kick out of seeing me taste the horses' salt lick, but how else are you going to find these things out?!

The Urchins were used to my weirdness because they'd been witnesses to it for such a long time. Years ago, on superhot Saturdays when Cricket was still alive, I'd bring a bottle of Gatorade with me. I don't do well in hot, humid conditions, and it's important to keep hydrated. I'd be standing around in the aisle, taking a short break from my poop-scooping duties, and swilling some 'Ade. Cricket would wander up and want to know what I was doing with the colored bottle. I let her sniff it once, and she decided that she liked Gatorade, so I tipped the bottle and let some run into her mouth. After that, any time I drank Gatorade, Cricket would find me and want a sip. That wasn't necessarily the funny part, though; the funny part was that after her tongue slobbered all over the bottle, I would wipe the lip of it with my dirty shirt, then have a sip myself.

"Whaaat?" I'd ask all and sundry when they looked at me with wide eyes. "How is your immune system going to keep the cooties out if you never expose it to any?" The Urchins weren't sure about this sketchy logic, but believe it or not, Wendy – who was a nurse by day – would actually nod in agreement: the immune system does, indeed, need new challenges in order to keep it working well. Still, no one else wanted to share their beverage – or any other ingestible, for that matter – with the equine residents. And who could blame them? Sharing with a slobbery donkey *was* kinda gross!

More Stuff

When I purchased that first bareback pad, I knew nothing about bareback pads at all, other than the fact that they existed. So it never occurred to me to ask any specific questions of the good folks at Sonseeahray – who know their products inside and out. All I knew when I bought that first pad was that it looked a little small. I used it a few times, but the tiny little triangle of padded fabric made me feel more than a little exposed and vulnerable. Later, I realized that I got that same feeling when I used an English saddle. At the time, I had no idea that bareback pads, like saddles, come in English and Western styles. What I had inadvertently bought was an English bareback pad. And I'll be honest with you: I really don't care for English-style tack.

If you're wondering whether there's an actual difference between riding bareback and riding with a saddle, I can assure that there is. In the first place, the saddle is constructed over a wooden "tree," which ultimately helps stabilize the rider. A bareback pad is just a bit of padding between your butt and the horse's back. It offers no stability whatsoever, requiring the rider to pay close attention to every move the horse makes. It's far more of a challenge staying on a horse when you're riding bareback than riding in a saddle, and far more difficult to maintain your balance.

It was while I was giving the English bareback pad issue some thought, and wondering whether another trip to Sonseeahray might be in order, that Dud and I discussed going to the annual Equine Affaire (spelling correct) in Columbus. I'd been hearing about the Equine Affaire for years, but usually dismissed it as something that actual horse people did – as opposed to the perpetually amateurish horse person that I felt myself to be. Perhaps it was time to reconsider.

From the descriptions of Wendy, and horse-boarder Sally – both of whom attended every year – the Affaire sounded like a cornucopia of venders selling all kinds of new and interesting horse-related products, and visiting trainers who gave free demonstrations on horses that they'd brought for just that purpose. For no specific reason other than that spring was taking its own sweet time in arriving after a particularly protracted and unpleasant winter, I thought that it might be fun to go. Given that Dud's eldest daughter happens to live in Columbus, we decided to kill two birds with one stone and make the trip.

We drove through several distinctly scenic and beautiful areas of out-lying Columbus. In doing so, I occupied myself with the burning question, *Does Eric Clapton live in one of these spectacular houses?* I'd read somewhere that Clapton's wife was originally from Columbus, and that they stayed in the area frequently enough to have bought their own property. Clapton is the one man on earth that I might consider leaving my dear husband for, so I popped a *Best of Clapton* CD in the player and amused myself with an informal search for the property until we found the Ohio Expo Center.

The Equine Affaire occupied several buildings throughout the grounds. Indeed, there were so many different things going on in the various buildings that there was no way we could see them all in a single two- or three-hour visit. We headed for the main building and found ourselves completely surrounded by vendors. We shrugged, randomly picked a direction, and started walking. We found some bareback pads at the second vendor we came to.

I had no idea what, exactly, I would need in a Western bareback pad, but when I saw what was on offer, I knew immediately that this was by far the finest I would find. For one thing, the pad had a much larger area than the English pad I already owned, and had considerably more padding. For another thing, the underside was comprised of a non-slip material that would help to keep it from slipping off the horse's back. It had no stirrups, a thing I was initially unhappy about until I read the attached tag which informed me that since there was no saddle tree to keep the pad from slipping over the withers, stirrups on a bareback pad could be dangerous. That made sense. The only thing left to do (even though we'd not seen the other 98% of the vendors yet) was to buy it. Unfortunately, they had every color of the rainbow *except* the navy blue that I wanted. The vendor promised to call me when the blue ones arrived in the warehouse, some 30 days hence.

I was beside myself with excitement: just because the English pad hadn't met my needs didn't mean that I wanted to give up on the idea of riding bareback altogether. If riding Bit bareback helped improve my seat, and alleviated some of the girth issues that generally upset him so, it would be a win-win situation, and nothing would make me happier than making Bit's life easier. So I tried to put my excitement on the back burner where it wouldn't drive me crazy, and attempted to wait patiently for the pad I wanted to come back into stock again.

In the meantime, we continued our Affaire adventure, looking in amazement at the products we didn't know existed (the electric poop sifter turned out to be our favorite), visiting briefly with Wendy and Connie, who were there representing Hilton Herbs, the dog and horse herbal supplements that they sell, enjoying a lovely visit with Dud's daughter, and buying some homemade sausage from a stand on the side of the highway. The location of Clapton's residence, alas, remains a mystery.

What If It Happened To You?

If you've read either of my previous two books, you'll know that Kenny the Tiger Guy is a local fellow who rescues unwanted exotic animals. He's done so for almost forty years. Twice, in the span of five-odd years, he's called Wendy at The Harmony Barn and asked whether she'd be willing to take a donkey that had been donated to him. The donations were intended to feed Kenny's critters, but Kenny didn't have the heart to slaughter healthy animals whose only crime was being unwanted. Both times, Wendy agreed to take the donkeys, and the barn volunteers spent a number of years enjoying their unique personalities.

Giving up the donkeys was a big deal for Kenny, a man of modest means who was forever seeking out donations to feed his collection of lions, bears, and tigers. While food wholesalers often donated tons of beef or chicken, Kenny could never count on having a continuous supply of food. Even so, he gave away two healthy animals that would have otherwise fed more than one exotic beast in his care. It's the kind of guy Kenny is.

I knew Kenny primarily through Facebook. Once, when I told him that I volunteered at The Harmony Barn, he invited me to stop by and pick up a bunch of horse halters that he didn't need; he thought maybe the Barn could use them. What I didn't realize until I went to get the halters was why he had them: because once they came off the donated horses that he slaughtered, he had no more use for them. While I was at his sanctuary, Tiger Ridge Exotics, I took a few minutes to look the place over. It wasn't a completely *ideal* set-up.

In the first place, there wasn't enough acreage to give the big cats room to run. In a perfect world, each tiger and lion would have their own acre to roam as they pleased. But Kenny didn't have a large enough property for that. What he *did* have was love in his heart, and a level of dedication to his animals that many pet owners don't.

In the second place, he cobbled his operation together as best he could, using whatever he had on hand: unable to afford customized metal signs, he posted hand-painted ones on the outsides of the enclosures, noting what species occupied the cage. It looked entirely amateur but he didn't seem to care. What mattered most to Kenny was that his animals were loved, well-fed, and happy.

Kenny and his critters remained on the periphery of my life for a number of years, until the day came that would haunt a good many animal rescuers, the day that Terry Thompson allegedly released a number of exotic animals that he owned, and then allegedly shot himself. I say "allegedly" because there are a number of people who believe that events didn't happen that way. Indeed, many believe that Thompson was murdered.

If you don't recall the incident in Zanesville, Ohio, what happened next was just heartbreaking. Not knowing what else to do – and no doubt having little to no experience with exotic animals – local law enforcement hunted them down and killed 50 of them. Ultimately, 18 tigers and 17 lions, among others, were killed by panicked officers who surely could've saved some lives had they bothered to contact any experts in the field.

According to the website www.earthintransition.org, plenty could've been done to avoid slaughtering 50 animals: "First, put out an emergency curfew to keep humans and their pets indoors, and have police patrols out to enforce the rule. Round up wildlife experts and trappers from across the country, and get them on the job fast. Have the AZA (Association of Zoos and Aquariums) and its zoos offer to pay for the operation. Most important, *take the killing option off the table* except in the unlikely case (the animals had all been fed) that someone is actually being eaten by a tiger. And finally, when the animals have been rescued, put all the resources of the AZA on the side of getting them out to sanctuaries, or at least to the best zoos in the country, so they can have the best life possible for the rest of their days." But it didn't happen that way, and seeing the corpses of so many beautiful animals lying around on Thompson's property made me want to weep.

Naturally, after the massacre in Zanesville. A number of Ohio politicians began to clamor for stricter rules and regulations for those who owned exotic animals. In fact, the laws were so strict that they were clearly the beginning of what was obviously a phasing-out of people's ability to own such animals. For those who already *did* own them, restrictions tightened like a noose around their necks, requiring a vast array of ever-changing updates to the cages in which the animals were housed. In Kenny's case, that meant $400,000-worth of updates to the fencing surrounding the enclosures. We won't even get into how much his new million-dollar liability insurance premiums cost. Suffice to say that the Ohio politicians who signed the new regulations into law were obviously trying to price small-time exotic animal operators right out of business.

This was no doubt a good thing, in some ways. Indeed, I'm sure that there were any number of roadside zoos that never should have been in business in the first place: dilapidated housing, and animals living in inhumane conditions, were just the sort of thing the new laws were meant to combat. But there were other, better facilities who were also under the hammer wielded by the Ohio Department of Agriculture (ODA), and somewhere in the middle, between those two ends, lay Kenny Hetrick's Tiger Ridge Exotics. The ODA pounced on January 29th of 2015 and confiscated 11 of Kenny's beloved animals.

Despite the fact that a local judge ordered them to return Kenny's animals, the ODA put up a hell of a fight. Instead, of giving them back, the ODA brought in their own legal team, threw up numerous roadblocks – knowing that Kenny could ill-afford a protracted court battle – and when it looked like they might actually lose the case, they started sending the animals to sanctuaries all around the US. It was a rotten, sneaky thing to do.

The main problem, though, was *not* necessarily the ODA. The main problem was actually Kenny himself: in setting up the new enclosure requirements, the new rules also said that exotic animal owners must file for their State of Ohio permit by a certain deadline. Since Kenny already had a Federal permit, he didn't think he needed to apply for the State one. Consequently, the application deadline came and went without Kenny so much as calling to find out whether he needed to get a State permit. The ODA used that fact against him in its proceedings. Meanwhile, they euthanized Leo the lion.

There was much back and forth in the press, not to mention Facebook, about Leo's death. Many so-called "experts" - who

I suspect were actually ODA employees hiding behind the guise of being innocent bystanders with an opinion – claimed that the lion was on death's door anyway, and had been scheduled to be put down by Kenny himself. Before going to bat for him in the local papers, I paid him a visit to find out what the story really was.

I had made a few comments in response to the Facebook "experts" before I realized that I didn't have as many facts at my disposal as I should've. So I sat down with Kenny, who was, at that time, constantly surrounded by a retinue of family and friends, and asked for the details. Everyone tried to talk at once, and I finally had to hold up my hand and say, "One at a time, please! Kenny – you first."

Kenny told me that while he had, in fact, scheduled the elderly lion to be put down before he'd been confiscated – and no one at the ODA gave him any advanced notice that they were going to come and take his animals – but he said that Leo had rallied, so Kenny called his vet and canceled the euthanasia. While that may sound farfetched to you, it sounded very familiar to me: more than once, during Macavity's last year, I had called the Vet Ladies and told them it was time. And more than once, I called them back and canceled. No one wants to put down an animal if there's even the smallest hope of reprieve.

So I took the information I'd garnered from Kenny and used it to fire back at all the folks who claimed to know what was going on. Kenny needed a voice, but he was not sophisticated enough to be that voice himself. I did what I could, for no other reason than that I couldn't begin to imagine how awful it would be for some State entity to swarm onto *my* property – at gunpoint, wearing masks – and watch helplessly as they took my animals away.

If the truth must be told – at least my own version of it; I'm sure Kenny and his retinue would strongly disagree – Kenny was probably the type of exotic animal owner that the ODA had in mind when it made the new regulations: there wasn't nearly enough acreage to keep all the animals comfortably, and his finances didn't allow for every possible contingency that might arise. Sometimes, loving an animal isn't enough; sometimes, loving an animal means letting it go somewhere where conditions are more optimal for that species's needs.

Having said that, the heavy-handed way in which the ODA pulled the rug out from underneath Kenny's feet, and the contemptuous way in which they treated him – they didn't even bother to let him know that Leo was going to be euthanized, let alone allow him a last visit - was cruelly unacceptable to anyone with any sense of decency. The ODA wasn't the least bit interested in working with Kenny. They simply swooped in, took most of the animals (not all of the species required permits), damaged much of the expensive fencing they'd ordered Kenny to construct, and didn't even bother to say "sorry."

From my relatively objective viewpoint, I could see both sides of the issue. But when I heard that the ODA had begun sending the animals to sanctuaries around the country – using the claim that their new, state-of-the-art Columbus facility was intended to be strictly temporary, while their case against Tiger Ridge was turning out to be anything but – I knew that Kenny wasn't going to get his animals back. It would be too costly to round them all up and return them, and it would be a win that the ODA was determined would not happen on their watch.

Don't get me wrong: the care and housing of exotic animals *should* be left to proper sanctuaries. And there was no doubt going to be a period of time – in Ohio, at least – where the transition from the animals being privately owned to living in State-certified sanctuaries would be a bumpy one.

But at what cost to a man's soul?

Boyfriend Duck

Having acquired a third female duck, a Pekin we named Daffy, we could only assume what a boost our small harem might've been for Boyfriend's ego. The name on my caller ID told me that Animal Control Officer Dave had a critter-related issue to discuss with me. It turned out that he'd received a call from a woman whose boys had managed to catch a Pekin duck down by the river. The fact that they'd actually caught the thing told me that either the duck in question was particularly slow and easily caught, or that the poor thing had been abandoned by people she'd grown accustomed to. Either way, the woman who called Dave did *not* want a pet duck in her back yard. Was there any way, he wanted to know, that I could take her?

Dud and I discussed the matter and decided that if the duck was male, we'd find it a home with someone else; Boyfriend's limp was getting worse, and he wouldn't be up to the hormonal turf wars that male ducks engage in every mating season. If the duck was female, though, we saw no reason not to take her. As it happened, Daffy turned out to be a charming girl, so we loaded her up in the critter carrier and brought her home. She happily assimilated into the our small gang and made herself right at home. The four ducks made the back yard their own, then, wandering here and there, back and forth across the property in search of the perfect worm. For a time, it seemed they led idyllic lives.

After enjoying over two years of relative – if rather gimpy – good health, though, I suppose it was inevitable that Boyfriend's condition would eventually deteriorate. I had insisted to Dud that we bring Boyfriend home in the first place because he had developed a serious limp in his right leg. Duck legs are notoriously fragile, and I knew that his leg would never heal sufficiently to keep him out of danger at McKinnon's Pond. So he and mate Ethel were rounded up and ensconced on our property.

Over time, we added not just a pen for Boyfriend and Ethel, but an in-ground pond, and the two female Pekins as well. The four ducks would spend their days roaming the fenced-in back yard, searching out worms, insects, and whatever other treats they could find. It was a peaceful existence even if the local birds of prey did do the occasional fly-by, taking stock as they did and assessing what their chances were of bagging an animal as big as our ducks. Raccoons made nightly visits, regardless of how well I sealed off the holes in our privacy fence, but they seemed intent primarily on the eggs the girls laid in various nests, and for two years, raccoons and ducks seemed to co-exist fairly placidly.

I was not happy about those nocturnal visits, though. I knew what raccoons were capable of, and I took every opportunity to discourage them: anytime I saw them in the yard, I would drop what I was doing, run out the sliding glass door at top speed, and chase them all the way to the back fence, clapping my hands and yelling the whole way, threatening serious bodily harm if I caught them.

The routine was virtually identical every night. "Raccoon! Get the FUCK off my property you BIG FAT BASTARD! I swear to GOD I'll tear you LIMB FROM LIMB!" The frightened animal would throw itself under the fence and race off into the weeds on the empty property behind ours. More often than not, as I walked back into the house, I'd see Dud relaxing in his recliner, bemused smile on his face and no doubt thinking that while my efforts were admirable, they were probably fruitless: those raccoons were tenacious, and if I didn't chase them all the way to the fence, they'd actually stop running when they got to the big pine tree, and look back to assess the seriousness of my threat. When they realized that I wasn't kidding, they'd begin to run again in earnest.

My main worry at that time was Boyfriend. Much to my horror, he developed a limp in his left leg, as well, only this one was much worse: for some reason, his left foot became completely limp and useless. In order to get around, he had to fling his leg forward from the hip and hope that he'd used enough force to make the left foot fly forward, too. Many times, it didn't work that way, and his left leg would be propelled forward but the foot itself would end up dragging along behind. It was hideously awkward. The first time I saw him do it, I immediately made an appointment with Dr. Sue.

My thinking was that if Dr. Sue amputated the useless foot, then Boyfriend could peg-leg around on his stump. I'd seen it before with wild Mallards whose legs had been cut off by fishing line. It was an awful thing to witness – and, I'm sure, a whole lot worse to experience – but eventually, the wound would heal and the duck would get around just fine. So my plan was for Dr. Sue to amputate the foot, but the plan was turned on its head when she nixed the idea.

"Amputation is a serious surgery," she explained. "And at fourteen years-old, he would never survive the anesthesia."

"You can't just give him a local and lop it off?" I asked.

"No. You could band him [in which you put a rubber band or string around the leg very tightly so that it cuts off the circulation, and, eventually, the leg, as in the case of those wild Mallards], but that would be cruel and painful and I wouldn't recommend it."

I looked at her, vexed. "So...? What *can* we do?"

Dr. Sue shrugged. "He won't last long like this," she replied, "I would take him home and let him be how he is until he can't get around anymore. Then bring him back in and I can euthanize him."

I nodded in agreement. There was nothing else to be done. I wasn't ready to put him down, and I didn't think that he was ready to go, either, so I put him back in the carrier, thanked her, paid the bill and took him home.

"Here ya go, Boyfriend," I said fondly as I pulled him out of the carrier and set him on the grass, "you can live here as long as you want!" I knew that Dr. Sue was right about there not being any other options, and about him not lasting long in his current gimpy state. Remarkably, he *did* manage to get around the yard surprisingly well. In the morning, he'd be lying in the grass over by the landscaped island in the middle of the yard, and a few hours later, I'd find him lying under the red maple tree a good thirty feet away. A while later, he'd be across the yard entirely, having a nap by the boxwood shrubs with his bill tucked into his wing. As long as he wanted to keep going, I was content to let him do his thing. After years of experience with various species, I knew that when the time came to euthanize, I would know, and so would he.

It didn't work out that way, though. A week or so after our visit to Dr. Sue, I found myself being awakened in the early hours of the morning by Dud, who was always up before sunrise. Agitated, he said, "Something got Boyfriend! It's not good!" Groggily, I followed him to the sliding glass door, reaching for my glasses and peering out to where he was pointing, over by that red maple tree.

"See that pile of feathers? Something got him there. They must've chased him then, because he's over by that pine tree."

"He's gone?" I asked.

"Oh, yeah," Dud replied.

Sighing, I grabbed a towel and Dud grabbed a garbage bag. We walked out to the pine tree. Poor Boyfriend had taken a beating but his body was pretty much still intact. It was clearly the work of a raccoon: for reasons I can't begin to fathom, they will kill ducks without bothering to eat so much as a nibble of the carcass. Birds of prey, on the other hand, will eat so much of the carcass that, frequently, too little is left to identify the specie or the specific animal. With the towel, I picked up Boyfriend's lifeless body and put it into the garbage bag. Dud took the bag away while I got some latex gloves and a small plastic bag and picked up most of the remaining feathers. I didn't want there to be any bits or pieces left to entice another predator.

The girls all knew what had happened to Boyfriend, but it was Ethel that I felt sorriest for: Ethel and Boyfriend had been a mated pair for over ten years. In that time, when they lived at McKinnon's Pond, they chose to make the back side of the pond their own, coming together with the other abandoned domestics for the winter, and then heading off to their own bit of real estate in the spring. During feeds, I would pour out some cracked corn for the ducks who hung out by the boat house, and then I'd make my way to the back side of the pond to feed my two favorites. "Ethel-Ethel!" I'd call, "Where's a pretty girl?" Sooner or later, they'd hear me and come running, just the way a dog does when you call it. I would pour out some corn for them, then sit down and visit while they ate.

"What a great day to be ducks, ducks!" I'd enthuse. "Blue skies, nice and warm! And the breeze brings the smells right to your nose!" Ethel would make small squeaky noises in reply, while Boyfriend looked on, waiting until she'd eaten her fill before he stepped up to the pile. It was that way for ten wonderful years.

Apart from feeling helpless that I couldn't prevent his untimely demise, I felt curiously little else. Regret, of course, that he hadn't simply died in his sleep as I had hoped. Melancholy about all those years of friendship at McKinnon's Pond. Sad for Ethel, who had been his mate for over a decade. And, as it turned out, sad for Dud, as well, who had no idea how much affection he'd invested in Boyfriend until Boyfriend was killed. Noting his sorrow that morning, he remarked with some surprise, "The little fuckers grow on you, don't they?!" Indeed, they do, Dud. Later that day, he sent me this text: "Im sad."

"Me, too!" I texted back, "me and Ethel and Boyfriend go back a long way! We gave him a good life, tho, with lots of worms!"

"Yes we did," was his response. "I love you and Boyfriend."

If you read the chapter in NBM called "We've Got Ducks!" you'll know that Duddy was *not* enthused about the idea of having pet ducks. "They'll wreck the lawn," was his first thought, followed closely by a second having to do with pet ducks costing money to care for. There was a lot of swearing involved as he built what turned out to be a fine duck pen, and there was a fair amount of swearing involved when I decided that we should get a third duck (although, curiously, there was considerably *less* swearing over whether to add the fourth!). Dud just couldn't see the value in pet ducks, and he fought me at every turn.

But somewhere along the way, something happened. Maybe it was how enthusiastically the ducks would approach him when he had worms to give them. Maybe it was the fact that they chose to spend the cold winter nights huddled in the pen he had built. Who can say? But somewhere along the line, something in Dud changed, and I stopped getting taken to task for all the money I spent on worms and minnows at the bait shop. Even more telling, Dud joined in the feeding fun by voluntarily giving out handfuls of his beloved Goldfish crackers! Time, and the ducks' own personalities, had changed Dud's mind, and while I saw occasional glimpses of that fact, it only really jelled with that short, sorrowful text, *Im sad*.

You might well be wondering why we didn't lock the ducks in their pen at night. The reason had to do with how overly-zealous I had been when we first brought Boyfriend and Ethel home. Every night, I had to chase them around the yard in order to get them to go in the pen. The process terrified them, and once I figured that out, I didn't have the heart to force them into their pen anymore. Consequently, they spent their nights as they spent their days: wandering around a yard that, in darkness, turned out to be very unsafe indeed.

Russell's Rabbits

I was on the front porch of the Critter Shack, painting an old wicker planter when I heard neighbor Russell calling from next door. Passing traffic whittled his comment down to one word: rabbits. Walking over to the fence that separates our properties, I gave him a stern look and inquired, "Russell, have you mowed another rabbit?" The previous summer, Russell had told me that he'd accidentally mowed over a small rabbit in his yard. He hadn't meant to do it, but it was a ghastly tale all the same.

"No," he answered, "I was weed whacking, though, and I think I might've whacked a baby bunny." He held up his hand, the thumb and forefinger millimeters apart, to indicate what a close call it had been. "I checked him over," he continued, "but it looked like he wasn't breathing."

I shook my head as we rounded the side of his house and walked toward the back yard. "What is it with you and rabbits?! You tell me a horror story about them almost every year!"

Russell grinned. "It's hard to see them!" he said defensively. He actually wasn't kidding. I frowned as I walked over to the spot he was pointing to. Indeed, it was impossible to see the tiny bunny unless you were right up on him. I bent over the little fellow.

"It looked like he wasn't breathing," Russell repeated. But I caught the thing that he had missed: while the rabbit's body was completely motionless, his little nose was wiggling. I reached down and made to pick him up, but at the last second, he sprang out of my grasp and hopped three or four feet away.

"Won't his mom reject him if he smells like a human?" Russell wanted to know.

"Nah, that's a myth," I replied absently as I followed the bunny, "and besides, once they've left the nest, they don't go back." When I tried to pick him up a second time, he dashed off and wiggled under an errant cinder block that had taken up residence next to Russell's shed. I'd seen no outward signs of injury, so I concluded that the small creature was simply trying to figure out what his next move should be; it was a big world, and he clearly hadn't had much experience in it.

Satisfied that he was o.k., we headed back out to Russell's front yard, at which point he asked whether I knew anyone who did landscaping work on the cheap. Russell had a solid wall out front comprised of what I referred to as "old people shrubs." You know the ones, the yews that everyone and their cousin used as landscaping fifty-odd years ago. They've fallen out of favor in recent years, but Russell had what looked to be a ten-foot high wall of them, running parallel to the street. And while Russell was a nice enough guy that he wouldn't say such a thing himself, the hedge spoke loud and clear, and what it said was, "Fuck off and leave me alone!" It was my kind of hedge!

Alas, I didn't happen to know anyone who could trim his privacy hedge, so we parted company and I went back to painting my plant stand. It was as I dabbed the brush on the legs that I thought about how satisfying it was when an animal crisis ended well, and I wondered absently where the next critter adventure might take me.

This Means War!

As it happened, the next critter adventure took me to a place I never expected to find myself: the battlefield. In the days after Boyfriend's death, Dud had begun to mutter oaths about shooting the raccoons who ventured onto our property. Initially, I gave him my stock answer, "No, we're not killing animals!" But something in me had changed, just a little, so that the next time Dud broached the subject, my answer became, "How are you going to shoot anything without a gun?"

"Bill Davis has a .22 rifle," he replied. That threw me for a loop. For one thing, Duddy had already discussed this with Bill? For another thing, Bill, and his wife, Carol, were two of the most decent, one might even say "genteel," people I knew. On the back side of middle-age, Bill was a lawyer while Carol had been an executive at a local corporation. They'd made enough money to design their own nice home in the posh Kensington Country Club neighborhood, and that nice home backed onto Kensington Lake. In other words, these were *not* the sort of people you would expect to own guns.

Even worse, Dud let slip that Carol had killed a squirrel with the very same .22! I couldn't even begin to imagine it!

I *did* give the matter further thought, though, so that the next time Dud brought up the subject, my answer was now, "If you're going to kill them, then *kill* them! I don't want any suffering! Agreed?"

"Agreed," he replied.

If you're wondering what brought me to the point where I was willing to sanction critter killing, it was this: we brought Ethel and Boyfriend home so that they could live safely in our yard. Boyfriend could be gimpy without having to worry about the usual McKinnon's Pond predators – hawks, dogs, coyotes and the like. But after two years of relative peace in the yard, we'd become lax, and a raccoon had ended what had otherwise been a quiet, easy life, and I was mad as hell. It was my fault that we had become lax, and it was my fault that Boyfriend was dead. Nothing would bring him back, of course, but maybe if we took out a few raccoons, Ethel and the Pekins would be safe. And so I agreed to let Dud shoot them.

His first attempt involved him sitting in a chair out in the back yard, lying in wait, as it were. I glanced out the window into the darkness and took note of his posture: sitting rigidly upright, I could tell even from behind that he sat there waiting with grim determination for whatever came into the yard. As it happened, nothing actually came into the yard in the hour that he was out there, so he came back into the house, announcing that he would try again the next night.

When the next night came, he tried a different tack: this time, he sat in the darkness of our spare bedroom, rifle aimed out the window onto the back patio. He would shoot through the window screen, he told me. That night, a raccoon *did* come onto the patio, and began to eat from the bowl of duck food we'd put out as bait. Dud took a shot but wasn't entirely sure that he'd hit the animal. It immediately ran off through the yard and under the privacy fence. We saw no sign of injury.

"I aimed at his head," Dud told me later that night. "It was hard to see in the dark."

Something jogged my memory, then, and I shook my head, telling Dud, "No, you have to aim for the heart, not the head. The head's too small. Aim for the heart."

Dud nodded in agreement. "That makes sense," he said. Who knew my Army training would come in handy thirty-three years after the fact?!

I know what you're thinking: *You were in the Army, Kelly?* The answer is yes. But only for a short while. As it turned out, I discovered that I was a dedicated peacenik who didn't actually *want* to "kill a commie for my mommy." I made it through Basic Training and Advanced Individual Training, but the Army proved too much for someone who already suffered from debilitating depression and a marked inability to get along with my fellow humans. I was granted a discharge well before I had finished my period of enlistment, but it must be noted that I was a hell of a good shot! I was equally adept with both the M16 and the .38 revolver that was issued to female MP's. I particularly enjoyed taking out an empty training tank once with a LAW – a Light, Anti-tank Weapon [basically, a hand-held rocket launcher]. And while the Army had some pretty cool toys to play with, the last thing I wanted to do was spend three years being owned 24/7 by a bureaucratic entity that was not known for gender equality. When my discharge was approved, I heaved a massive sigh of relief.

I hadn't had anything to do with guns in the intervening years and, initially, I didn't want anything to do with Bill Davis's rifle; I was content to let Dud do all the killing. But Dud had plans to go up to Michigan to help his buddy Tommy open the family cottage for the summer, which meant that I would be on my own for five days, and the neighborhood raccoons would be coming and going with impunity. "Screw that!" I thought. I knew how to shoot a gun, and I didn't feel like sitting on the sidelines while Dud was gone. So I asked him to show me how the .22 worked and he gave me quick tutorial. Thinking about what must've been a horrible death for Boyfriend, I gritted my teeth and pumped myself up with the thought, *"This means war!"*

THE KILL ZONE

The first night that I tried my hand at raccoon killing, I set out a bowl of dog food near the back fence. As I sat staring at it in the gathering darkness, I realized that once nightfall actually fell, I wouldn't be able to see the bowl anymore. Rummaging around in the bits and pieces that Dud had tossed behind the shed, I found a short length of board that was painted white on one side. I propped the board against the fence, the white side facing me as I sat in a deck chair some twenty-five feet away.

I had dressed for mosquito weather: socks, jeans, a zip hoodie with the hood up. I doused myself with *Deep Woods Off,* because we'd had a lot of rain lately and the little bloodsuckers were out in force. I didn't want to be distracted by bugs and possibly miss my chance with a dog food-eating raccoon. Once I was settled in, I sat the rifle across my lap and waited quietly as the darkness began to gather around me.

My posture was much the same as Duddy's had been, that first night he waited in the yard. I felt the same grim determination that he had, and one thought kept racing through my head: "Bring it on, you bastards!" Never in my life had I wanted something more than I wanted to take out the murderous beast that had killed my duck.

You mess with my duck and you mess with me!

It must've been about twenty minutes after I sat down that I saw the dark shape moving near the bowl of dog food. Instantly, I was on alert, raising the rifle slowly to my shoulder and squinting through the scope into the darkness. I could just make out the large, familiar rounded raccoon shape. I took a deep breath, and, remembering more of my Army training, slowly exhaled. You're meant to shoot on the exhale, not the inhale, because your body is more relaxed on the exhale. Inhaling creates body tension, which can throw off your aim. I inhaled once more, and as I exhaled, I squeezed the trigger. The .22 wasn't particularly loud, but the noise shattered the evening quiet all the same. I wasn't sure whether I'd hit the raccoon or not until I saw that same shape run, awkwardly, flailing a leg, back the way he'd come. When I swept the area with a flashlight, he was gone. I had no way of knowing whether I'd fatally wounded him or not.

My conscience was surprising quiet on the subject of having shot an animal. I didn't lose any sleep that night, or any subsequent nights. Indeed, once the first shot had been fired, I felt comfortable moving forward with another attempt the following night.

The next evening, I changed the location of the Kill Zone. I didn't know whether the raccoon I'd shot would come back, but if he did, it was a safe bet that he wouldn't want to revisit the site that had frightened – and possibly wounded – him. So I put the white board up against the fence between our property and neighbor Russell's. I set the same bowl of dog food against it, then moved my chair into another area of the yard. I was fairly optimistic about this new Kill Zone. At least for a few minutes.

As I sat again in the gathering darkness, my mind wandered off into several different places – none of them important – before I suddenly realized that if I took a shot from this trajectory and missed, the bullet might well go straight into Russell's above-ground pool. I grimaced as a picture came to mind, that of pool water slowly leaking from a bullet hole, and a discussion with Russell about what brand of replacement pool we'd be buying him. "Crap!" I thought, "That would *not* be good!" I got up and rearranged the Kill Zone, but to no avail. No racoons came by in the hour that I sat waiting. The next few nights, it rained, and then Dud came back from Michigan. I had hoped that he would take up the raccoon hunt again and let the Critter Lady off the hook, but he seemed to tire of the mission; there were no more grimly determined hunts.

About a week after he came home, I decided to have at it again, and created a third Kill Zone. This one would be slightly different, though. This time, I strung an outdoor extension cord from the duck's pond (where we had an aerator plugged in) to the back side of the shed. I strategically placed the white board and set the bowl of by-now rather moldy dog food in front of it. My deck chair ran parallel to Russell's fence, and there was a shrub between myself and the bowl of food that was meant to partially obscure my view of the raccoon (and his of me). To top off the arrangement, I brought out a small nightlight and plugged it into the end of the extension cord. It produced a small amount of light – just enough to enable my 52 year-old eyes to see what I needed to see. I sat quietly for over an hour before calling it a night. Either the racoons were coming later at night (because *something* was still stopping by to steal the eggs from the girls' nests), or they were taking time off from nocturnal visits altogether.

When I decided to have another go at my third Kill Zone a few days later, I noticed that the rifle was gone. I asked Duddy where it went, and he insisted that Bill Davis wanted it back, which may or may not have been true. A part of me suspected that Dud worried that I might, in the midst of one of my depressive episodes, actually use it on myself. I gave that idea some thought. I got as far as picturing myself with the barrel in my mouth, pulling the trigger, before I shuddered involuntarily at the whole idea. *No*, I thought, *not going to happen!*

In all my thoughts – and there had been many – about attempting suicide, none of them had ever involved using a gun. The possibility of not actually dying but rather, rendering myself helpless to ever do more than breathe on my own again was simply too frightening to risk. No matter how awful my life had been, no matter how deep the pit of depression, I never considered using a gun to kill myself, and that certainly wasn't going to change now.

Interestingly, I once shared space in a hospital psyche ward with a woman who *had* shot herself in the head. The story I heard (from a reasonably reliable source) was that she had put the gun to her forehead, pulled the trigger, and ended up in the ER. I don't know whether the ER docs succeeded in removing the bullet from her head, but from the look of the no-doubt purposely-large stitches they left after their attempt, it was immediately clear that they hadn't bothered to bring in a plastic surgeon to close the wound; Old Bullet Head (as I privately called her) would be forever marked by that large X of stitches in the center of her forehead. It was a cruel thing to do, but I've learned that there are a number of people working in emergency medicine who have no empathy whatsoever for troubled minds.

If you're wondering how Old Bullet Head survived the attempt, I can say only this: I don't know what sort of personality she had before, or whether the attempt gave her a self-inflicted lobotomy, but when she arrived on the psyche ward, she approached me and asked if the food was any good. In fact, she was walking, talking evidence that if you're going to shoot yourself in the head, you should first do some research about *where*, precisely, to aim the gun.

In any case, I brought the subject of gun ownership up to Dud more than once. If Bill Davis did, indeed, want his gun back, then we were going to need something for raccoon control. After experiencing the awkwardness of a gun stock made for a man (meaning that it was larger, and more difficult to use, than one made for the smaller body of a woman), I decided that I wanted a handgun. A small caliber would do fine, something without much kick that would take out a raccoon at 25 feet or less. When I'd made it clear to Dud that I wasn't going to let the subject slide, he finally promised that when he made some money (his work, being seasonal, was somewhat unreliable), we would buy one. I aimed (if you'll pardon the pun) to hold him to that.

They Have an App for That!

I've been seeing my current shrink since 1998, and because the boundaries had become somewhat fuzzy after so many years of rather intimate familiarity, I know more about her than most people do about their next-door neighbors. Still, there was plenty that I *didn't* know, which made it all the more surreal the day that we sat in her office talking guns.

I'd been telling her about our attempts to thin the local raccoon herd, and how awkward the .22 rifle had been for me to use. The scope was nice, but trying to jam that gun stock into my shoulder and aim effectively was tricky. I mentioned Dud's comment about us buying a gun. "I want a handgun," I told her. "Something small without much kick to it." To my considerable surprise, she remarked, "I've got a nice little .22. I think it's a Ruger." My eyebrows rose to the ceiling.

"Wait! What?" I said with some confusion. "You own a gun?"

"Yep," she said, as though I had just asked whether she owned a car.

"*You! Own a gun?*" This was really big. I knew her politics were a little conservative, but this was...you know...*big!* "Why?"

"Are you kidding?" she asked incredulously, "I work in dodgy neighborhoods!" She wasn't wrong. Lately, in addition to her everyday work counseling sexual abuse survivors, she'd taken up the cause of human trafficking. At first, she was asked to be on the board of a local rescue group. Then, because of her connections, and pit bull-fierce[2] determination, she'd been appointed director. If anyone could rescue a human trafficking victim from the clutches of scummy pimps, and the horrors that went with being bought, sold, and traded like chattel, it was my therapist!

"How do you know where to find the pimps?" I asked. "How do they end up here?"

"I-45," she said. "They kidnap them in Tennessee, Kentucky, wherever, and drive them up here. They keep them pliant by making them take drugs every day, pass them around to paying customers, then maybe take them to Chicago for a while, bring them back via Detroit. They use I-45 the same way drug runners do."

While the Interstate 45 corridor was the known north-south drug-running route in this part of the country, I'd had no idea that people were trafficking more than just drugs. But my shrink knew. She knew where the local stash houses were, and generally had her finger on the pulse of what was

---

[2] My apologies for perpetuating an unfair stereotype about pit bulls. In fact, if you're not Michael Vick, training dogs to fight for you, pit bulls are as loving and friendly as any other breed of dog. I simply wanted to create an image of my shrink as a woman with a level of tenacity that makes grown men nervous.

going on in any given part of town. And she was right: it was all extremely dodgy.

She told me a story, then, about how they'd rescued a girl and taken her to a safe house a couple of towns away. The safe house was run by nuns, which apparently was not a good fit with the rescued girl, so they moved her to a safe house closer to where her sister lived. The girl asked to be allowed to visit her sister. They dropped her off up the block from her sister's house, not knowing that the pimp had a satellite house nearby. The pimp saw the girl, dragged her to the satellite house and beat her to a pulp. He also set his dogs on her. It was a miracle that she survived. In one of those instances where the system fails miserably, no one in the local law enforcement community did what they were supposed to do, and the pimp essentially got away with the beating. Until my shrink heard about his dogs.

The pimp had two adult rottweilers and nine puppies, the rescued girl told her. The shrink chewed on that for a while. She happened to be downtown at the local farmer's market a week or so later when she realized that the Perry County Dog Warden's office was just a few blocks away. Off she went, to report a vicious dog attack. The dogs were confiscated a week later. One way or another, my shrink was going to put a dent in the lifestyle of the human trafficking pimp.

"Have you shot the gun?" I wanted to know.

"Yes," she replied. "There's a range in Mansing." Mansing was the next town over. Boy, the things you find out about someone! I didn't even know there *was* range in Mansing. She pulled out her cell phone.

"I'm *not* a member of the NRA," she said emphatically, "but they have this free app. Check it out!" She handed me her phone. The next thing I know, I'm deciding whether I'm 'shaky' with a gun or a 'dead eye,' then trying to shoot the targets that were jumping all over the phone's screen.

"How are you supposed to hit these?" I asked in frustration, "They keep moving around!" She came over and sat down beside me, taking her phone back and rapidly touching the screen again and again. By the looks of it, she was clearly a 'dead eye'! I watched, amused. Even after seventeen years, and all the insanity we'd been through, the last thing I expected was to find my shrink showing me what a good shot she was on the NRA's free shoot-'em-up app!

But there was more to it than that. Indeed, after all those years of insanity, it was extremely telling that she never once voiced any concern about what else I might do with a loaded gun. At one point during our session, she even texted her gun-owning brother to find out what sort of thing might prevent me from buying one. Suffering from depression? Apparently not a problem. Multiple hospitalizations? Definite roadblock. And my one psyche ward stay didn't count as 'multiple.'

"Well, there you have it!" I remarked, steering her back to the subject of my lingering guilt over Boyfriend's death before our session ran out. "I should've done something!" I insisted.

"It's not your fault," she replied.

"Either way, he's still dead." I said morosely. "And it happened on my watch."

"No matter how they die, you're going to grieve. There's no getting around that. But the guilt isn't doing you any good." As usual, she was right.

What Does a Dying Walrus Sound Like?

I was in the back yard hosing down duck poops when I heard the noise. It sounded like the agonized groans of a dying walrus, and it was coming from neighbor Russell's back yard. I peered through the hole in the privacy fence but saw nothing amiss. Still, the noise persisted, and it was clearly coming from the vicinity of his pool. I shrugged and went back to my duck chores.

As luck would have it, I ran into Russell later that same day at Maytag's. You may recall that I worked as a greeter for a time at Maytag's; it's where everyone on the east side of Whoville takes care of their grocery, health and beauty, clothing, computer, and various other needs. Russell was standing in line at the check-out when I accosted him with, "Russell! What the *hell* is that awful noise coming from your pool pump? It sounds like a dying walrus, for God's sake!"

"I know," he grinned sheepishly, "something's wrong with the pump. I had to turn it off."

"How's the water?" I inquired, hoping he'd extend an invitation for a swim.

"Seventy-four degrees," he reported. My hope flagged, then; invite or no, there was no way I was going in water that cold!

"Hmm," I replied, "too cold for my liking!

"Me, too," he said. "Hopefully this warmer weather will heat it up!"

"Any more rabbit problems?" I asked. I figured that while I was standing there, I might as well get up to speed on any recent mower massacres.

"No," he laughed, "none this week!"

"Thank God for that!" I exclaimed. I gave him a wave and walked on, knowing that at some point in the near future, there would be both rabbit issues and pool invitations coming our way.

Back to Basics

In keeping with my on-going bomb-proofing training, I continued to look for opportunities to teach Bit new things. This was quite a challenge given that we never left the property, and that he was pretty much familiar with everything about it at that point. He knew there was a giant poop pile next to the track; He knew where the dips in the ground were in the back pasture; He knew that there were cars and dogs and kids and the occasional visit from the UPS guy up by the front barn. So teaching him anything new required a fair amount of intrepidity on my part. Sometimes, though, the ideas were painfully obvious, like the monsoon rains that left a record amount of water all over Northwest Ohio.

There was an entire day of rain, the last week of June. Weather forecasters warned of flash floods and possible wind damage, but you know know how inaccurate they can be. Unfortunately, this time they were right on the money, and over a period of 12 hours, six inches of rain fell in Whoville.

The ducks had a field day. They swam happily all over the back yard, darting here and there as they spotted worms floating in what was by then a giant, half-acre lake. Ethel, who was nesting, chose to ride out the weather in her pen, but Penny and Daffy made the most of the opportunity to feast on something other than corn and duck pellets. And while the deluge inched ever closer to the Critter Shack, it never actually breached the foundation, and by the very next day, the water in the yard had receded considerably.

I had watched the rain with a certain inner misery: all this flooding meant that the track outside The Harmony Barn would be one big lake for who knew how long. I'd either have to ride in the arena (boring!) or not ride at all until Lake Harmony dried up. Neither option appealed to me, particularly because I'd be paying Bit's lease whether I rode him or not. Staring out at the rain, the hamster in my head doing fast laps on his wheel, the solution eventually presented itself: ride Bit in the puddles.

O.k., so it seemed obvious to you; sometimes these things elude me! And while you may think that walking through puddles has no bomb-proof training value at all, it would actually prove to be just the sort of challenge Bit needed to overcome.

Given that horses are prey animals – meaning that predators eat them – many horses are skittish about things that don't even make sense to you or me, like puddles. Riding instructor Connie told me it's because they can't tell what's under the water, which means that that innocent looking puddle could be hiding a terrifying horse-eating Thing. And while a good many horses don't give puddles a second thought, the minute I aimed Bit toward one, he let me know that he wanted nothing to do with it. It was time to whip out my Wellies and show him that puddles were not his enemy.

More often than not, I have to walk Bit through whatever thing he finds objectionable. In this instance, I literally had to walk through every single puddle myself before he was willing to try it. I would plunge right in, stomping my feet around and splashing both of us in the process. In one especially deep puddle, I lost my balance and almost fell over. Water went up, over, and into my boots, and at that point I could either get angry about the situation or laugh. I laughed. "See, Bit? It's just water, Bubby!" I leaned against the back pasture fence and tried to remove my boot. The water had created suction, and it took a few tries before I got the boot off and emptied. By then, Bit had become more or less inured to the whole water thing, which meant that it was time to get in the saddle.

I was using my new bareback pad more or less all the time at this point. I was still having balance issues that I wanted to correct, and it seemed like Bit didn't find the pad as objectionable as his usual saddle. I'd gotten into the habit of tying the reins to the loop on the pad, and then taking one rein in each hand to steer. It was a lazy thing to do, and it took me a couple of weeks (in which it rained several more times, topping off the puddles in the process) to realize that my lazy approach was creating more problems than it solved.

I noticed the issue as I guided Bit through a particularly large puddle. There was a tiny pond on one side of the back pasture, and the monsoon caused it to breach its banks. By the time I started riding, rather than walking Bit through the puddles, the tiny pond and one of the track puddles had merged. This created an incredibly dangerous situation that only I was aware of. Bit had no idea where the pond's bank ended and where the puddle began, he only knew that he didn't want to get too close to the arbor vitae that bordered that stretch of track. So he veered to the left, and I suddenly realized that at any moment, he would find himself sliding down the bank of the pond.

It's important to keep in mind that Bit has EPM – a neurological disease that affects his balance. Bit would have no doubt slid around on that hidden bank, and probably have fallen down into the pond, as well, if he had continued his leftward-leaning trajectory. I quickly tugged on the right rein, pulling him toward those dreaded shrubs, and it was then that I noticed what I had failed to see for the past two weeks: I wasn't guiding Bit as much as I was pulling on the reins one way or the other, no doubt confusing the hell out of him while at the same time, creating a very uncomfortable situation in his mouth.

Reining properly is an art form. You're not actually *meant* to simply tug on the left rein or the right rein. What you're meant to do is a subtle dance of the hands in which you signal your request by lightly touching his neck with the rein. In this way, if your right rein touches the right side of his neck, he knows that he is supposed to turn left. And vice versa. All of this came back to me later, after I'd put Bit back out with the herd and given myself time to chew on my observation.

You may recall from NBM that I once paid an animal communicator to see whether Bit had anything to say that I needed to hear. After our discussion, I was no wiser as to whether the woman actually *could* communicate with critters, but even now I remember that she remarked, "You have soft hands." I had no idea what that meant, and asked her to elaborate.

"You're gentle with the reins," she replied, "You don't hurt his mouth."

Hmm, I thought. *Good to know.*

I thought now about how my lazy rein use was actually pretty rough on Bit's mouth, and I felt awful. I also felt like a rank amateur who had forgotten all of her training. At Bit's expense. *Dammit!* I thought. *I need to do better than this!* I immediately resolved to get back to basics, then, and do things the way they were supposed to be done.

In my daily surf around the waters of Facebook, I almost always see links to Stacy Westfall's blog. Stacy Westfall is an internationally known horsewoman. She studied at Ohio's own University of Findlay (which has a renowned equine program), and has competed, and trained horses, for years. Her blogs are a great way to learn from a true master for free, and I almost always bookmark the links and read her blog entries later when I have time. I would recommend her blogs to anyone who wants to learn more about how horses think, and how you can improve your horsemanship.

One particular day, though, I came across a link to a blog by a woman I'd never heard of, Anna Blake. When I went looking, I found a website with a lot of blog entries about horses, and one in particular caught my eye. She was writing about what she called "calming signals," things that horses do to calm themselves in stressful situations, and how horses send those cues to humans. This was the part that really interested me:

"When a horse looks away, either with his eyes or whole head and neck, it's a calming cue. He uses a signal like this when he feels pressured and wants the rider to know he senses the person's agitation or aggression. In the horse's mind, he is communicating clearly and with respect."

How many times has Bit done this? I wondered. *And I ignored or misread it.*

Indeed, Bit looked away frequently when I had him in the cross-ties and was about to saddle him up. Bit had been "girthy" for years – more years than I had known him – and I tried to be as gentle as possible, but there was simply no way to avoid tightening the girth if I wanted to stay on his back. I would tighten it in increments, distracting him in between by giving him a snack, or moving the mounting block into position. But no matter how carefully I tightened that girth, Bit always reacted with head-tossing, attempts to bite me, and all that looking away that Anna Blake was talking about. I started chewing on this information, as well, and came to the conclusion that I really needed to make some changes in that routine I'd fallen into.

The first thing I did was resolve to start using the reins properly again. I would tie them to the loop in the bareback pad only long enough to get on Bit's back. Then I would take them properly in hand and get back to being the light touch that I used to be. Secondly, while there was no way to tighten the girth other than the careful way I'd been doing it, I could certainly change my overall demeanor from one of impatience (*"Bit! Knock it off!"*) to one of empathy (*"I know, Bubby. I'm really trying to be careful!"*). Bit might not understand the words, but he could certainly grasp the tone of voice.

When I put my plan together, the very next day, the results were immediate: Bit went where he was directed to go, when I directed him to do so, and his behavior in the cross-ties improved in equal measure to the vibe I was putting forth. He still acted up, letting me know that he didn't like the girth being tightened, but the degree to which he did it lessened considerably. For once, the fix had been relatively simple, and, even better, I'd managed to figure it out for myself. Hopefully, amping up my respect for Bit would ultimately help amp up his for me.

Ethel

In the months after Boyfriend's death, Ethel's own health began to deteriorate. The slight limp she'd developed over the years (which was probably due to old age) increased significantly, to the point where she now used her tail as ballast. Instead of her tail feathers waving upright as she walked, they now shifted, down toward the ground, left or right, depending on which leg she was walking on. It was meant to keep her from toppling over, and much of the time, it worked. Still, it didn't fix the original problem – the pronounced limp – and that limp ultimately kept her from walking as much as she should have to keep her legs from deteriorating even more. Because of that decreased activity, her legs weakened to the point that, in order to lift herself up from a sitting position, she fell into the habit of pushing the end of her bill against the ground as a boost. Ethel had clearly reached advanced old age.

Late that summer, I noticed that a cloud had developed over her left eye. It looked like a cataract, and it rendered her completely blind in that eye. This was really bad: Ethel needed two good eyes to keep a lookout for raccoons. She obviously wouldn't be able to out-run them anymore, but she needed two good eyes just the same. There was nothing to be done for it except to start wondering whether it was time to euthanize.

We'd already been putting her in the pen at night for safekeeping. After Boyfriend died, and I was in the middle of a period of abject misery over my inability to have kept him safe, I texted Duddy with the decision, "We're going to put Ethel in the pen at night. That's what it's for and we're going to use it." Surprisingly, after all the terror she and Boyfriend had originally experienced over being put in the pen at night when they first came to live with us, now Ethel was almost agreeable to the idea, and it took very little effort on my part to get her to go in it at night. Indeed, all I had to do was slowly walk up behind her and say, "In the pen, Ethel, in the pen!" As long as I kept walking behind her, aiming her in the direction I wanted her to go, she would keep walking until she'd walked herself right up the ramp and into the soft pile of straw that I fluffed up for her every day. I would offer her a few worms, then add her food and water, telling her, "Here's your corn, Ethel, and here's your bucket! You have a good night, Ethel. I love you and I'll see you in the morning!" And then I'd closed the pen door and lock it. Ethel would offer up a few quiet squeaks as I walked away. It was the same routine every night.

I didn't mention my private wonderings about whether it was time to euthanize, but apparently, Dud was thinking along the same lines.

"Should we put her to sleep, do you think?" he asked one night.

"I've been wondering that myself," I replied. "My usual criteria is suffering. Do you think she is?"

"Well, she's *got* to be uncomfortable with that limp, and she's half-blind..." he trailed off, clearly unsure what his own criteria should be.

"Yes," I acknowledged, "but every single day, she comes out of the pen, and walks around the yard. Every time I look out there, she's someplace different than the last time I looked. So she's still choosing to participate in life."

"She won't make it through a cold winter, though," he remarked. I nodded in agreement.

"Probably not, but it's only August. We've got a while before we have to worry about that."

"True," he said, and made no further comment. Apparently, we had silently agreed to take a wait-and-see approach to the end of Ethel's life.

As it turned out, we never had to make the decision. Toward the end of August, as I opened the pen one morning, I saw immediately that she was gone. "Oh, Ethel," I said sadly as I smoothed her tail feathers. I went into the house and texted Dud with the news, choosing not to disturb her body until he'd come home to say good-bye. There was no real rush to do anything at all since the worst had already happened. I gave some thought to what we should do with her body – Boyfriend's had gone out with the trash – before Dud got there, and decided that I wanted Ethel cremated, and I wanted to bring the ashes home. I'd had three cats and Pretty Boy Duck cremated, and their ashes had come with me wherever I moved. I liked the idea of their portability, the idea that even if they were dead, some part of them remained nearby. And so it would be with Ethel. When Dud asked, I told him that I wouldn't make that same request about either of the Pekins. "But Ethel, I want her here with me," I said. Dud nodded his assent.

After a time, a few hours in which I resisted facing the fact of her death, I took a towel and went out to the pen. I wrapped Ethel up, with only her head sticking out, and sat down on a chair nearby, cradling her in my arms. "I'm going to miss you, old girl," I told her. My mind couldn't take in the enormity of the loss. That decade in which I'd known and loved her seemed like a blur that had taken place over a matter of minutes rather than years. I *knew* her time was coming, but only in that abstract, it'll-happen-one-day kind of way that always ends up setting you up for complete devastation when it actually happens.

While I sat with Ethel, Penny walked up. She stood a few feet away, looking at us.

"Want to say good-bye, Pen?" I asked, laying Ethel carefully on the ground in front of my feet. I watched Penny watch Ethel, then. She would tilt her head down to get a good look, then glance away for a minute, as if trying to digest the fact of Ethel's death. Then she would tilt her head and look again. She did that several times before turning and walking away. It was time to go.

It was as I was driving home from the vet's office – hell, I didn't even make it out of the parking lot first before bursting into tears – that the grief really hit me. Ethel had been the last in a long line of ducks that I had lovingly cared for, over the years. I couldn't begin to remember how many there had actually been at McKinnon's Pond, but due to the rescue efforts of Aimee Van Staten, Ethel had been the final link to that time in my life. With her passing went an entire decade of purpose-filled love and care on my part, a decade in which I had a reason to get out of bed, fight past some Godawful days/weeks/months of debilitating depression, and define not only who I was, but who and what I was meant to be: I was the Critter Lady, the one who cared for critters that no one else wanted. Those McKinnon's Pond ducks had been my cause celebre, and through my writing and my pleas for assistance, I'd managed to acquire quite a following of locals who regularly donated food for them, as well as vets who willingly lowered their fees when those ducks needed medical treatment. It had been a noble cause, and now it was over.

I hadn't forgotten the two remaining Pekins. I had taken them on for their lifetimes, and they would stay in our back yard for however many years that turned out to be. But they were strangers to me, by comparison. Ethel and I had a long history; the Pekins and I did not. A number of nights, I lay sleepless in bed, thinking about that very thing, and wondering whether I'd *ever* have the kind of friendship with them that I'd enjoyed with Ethel. To that end, I realized, I would need to actually *cultivate* one, do more than just hose down their poops and refill their food bowl. I would have to do what I originally did with the ducks at McKinnon's Pond: I would have to get to know them. It wasn't something I particularly felt like doing, in the midst of grief, but I decided to do it anyway.

Skunky

In the weeks after Ethel's death, a new raccoon showed up on the property. He was so small that I considered him a juvenile, and he was so unafraid that I didn't know what to make of him. I would try to chase him off the back patio, but he never actually *ran* anywhere; his usual speed was an unhurried walk. I'd clap my hands and yell at him – often getting within touching distance in the process – but nothing seemed to faze him. Even when I tried to scoot him along using the snow shovel that had spent the summer leaning against the side of the house, he merely looked up at me from under the yew shrub. I would stand over him, completely vexed, having no idea what to try next.

"Just whack him over the head with the shovel," Dud suggested.

I looked at him incredulously, then looked at Junior Raccoon, considering the prospect. I looked at his stupid little expressive eyes, and his stupid little cute twitchy nose, and I looked back at Dud and said flatly, "There's no way I'm doing that!" Shoot him with a gun, yes. Smash his head in with a shovel, no.

Regardless of his diminutive size, Junior scared hell out of the ducks. Dud heard them quacking in the middle of a September night and said, "The ducks!" loud enough to wake me. Blindly, I jumped out of bed, raced to the family room and threw open the sliding glass door, intent on surveying the yard. But before I could even set foot on the patio, both girls came racing toward the house. They were so terrified that they actually ran right into the family room!

Try as I might to bribe them with worms, in ordinary circumstances, neither Pekin was willing to come any further into the house than was necessary to grab the treat, and the moment they had it in their bills, they would immediately run back outside. For them both to come all the way into the house and stand there was unprecedented, and spoke volumes about the level of their fear.

Dud and I stared down at them, unsure how to proceed. In their turn, both girls looked at us and it was clear they were wondering what their next move should be. I sat down in a chair and talked softly to them, trying to reassure them that they'd made the right choice by coming in. After a couple of minutes, Penny pooped on the rug. It figured! It was about that time that Dud announced, in the bossy way he has when he thinks he can get away with issuing an edict from on high, "Well, they're *not* spending the winter in here!"

"No one said they were, Dud!" I sighed, "but they clearly don't want to be outside right now, either!"

Fifteen-odd minutes later, both ducks felt sufficiently safe to go back out. They were on the patio for less than a minute before they came running back to the step. Again, I slid the door open, and again, they walked back into the house. This time, though, while Dud and I were debating what to do with them, they managed to wander through the kitchen and dining room before finding themselves in the dead-end that is the laundry room. It finally hit me that we could lock them in the duck pen that hadn't been used again since Ethel died. I grabbed Daffy and put her in Dud's arms, and grabbed Penny for myself, and we closed them into the pen. Finally satisfied that neither duck would meet an untimely demise that night, we fell back into bed.

I mentioned our on-going raccoon problems to Barn Urchin Lydia, who had done a bit of duck sitting for us earlier that summer. She had been tasked with getting Ethel into the pen every night, and letting her out again every morning while we went on vacation. Now she was back, getting the lowdown on the house/duck/cat sitting we would need her to do come Thanksgiving week. It was as I was outlining some of her responsibilities that I happened to mention the raccoon.

"He's either really dumb, really acclimated to humans, really deaf, or I don't know what!" I remarked. "In any other circumstances, he'd be a cute little bugger, but as it is, he's just a threat to the ducks!" Lydia responded by saying that her dad had a humane trap she thought we could borrow, and I said, "Great! Feel free to use it while you're house sitting!" But Lydia was even more helpful: a few days later, after my sorry little brain had totally forgotten our conversation, Dud stuck his head out the patio door and hollered, "Company!" I had no idea what he was talking about – we never have company! But sure enough, out onto the patio stepped Lydia, holding the humane trap she'd mentioned.

"Oh, *cool!*" I said enthusiastically, "Thanks so much for bringing that!" After she left, I went to the store and bought a can of cat food while Dud figured out how the trap worked. Since every raccoon we'd seen in the yard had been brave enough to walk onto the patio, that was where we set the trap. I was sure we'd get great results with it, but much to my surprise, I turned out to be wrong.

Several nights in a row, we set the trap in different areas of the yard. And several days in a row, we went out to find that the only thing in the trap was the ants who'd made themselves at home in the can of food. Puzzled but undeterred, I tried yet another area of the yard, by the back fence, near the hole I'd seen raccoons running through when I chased them. Sooner or later, I was sure, *something* would find its way into the trap.

In the meantime, I made the decision that the two Pekins would now spend their nights locked in the pen. To my great surprise, they proved much easier to catch than I had expected. This had a lot to do with *where* in the yard they were when I grabbed them. I found that cornering them literally in the area where our fence met neighbor Russell's garage wall, while using the pond skimmer to herd them, made it very difficult for them to get away, and consequently, very easy for me to grab them one at a time. I would hold the duck in my arms for a minute or so, telling her what a good girl she was and trying to get her accustomed to being handled in the process. Once both ducks were in the pen, I put a bucket of water in with them, locked them in in a fashion that even a genius raccoon wouldn't figure out, told them good-night, and went to bed with a level of peace of mind that I hadn't enjoyed for quite some time.

I'm sure there are duck pen experts out there who believe that there's no such thing as a raccoon-proof pen, but I feel confident that Dud built just that. Using quality lumber, and ancillary materials, along with the specifications I gave him based on the experiences of people I'd known who'd suffered the anguish of a raccoon attacking their animals, Dud built a strong, safe pen. And while I'm sure that raccoons looked in on the ducks every night via the screen window we'd put in the east side of the structure, there was no way for them to *get* in. I like to think that fact gave the girls some sense of security.

Meanwhile, on the fifth morning of Operation Critter Catch, when I went out to release the girls from the pen, I noticed that something had finally sprung the trap. Walking over, I was surprised to see not a raccoon but a rather small skunk, curled up in ball, asleep, the empty cat food can by his head.

"Skunky?" I inquired gently, "are you o.k.?" Around the outside of the cage, I noticed evidence of considerable digging. Whether it was caused by Skunky originally trying to find a way in to the cat food, or a raccoon trying to find a way in to Skunky, I couldn't say. Eventually, Skunky lifted his head and peered out at me. *Aww!* I thought, *what a cute little booger!* Carefully, I reset the trap, then piled up some landscaping bricks in such a way that when the trap was tripped as Skunky tried to get out, the door wouldn't shut on him. After that, I went back in the house and almost forgot about the little guy.

When Dud came home from the gym a short time later, I remembered Skunky and mentioned him to Duddy. "I piled up some bricks so the trap wouldn't close on him again," I told him.

"You don't have to set the trap,' he replied, "you can set the door open without putting that release bar on it." That hadn't occurred to me.

"Will you go out and fix it?" I asked. I was in the middle of something on the computer at the time.

Dud scoffed. *"No way!"* he said.

"Oh, come on, you big wuss! It's just a baby skunk!" But he absolutely refused to have anything to do with it. Sighing, I went out and fixed it myself, approaching slowly and talking softly the whole time. I explained to the little fellow what I was doing, and he seemed to take it all in stride. At no point in our transaction did I feel that I was in danger of being sprayed. As I turned to walk away, I saw Dud going into the house. He was so sure that I'd get sprayed that he'd come out on the patio to watch! With a measure of smugness in my voice, I called after his retreating back: "Wuss!"

The Open House

In early October, The Harmony Barn held its annual Open House. This was an opportunity for the 501(c) charity to bring in some much-needed funds to pay for the additional costs accrued by the rescue horses, who were frequently in poor health. Fliers were passed out, the local print and news media were notified, and although the Weather Gods could surely pass a small miracle and arrange for decent weather for a few hours once a year, they seldom did. The day was almost always cold, wet, and miserable. This hardly dampened the spirits of the visitors: we volunteers were used to showing up in any weather, of course, and a surprising number of hardy souls turned up as well, curious to see the animals, and possibly win something, too.

I was reminded of my barn friendships before I'd even left the house that morning. "What time will you be there?" came the text from Mandy, who would be fitting the Open House into her already-packed schedule of last-minute wedding planning. Her wedding was a mere month away, and almost every day brought frustrating new problems and discrepancies to light. It seemed like nothing was destined to go smoothly for her. Meanwhile, Lydia – who never calls me for any reason – called while I was en route, asking whether I'd be attending. "I'm on my way," I told her as I headed up the road. It sure was nice to feel wanted, and I looked forward to visiting with both women.

For a small mom-and-pop operation, the Barn was always on the receiving end of some pretty cool donations: for the silent auction, there were charming George Carruth sculptures, gift certificates for equine and human massages, baskets of food, books, Mary Kay products, jewelry and more. The raffles had nifty stuff, too: crock pots with packets of gourmet soups, original artwork, items for the garden, and large stuffed toy horses. The Barn also offered light refreshments for sale, pumpkin decorating for children, and fun horse games for whoever wanted to participate. It was also a time to visit with volunteers we hadn't seen in a long while, and a chance to spend some quality time with Dud's grandchildren.

We brought Dud's daughter Lauren with us, along with three year-old Liam and baby Stella. As we all piled into the barn, Dud issued the edict, "Don't. Buy. *Anything!*" His seasonal roofing business was winding down, and he was understandably concerned about whether we'd have enough money to get through the winter. Still, my prevailing thought was, "How little you know me!"

I had already formulated my plan: enjoy the Open House with Dud, Lauren, and the kids, get photos of Dud, Lauren, and the kids (alongside Handsome Harry the donkey), go home and wait for Lauren to leave, and Dud to drive off to the gig he had scheduled that night, then get myself back to the barn and proceed to bid on the three silent auction items that had caught my eye. Which is exactly what I did.

To kill time waiting for the auction to end, I wandered around the barn, visiting with volunteers I knew but hadn't seen in a while.

"So how goes the wedding planning?" I asked Mandy.

"Oh, my God!" She replied, rolling her eyes.

"That bad?" Just as the words left my mouth, Wendy walked up to us. Mandy asked whether Wendy was going to RSVP anytime soon, and Wendy responded by telling Mandy that her invitation didn't include an RSVP card. Mandy's lips tightened.

"This is just what I'm talking about," she sighed.

"Who did you delegate the invitations to?" I inquired.

"My aunt and my 88 year-old grandmother," Mandy replied.

"Maybe don't do that next time," I remarked thoughtfully.

"*Thanks!*" Mandy gave me that look she gets when I've been excessively irritating. "Not helpful!"

"I'm sure it'll all work out fine," I told her, although in truth, there was no actual way to be sure about the outcome of such a major catastrophe.

"I'm sure it'll be fine," said Wendy as she walked away. Wendy was ever the optimist.

"Thanks," Mandy replied with genuine feeling.

"*I just said the same thing!*" I exclaimed, "And you dismissed me!"

"I believe Wendy!" she said, "you, not so much!" All I could do was laugh: this was the kind of friendship we had.

I spent a few minutes, then, helping Liam decorate a pumpkin with scary stickers as Mandy looked on.

"I can't believe you're actually doing the grandmother thing!" she remarked, amused.

I grinned. "I know, right? You never thought you'd see this side of me, did you?!" She shook her head. Given that we'd begun our friendship trading insults, it wasn't surprising that she hadn't anticipated my having a maternal side, however small that side actually was. In truth, while I was genuinely fond of all of Dud's grandkids, I liked even better embracing my own childlike nature, getting down on the ground to the same level the kids are, and throwing myself wholeheartedly into whatever fun thing I was technically supposed to have outgrown by 52. In this instance, it was pumpkin decorating.

"Wow, Liam! Check it out: horrible green scars we can put on the pumpkin!"

"Yeah!" the little guy replied, "scars!" He was easy to amuse. We spent a few minutes sticking scary things on his little pumpkin, and then it was time to play a game.

Spotting Lydia and Allen out in the arena, I jogged over to join them. There were other folks milling around, too, curious to know what kind of game you could possibly play with a horse. Whatever Wendy thought up, it was bound to be a hoot. We all gathered around her to hear the rules.

"Your team all have to hold hands. No touching the horse, no bribing ("Dammit!," I said to Lydia, "I've got all kinds of good shit in my pockets!" And proceeded to show her the apple and horse cookies I'd brought with me), and no talking to each other or the horse." I don't know why Wendy always looks at me when issuing the rules, as though she fully expects me to be the one to break them. You bend a few rules and you're marked for life!

The task was one I hadn't done at the barn before, that of getting the horse to walk over a "jump" - a length of PVC pipe held up about eight inches off the ground by a couple of square plastic containers. The horse she'd chosen for this task was an ancient mare named Precious Winnings, or Winnie for short. I knew Wendy well enough by now to know that she had chosen Winnie specifically for this task, although the reason itself eluded me. Wendy was like that. She liked to throw us curve-balls: back when Miss Blonde was still alive, Wendy would use her because she had food issues. If you put hay in front of her, Blondie would focus on it to the exclusion of all else, completely vexing our attempts to get her to move. Initially, we didn't know that about Blondie, or the fact that all you had to do was take the hay away from her to get her attention. But Wendy knew things like that, and would choose the horses accordingly.

Allen and Lydia were team captains for this task, and I happily joined Lydia's team. There were three other adults on our team, and a couple of children. We watched as Allen's team went first, and we noted how they kept getting in the way, standing in front of Winnie so that she had nowhere to go. When they finally got her moving toward the jump, she veered away at the last minute and walked around the end of it.

As I studied Allen and his team, I came to see that the task would probably prove impossible to accomplish for that very reason: because the team couldn't close off both ends of the pipe at the same time, not while they were all holding hands. If the team was able to split itself in two, then the task would've been immediately do-able. But not the way Wendy had set it up. We took note of the problems Allen's team had, and tried to correct them in our own attempt, but the task was timed, and we ran out of time without succeeding.

Happily, Wendy relaxed the rules for the second attempt. This time, you could use anything in the arena to aid you in your attempt. Other things in the arena included more PVC pipes, and a couple of mounting blocks. When Wendy wasn't looking, I took a horse cookie from my pocket and rubbed it all over my coat sleeves. "Can't hurt!" I said as Lydia looked on, laughing.

I chewed on the problem of herding an unwilling horse over a jump while your whole team is tethered to itself while

I watched Allen's team take up a couple of lengths of the pipe to use as extensions of their arms. I had had the same thought myself before the light bulb went off in my head. Turning to Wendy, I asked, "Can we move the jump?"

She looked a little surprised before shrugging, "Sure."

When Allen's team failed at their second attempt, our team proceeded to implement my idea: move the jump so that it was bordered on one side by a stall. That way, all we had to do was curl around behind Winnie, and cut off her ability to go around the other end of the jump; she would be forced to go over it. And go over it, she did. *"Yeah!"* I hollered, pumping my fist in the air and grinning at Lydia.

Our team was exceedingly pleased with ourselves, and taunted Allen's team when, in their third attempt, they tried things our way and also got Winnie over the jump. "Copycats!" we yelled. But we were good sports about it, too, happy that everyone had succeeded at the task. As a reward, Wendy handed out ribbons with medallions on them, a horse's head decorating each medallion. I immediately put mine around my neck and strutted about like an Olympic champion, making everyone grin.

With the game over, we still had some time before the end of the silent auction. I leaned in toward Lydia and Allen and asked conspiratorially, "Did you guys see Casey?"

Lydia nodded. "I didn't recognize her," she said.

"I didn't either," I replied. "I'm thinking either eating disorder or meth."

"Meth," she and Allen answered in unison. We weren't joking. Something was very wrong with Casey, a volunteer we hadn't seen in quite some time.

Casey had come to the barn with plenty of horse experience under her belt. She was one of the few who enjoyed riding the skittish rescue horse, Sis, while the rest of us shook our heads and watched, waiting for Casey to go airborne. It only happened once.

Casey had had a spot of bother in college, getting busted for a DUI. There had apparently been problems after that, too, because she stopped coming to the barn some time ago. Seeing her at the Open House wasn't particularly surprising, but her appearance was: the once-chubby girl was now emaciated, her face pale and sharply angular. It didn't help that the fellow with his arms wrapped around her looked equally drug-thin. The two of them had been on Lydia's team for the horse game, and although I hoped that I was wrong about them, I was glad nonetheless that my purse was strapped firmly across my body where thieving drug users couldn't get at the contents.

"I can't decide which would be worse," I remarked to Lydia quietly, "an eating disorder or a drug addiction."

She shrugged, "Either one would suck." She was right, of course.

By this time, the silent auction was winding down, with only a few minutes left before winners were announced. Lydia and I had both bid on things, and were both determined that this year, we would not be outbid. So we hovered. And, glancing at each other, we giggled.

"Keep an eye on that Carruth for me, would you?" I asked her. She was closer to the auction form than I was; I hovered at the other end of the table, near another item I wanted. She had to bump up my bid once, but only by a dollar – we'd both figured out that it was unnecessary to bid up any more than that, and ultimately, we both won the things we'd bid on. "It pays to hover!" I exclaimed. She laughed in agreement.

Suddenly, I was aware of the kinship I'd been missing since I stopped volunteering on Saturdays. A newly developed lung ailment, in which I coughed excessively day and night, meant that I needed to cut back on the amount of time I spent breathing in the barn dust. Since I wanted to spend time with Bit as often as I could, cutting out my Saturday volunteering was the only other way to spare my lungs the aggravation of all the dust that swirled continuously around the barn.

In truth, though, I was no longer the only one absent. Now that she'd graduated high school, Lydia had a job that occupied a fair amount of her time. Olivia, while still in school, was busy with numerous family and artistic activities, and Mandy rarely made it out to the barn anymore. In January, Allen would go off to a college two hours' drive away.

I hate change. And this kind of change was the worst. It had taken years – literally – to get used to the Barn Urchins, never mind actually enjoying their company as I did now. I had known, in that vague, who-knows-when-it-will-happen kind of way, that they might grow up and get a life one day. I just didn't realize that the day had actually come.

I gave Lydia a firm hug as I said good-bye. I would see her again fairly soon as we were planning to do more bomb-proof training when she had time. But the hug, whether she knew it or not, was more about saying good-bye to the past than it was about see-you-soon. I had no doubt that we would carry on some form of friendship outside the barn, as Mandy and I did, and that was fine. It was just that the dynamic I had grown to love was changing, and I had no control over that.

Although there would ultimately be another group of kids doing poop duty on Saturday mornings, *this gang*, like my classmates in high school, was the one I had grown with, learned with, laughed with. We had grieved together for our common losses – Cricket the donkey, and Ruckus the riding horse – and had encouraged each other through tough times with family and friends. A gang like ours didn't come along very often; it was a once-in-a-lifetime group of people. I feel honored to have known them.

Gotcha!

After a few false starts involving the skunk, a feral cat, and a rather large opossum – not to mention a surprising number of nights in which nothing could be tempted to enter the humane trap – we finally caught a raccoon, and a big one, at that. Dud came out to see it with me, the next morning, but absolutely refused to get any closer than eight feet away. "Careful!" he admonished, as though the critter was going to somehow escape the confines of the trap and savage my ankle.

"He's only growling because he's scared!" I responded. I had leaned into the shrubs to get a look at the raccoon, and he'd looked up at me and growled. I understood: he was trapped, he didn't understand what was going on, and he didn't know what our intentions were. So I told him.

"When it gets dark out, we're going to take you somewhere else and let you go. Just hang in there. Take a nap or something."

Dud shook his head at this bit of what he saw as nonsense. "Just be careful!" he repeated, as though talking alone would somehow cause the transference of any rabid cooties from the raccoon to myself. How little he understood the Critter Lady!

The question of where to dump Rocky had initially seemed a simple one: we would drive out into the Whoville countryside, pick a secluded spot, and turn him loose. Or so we thought, until we happened to mention the prospect to Animal Control Officer Dave.

We'd run into Dave at the Whoville Public Library's 1st Annual Local Author Fair. They'd set up tents for the thirty local writers who'd signed up for the event, and scheduled it during one of Whoville's weekly Farmer's Markets in the hopes of attracting some of the Market's pedestrian traffic. To keep things interesting, I would call out to people as they walked by, inviting them to come over and talk to me. I was in the process of calling to a couple I'd seen coming out of the corner of my eye, and it was only after I'd turned to face them that I realized it was Dave and his wife, Jan. Dave looks completely different when he's out of uniform. I've run into him before on his off time and had trouble recognizing him. I grinned, and waved them over.

"So how did you like the book?" I asked Dave. I'd given him a copy of NBM when it first came out. To my surprise, he looked uncomfortable as he replied, "It was a little close to home."

"But I changed your name, *Dave!*" I remarked, pointedly emphasizing the name that is manifestly not his in real life.

"Yeah, *Dave!*" his wife chimed in.

When I thought about it, though, I recalled a conversation Dave and I had had a number of years ago. I had written one of my animal-related letters to the *Whoville Journal*, and it had mentioned Dave by name. Not long after that, Dave told me that the Chief of Police had pulled him aside and warned him that, as a City employee, he must maintain the appearance of impartiality, rather than seeming to take anyone's side – even it *was* a Critter Lady. Indeed, Dave's need for impartiality was one of the main reasons I chose to change several revealing details in NBM, to avoid Dave getting into trouble at work. That was no doubt what concerned Dave now. That, and the fact that he probably had no idea whatsoever that he would end up a featured character in someone's book!

The subject veered briefly away from books and animals as Duddy remarked to Jan that he had done some work on their house, years ago. "And a charming house it is, too!" I observed. I drove from Middlebridge to Whoville on an almost-daily basis, and, because Dave and Jan lived on the main North-South drag into town, I passed their house all the time. It was a snug yellow farmhouse set on 10 acres of township land, with tasteful landscaping, a huge sycamore tree up by the road, Dave's crittering truck in the driveway during his lunch hours, and an impressively-sized treehouse out back. Their children were grown and gone, now, but the fort remained. "Cool tree fort," I added.

"The tree is dead, now," Jan replied. You could see the truth of her words from the road: while there were several large branches protruding up through the roof of the tree-house, they were all in fact quite bare. "A raccoon lives there," she added absently. The casualness of her remark almost made me miss the significance of it.

"Wait!...What?...A *raccoon* lives in your kids' old tree fort?" I asked. Jan nodded.

"Let me get this straight," I stated, trying to get my mind around it, "Whoville's Animal Control Officer has a *raccoon* living in his kids' old tree fort?"

Dave grinned. Shrugging, he answered, "He doesn't bother *me!*"

I grinned back. "This is *so* going in the new book!" I announced.

It was around this time that Dud mentioned our raccoon trap-and-release plans. Dave gave us a look. "Careful," he made a point of saying, "dumping raccoons is illegal."

"Rabies?" I inquired. Dave nodded. We already knew we were in no danger of being busted by him: Dave's jurisdiction was the City of Whoville, while we lived in Whoville Township. But who knew whether or not the Township police were aware of the laws regarding dumping raccoons? Dud and I glanced at each other, and the look said, "We'll need to think about this a little." Which is what we did.

By the time we'd actually caught the raccoon, we'd already decided on our plan of driving out where the houses were sparse and there were plenty of wooded lots just asking to have a resident raccoon. We had debated various ways of transporting the cage to the back seat of Dud's car. We agreed that a length of rebar would do the trick: we'd slide it through the holes of the cage and we'd each carry an end. Simple enough, but when I went to lift the cage out of the shrubs, the raccoon turned out to be surprisingly light in weight. Given its' size, I had assumed that it would weigh considerably more than it actually did. Walking across the yard, I decided that it was light enough for me to carry on my own, although Dud hovered nearby, making concerned noises and saying, "That's gonna be too heavy for you to carry by yourself...well, o.k....you're already doing it by yourself..." To which I responded by suggesting that he open the car door for me. We got the cage settled on the back seat, climbed in, and drove off.

In a nod to Temple Grandin, who believes that animals communicate using their own form of music, changing the tone and pitch of their barks/meows/what have you as the situation dictates, I started singing The Beatles' *Rocky Raccoon* to our captured critter. It was one of my favorite White Album songs, and no harm would come of singing to a wild animal, so why not? As to whether it had the intended soothing effect, though, I cannot say, as the cage was covered by a large beach towel.

It was as we drove down Middlebridge Quarry Road that we saw the train coming. It was dark. It was cold that night. And Dud's reserves of patience – always in short supply anyway – were running low. He didn't want to wait for a train. So he veered off into Whoville Township Cemetery.

Well, why not? The occupants weren't likely to object.

He drove slowly toward the back of the property. We were approaching an area with tall pine trees, when I saw what looked to be a brick ranch house up ahead. "A *house*? In a cemetery?" I asked in confusion. "You'd better pull up there by those pine trees."

"Hurry up! Just dump him!" Dud said impatiently from the comfort and safety of his car, while I wrestled the trap out of the back seat.

"I'm going to let him loose over by those trees," I replied, feeling my own sense of urgency over that mysteriously-located house. What if someone was watching us? Or worse – calling the cops? Even so, I was not content to simply dump Rocky just any old place; I wanted him to have some shelter, and the pine trees offered that to a small degree.

It wasn't until I was satisfied with the location that I saw the problem: I hadn't brought along anything to prop the trap door open with; I would have to stand there actually holding the door as the raccoon walked out. Happily, this turned out not to be a problem, as the minute I opened the door, the raccoon bolted, making a fast beeline for the trees. As we drove home, I felt a measure of satisfaction that we'd disposed of that particular nuisance in a humane manner. Shooting may have been easier, but re-homing was kinder.

It was only a matter of days before we caught a second raccoon, although this one turned out to be considerably heavier than the first. I was able to carry the occupied trap to the bed of Dud's truck – just – but my arm muscles screamed in protest. As with Rocky, we waited until after dark to move Rocky II, and in the meantime, I took a leisurely daylight drive through the cemetery, determined to find out *what*, exactly, was on the property. To my surprise, rather than one ranch house, there were two ranch garages, with three bay doors each. It made sense on one level: the cemetery no doubt needed a place to store the hole-digging vehicles. But just *how many* hole digging vehicles did one cemetery need?

Relieved that we weren't going to be busted by some ghoulish live cemetery residents, we took our time driving back to the same clump of trees where I'd dumped the first raccoon. Again, I opened the trap door, but was surprised when my quarry refused to leave. "You've gotta go, now, buddy," I informed him. It was only when I tipped the back end of the trap, forcing the raccoon toward the door, that he got the hint and took off at a gallop, racing toward the same trees that the first Rocky had run to a couple of days before. *Two down, how many more to go?* I wondered.

As it turned out, the next critter(s) to have a go at the trap were exceptionally gifted: on three successive nights, both the cans of wet cat food and the bowl of dry cat food had not only been eaten, but they'd been removed from the trap beforehand, by an animal of such skill that the trap never closed. All three times, the morning after, cans and bowls lay a few feet away from the trap, mocking me with their emptiness. "We need to get smarter than the critters," I told Duddy. He gave the matter some thought before announcing, "tent stakes."

It made sense: I would dig a small hole in the ground, place the can of cat food in it, then put the trap over it, and secure the trap with tent stakes to that the trap couldn't be moved out of the way by a critter determined to get at the food. We picked up a set of four such stakes at the same time that we loaded up on more canned cat food. The first night we put the new plan in action, we caught an opossum. It wasn't the raccoon I was hoping for, but it showed us that we were definitely on the right track. It was now only a matter of time before we caught more Rockys.

Going Solo

It was as Bit and I were walking the track on Wendy's property for the umpteenth time that I began to feel the call of new adventures, and a desire for more training challenges. For three years, we had worked on bomb-proofing with a view to making Bit a competent trail rider. Now, it felt like we had accomplished all that we could on the property, and given that the neighboring farm fields had finally been cleared of their crops, I started lusting after an off-site ride.

This was no small consideration. Although Sally had taken Big William for numerous off-property rides, she actually owned William and was therefore free to do as she pleased with him. But Bit was owned by Wendy, and I'd already scored some major black marks with her by taking an impromptu lope through her next door neighbor's field, a year or so ago. The crops had been cleared but that didn't matter to the owner, who was, apparently, a grinch beyond measure: Wendy once told me that the man actually rode a four-wheeler around his property line, checking for the hoof prints that would tell him that someone had trespassed.

At the time, I'd had no idea that Wendy, Ron, and Wendy's daughter (and my riding instructor) Connie all had eyes in the backs of their heads. No idea at all until Ron approached me a few days later and gave me the sort of ass-chewing generally reserved for recalcitrant teenagers, not women in their 50's. I ran crying to Wendy and apologized profusely. I've made a point of asking about every little detail ever since.

In any case, I decided to ask Wendy whether Bit and I might start doing some off-site rides. These would not be on the land owned by Mr. Grinch. His property only bordered one side of Wendy's land; the other sides were owned by people who didn't seem to mind hoof prints in their dirt, provided there were no crops to contend with. This left Spring, Fall, and any part of Winter that wasn't a sheet of ice, ripe for rides that were considerably longer than the track we'd been using for the last three years. And while I'd been on numerous off-property rides with Connie and my old lesson horse, Ruckus, I'd never done any solo, and something told me that Wendy was going to object.

I'd already spoken to Sally about whether she and Big William would be willing to accompany us, and I'd consulted Wendy's niece Alex, as well. Alex had been doing 4-H competitions for several years now, and was a reasonably accomplished horse girl, given the fact that she was just a teenager. Both Sally and Alex said they'd be more than happy to do rides with me, and I suspected that having someone ride along would make Wendy more agreeable to my request. As a last resort, I planned to ask her, "What needs to happen for you to be o.k. with the idea?" At this point, I was desperately keen for her to say yes, so I was prepared to agree to just about anything.

Having resolved to ask, I headed out to the barn one dark October evening around feeding time. I chatted with Wendy while I helped her feed the horses, then followed her around as she topped off the water buckets. We talked about a range of subjects, most having to do with Bit's EPM and her belief that the change of seasons tended to bring his symptoms to the fore. It was as we discussed Bit that I casually remarked that I'd like to take Bit on some off-property trail rides. I was 99% certain that the answer would be 'no.'

"Take your phone with you," she replied. I blinked. This was not the answer I was expecting.

"O.k.," I said.

"If you want a longer ride, you can go around and up the other side of the creek," she added. That was *way* more than I ever thought she'd say! What she was suggesting – something I'd never even considered, but that Sally had apparently done with William, was follow the creek all the way til it met Hauzlander Road, cross the bridge and take a left to follow the other side of the creek as it meandered back toward Middlebridge Creek Road. To understand what a considerable ride that actually is, you need to know that just riding to Hauzlander Road and back takes the better part of an hour. This was so much more than the pokey rides around Wendy's track, which generally took no more than fifteen minutes. What she was offering now was the sort of trail ride I'd originally had in mind for Bit, but never imagined we'd actually be allowed to do. I drove home on cloud nine! *Tomorrow!* I thought.

The next day broke cloudy and a little chilly but it didn't dampen my spirits. Keenly, I wondered whether Bit would even be willing to leave the property, and how I would handle a refusal. I decided to take my flag along with me.

The flag had been a freebie from horseman Carson James, who I think was trying to build a following by offering free flags and a training DVD to boot if you just ponied up the shipping fee. As it happened, I was in the market for something very like his flag, so I paid the shipping and got the goodies. I tied the flag to the riding crop I'd been using during Bit's training sessions, giving myself an even more emphatic way to enforce my commands. Never – and I do mean **_never_** – have I used that crop to hit Bit. And I never will.

It would be the first time in a long time that I'd be using a saddle. I'd been riding strictly with the bareback pad for over six months. I had considered using it on the trail ride, but then realized that if I needed to dismount for any reason, I wouldn't be able to remount a bareback pad that had no stirrups. As it turned out, all those months of riding bareback had improved my "seat" - the proper way to ride a horse – considerably, which pleased me no end. Having a poor seat was not only uncomfortable for the horse, but for the rider as well. I was glad to find that we'd both be enjoying a better ride now.

When I led Bit off the property, he went willingly. *Any minute now, he's going to stop,* I kept thinking, but it never happened. He didn't fuss, he didn't refuse to move. I was amazed! He kept walking the entire length of the creek, and didn't balk once until we made it to Hauzlander Road. The bridge was apparently more than he had the courage to do, and he stopped a few feet short of it. Nothing I said or did moved him sufficiently to continue walking.

I hadn't anticipated this, but a day or two later, when I was consulting a book on horsemanship by world-renowned horseman Pat Parelli, I learned that horses have poor depth perception. To them, it's difficult to tell where the bridge ends and where the drop-off begins. This explained much, but at the time, all I knew was that we were never going to see the other side of the creek if I couldn't get him over the bridge. After a bit of head-butting during our next ride – in which he refused to cross the bridge again, I asked him to do some backing up. It's important that you give the horse a chance to succeed at a task, and since Bit wasn't going to succeed at crossing the bridge that day, I gave him the task of backing up instead. Once he did what I asked, I rewarded him by turning him in the direction of home. We would not be crossing the bridge that day, either.

As it happened, the creek also intersected Middlebridge Creek Road just a few houses up from Wendy's spread. When we returned to her property, I aimed Bit out toward the road with a view to schooling him on that bridge. Bit was in no mood for any bridge, though, and I had to dismount and walk him back and forth across it from the ground. This was not as easy as it sounds: Bit's distrust was clear on his face, and he kept sniffing the air suspiciously.

Only with a great deal of insistence on my part would he walk across, eyeing the guardrail as though it were a snake poised to strike. Back and forth we walked across the bridge. I would make him stop and stand in the middle, and I'd walk him near the edges so that he could see the creek. Then I walked him back to the mounting block at Wendy's, climbed back on, and directed him up the driveway and out onto the road.

He walked about five feet up the street and stopped. He was having none of this easy acceptance of something new – why I thought he would is anyone's guess; nothing new ever came easy with Bit. So I dismounted again, walked him up to and over the bridge, and then back to Wendy's once again. That seemed like enough work for one day. Time to let him rest. The next week promised to be warm and sunny. We'd pick up where we left off then.

Rocky III

After a couple of quiet nights in which nothing entered the trap, Rocky 3 made his way in. When I checked the status of the trap the next morning and found it occupied, I told the critter reassuringly that once it got dark out, we'd move him somewhere else and let him go. He seemed to digest this will little apparent concern. To make him feel less vulnerable in the cage, I threw one of my large beach towels over it and left him to pass the time in whatever way he saw fit. When darkness fell, I went out to retrieve him.

The light from the patio spilled out into the yard, but didn't reach behind the shed, so I couldn't see what had happened to my towel; I knew only that it had moved considerably from where I'd originally placed it. I felt around in the dark for it and could only find bits and pieces. Puzzled, I picked up the trap and carried it out into the yard. By the patio light, I could see that Rocky had kept himself busy that day by pulling the towel in through a multitude of cage bars. I laughed so hard I had to put the trap down.

"What did you *do*, Bubby?!" I asked him. He peered around a bunching of the towel and I could see that his expression said, *Is it o.k.?* I think he was a little worried that I'd be mad.

"You're fine, Bubby!" I replied.

At this point, Dud appeared by the fence gate and said irritably, "Hurry up, will you?"

"Oh, relax, Grumpy!" His irritation was *really* irritating! How could he not understand by now that it was important that The Critter Lady commune with her charges?

"It's time to go, now, Bubby. Just a short ride in the truck and then I'll let you go."

As with the previous two, we then drove him to Middlebridge Cemetery and dropped him off.

BEST. TRAIL RIDE. EVER.

It soon became apparent that if I wanted Bit to cross either the Middlebridge Creek Road bridge, or the Hauzlander Road bridge, I'd have to dismount and lead him across from the ground. Mind you, this only applied to the outbound crossing; heading toward home, Bit was more than willing to cross the very same bridges that terrified him so when going in the other direction. The problem with dismounting, though – which I was perfectly willing to do – was getting back on Bit again afterward.

Ten years ago, when I was taking lessons on Ruckus, I was not only younger and sprightlier, but about 25 pounds lighter, as well. These days, even if Bit *was* willing to stand still long enough to be mounted (and he wasn't, unless I was using a mounting block), there was simply no way I could get back on him from the ground.

This didn't necessarily spell defeat. If you've read NBM, you'll recall that I told Mandy that I was training from both sides, which means I was mounting and dismounting from both his left, and his right side. Pat Parelli isn't the only horse expert to endorse this kind of training – Stacy Westfall encourages it, too.

The main benefit of training your horse to get used to being mounted and dismounted from both sides is that if you happen to be, say, trail riding on a horse that doesn't want to cross a bridge, and you don't want to have to walk all the way back to Wendy's property to use the mounting block, then you can, with any luck, remount in some other fashion with what's available on the trail.

In this case, what was available was the guardrail used to keep cars from driving off of both bridges. That railing extended out far enough away from both sides of the bridges that I was able to steer Bit close to it, stand up on the railing, get a foot into the stirrup, and hoist myself onto his back. Happily, due to that both-sides training that Mandy didn't think I needed, Bit was sufficiently accustomed to my doing things on his right side that he was willing to stand still long enough for me to remount. This meant that we could go much farther than the bridge, and on our third trail ride, we did just that.

Bit was more or less willing to plod his way up Hauzlander Road, although he shied away from areas where street workers had used an excess of tar. I think he thought they were bottomless holes. He'd veer off onto the grass shoulder – what there was of it – until he'd safely passed whatever danger he'd thought it was. We passed an oddly-shaped house on the right (empty fields were on the left) and as we got farther down the road, we discovered that there was a pasture behind a treeline, with five horses in residence. I didn't know what Bit would make of this. I didn't know if he was aware that other horses, and other herds, existed outside of his frame of reference. For their part, the five in the pasture all came trotting to the fence to have a look.

I say, Bit called out to them. *Are you-all horses?*

Why, yes! They replied. *Yes, we are! And you?*

Yes, Bit answered. *I'm a horse, too!*

And that seemed to be the long and short of it. Bit walked on, then, almost to Faust Road. He didn't actually want to walk anywhere too close to Faust Road, so we had to butt heads about where, exactly, we would be turning back. It's important to make the horse think that he's doing what *you've* asked him to do, rather than letting him think that he gets to decide things for himself. So we had some back and forth in which I encouraged him to take a few more steps in the desired direction, and then I rewarded him by allowing him to turn around and head toward home. Notably, he was perfectly willing to cross the Hauzlander Road bridge without hesitation on the way back!

We hadn't actually reached the bridge yet when I looked up and saw the school bus coming. *Oh, man!* I thought, *this is not gonna go well!* Bit had never encountered a vehicle that big before, and at this point, Hauzlander had narrowed to literally one lane. The grassy shoulders were narrow, and ended in a good two-foot drop-off that I wasn't confident that Bit could navigate. Doing my best to remain calm and collected, I steered Bit toward the side of the road. If he only knew that the picture in my head was of him panicking and running right in front of the bus! The bus approached us ... and passed without incident. You could have knocked me over with a feather! *So...big yellow buses are o.k. but tar puddles schmeared across the road are terrifying?!* There was no logic in it whatsoever. I said a silent prayer of thanks to the Gods, and urged Bit forward.

It was as we headed back up Hauzlander, and turned onto the field beside the creek that I realized that all our patience and training had paid off. *This* – our off-site trail ride – was the culmination of two-years-worth of groundwork, nervous grass-eating, more groundwork, more nervous grass-eating, and finally, all our treks around the track behind the pasture.

Bit had started out as such a Nervous Nelly that Wendy had seen fit to put him on an herbal supplement (which worked a treat, by the way). Bit was by nature such a panicky horse that he startled at the sight of his own shadow. Indeed, he was *so* panicky, I didn't feel safe riding him on that track until we'd done a year's-worth of groundwork on it first. We then spent a year getting used to riding the track. These trail rides were my reward for all the hours I'd put in waiting for Bit to figure out that the whole world was *not* actually trying to eat him. It was an incredibly satisfying feeling, knowing that even though I'd made up a great deal of our training as we'd gone along, it had worked anyway. And now, here we were, doing the one thing I'd wanted to do most, wandering off-site, having new adventures to enjoy.

Things didn't get any better than this!

A Barn Christmas

Because the northeast area of the country had been enjoying record-breaking warm weather for a couple of months, the weather on the Saturday before Christmas – in which the temperature decided to plunge from the high 40's to the low 20's overnight – came as a rude awakening. Wendy was holding her annual Christmas gift exchange party for the volunteers and the folks who boarded, and although I had dressed accordingly, the walk from my car to the barn threatened to turn me into a popsicle. It was the wind that really made me miserable: there were no suitable windbreaks on Wendy's property, so when it blew, that wind blew right through to your bones. Thankfully, the viewing room was heated by a plug-in radiator.

"Man, it's fucking *cold* out there!" I announced to the room at large. Urchins Allen and Olivia had already arrived. They would expect nothing less than some cheerful profanity from me. I looked around, taking in the table laden with gifts, and the sideboard laden with food.

"Lydia's not here?" I asked.

"I think she had to work," Allen replied.

Other people started coming in, then. Some I knew, some I didn't know, and at least one I didn't like. I realized that there were going to be a few who wouldn't be getting the customary Kelly gift of a framed photo. I would have to say something; I didn't want any hurt feelings. After a few minutes, Allen checked his phone and announced that Lydia was on her way. It wouldn't have been the same without her.

Wendy came in and urged us to start eating. There was quite an array of goodies – much more so than in previous years: there were deviled eggs and veggie trays, shrimp cocktail and sugar cookies, and when Lydia arrived, a mint chocolate ice cream cake, as well. We all began munching while Wendy started passing out the gifts.

"Handsome Harry did all the shopping," she announced, "and he was up *very* late last night, wrapping!"

"That's one intrepid donkey," I mused in response. Wendy was always saying things like that, that one of the equine residents had done this, or said that. I looked on in amusement as she handed Allen (who was the only male in attendance) not a wrapped gift but a small envelope.

"Harry decided that you were hard to shop for, so he got you this instead!" It was a gift card to one of the local stores. Allen accepted it with good humor.

Handsome Harry's gift to me turned out to be a rectangular wooden frame that held five photos – some with me in them, some with Bit, and one of me and Harry. It was a lovely gift and as I hugged Wendy, I asked her to extend my thanks to the donkey, as well.

Wendy handed me a second gift, saying as she did, "This one's from your boyfriend!" She meant Bit, the other man in my life. I couldn't imagine what Bit might've thought of until I unwrapped the box and peered inside. It was a huge blue rosette, with two exceedingly long blue ribbons trailing beneath it. It took me minute to realize that the long blue ribbons weren't meant to hang under the rosette in the traditional fashion; the long blue ribbons were meant to fasten around a horse's neck via the small bits of Velcro on the end of each ribbon.

"Let me try this out on you," I said to Allen as I reached around to the back of his neck. I fastened the ribbons and then stepped back: the large blue rosette hung down to his belly, and one of the ribbons was emblazoned with the legend *BEST HORSE EVER*. Bit had indeed found the perfect gift for me! I couldn't wait to put it on him and take some pictures!

Grinning broadly, I said to Wendy, "This is *perfect!*" I loved that she got into the spirit of the whole blue ribbon thing – that just because Bit hadn't competed didn't mean that he hadn't accomplished a hell of a lot. Even Carol took a minute to remark on that.

"I saw you two out on the road the other day," she told me. "You've really made a lot of progress with Bit!" Carol owned the soon-to-be 36-year old Keeper. Keeper was a cantankerous old geezer who would kick anyone that dared to talk to Carol while she was grooming him. Keeper figured that that was his special time with her and everyone else should just fuck off! As for Carol, I had no idea that she'd seen Bit and I doing anything, let alone walking up Middlebridge Creek Road. Isn't it funny how you go through life feeling invisible and assuming that no one knows what you're up to, until someone comes along and says, "I saw you..."?!

The praise was good to hear, though. Carol and Keeper had been at The Harmony Barn for many years; they knew what a big stinker Bit used to be before he had a human companion to teach him things. I told Carol the story about Bit and the school bus, finishing laughingly with, "So a giant school bus is o.k., but the tar on the road is apparently terrifying!" Carol and Wendy joined in the laughter; they knew how arbitrary horses could be.

At that point, Allen started handing out his gifts. This was a first for him; usually, Olivia the artist was the only one who gave us anything. As it turned out, Allen had given his ideas some thought: his gifts were individualized, personalized clear-glass Christmas tree ornaments, each one bearing the name of the human and their particular horse (or favorite horse, in the case of non-horse-owning volunteers). Inside the glass sphere was a collection of items: some of the sawdust Wendy used as bedding in the stalls; a small piece of wood; some grass; and, in mine, a handful of hair from Bit's tail.

Grinning, I asked him, "So...what? Did you go around with scissors, giving all the horses a haircut?!" Allen laughed as he explained that in the case of Handsome Harry – whose hair featured in two ornaments – one of the volunteers had just finished grooming the white donkey, which meant that there was a considerable amount of shed hair for the taking. It was a very thoughtful gift, from a gender not always known for its thoughtfulness, and I was really touched.

I began handing out my photo gifts, then, after I'd made an announcement.

"Folks, I have a brief announcement," I announced.

"Uh-oh!" Came Wendy's teasing voice from somewhere in the throng of people. "She's going to make an announcement!"

"That's right! I am!" I replied. "I don't have a present for everyone because I haven't been here much this year. So if you don't get a gift from me, it's nothing personal!" As I distributed the gifts, I gave my usual little speech: "As always, I used my finest wrapping paper, because that's the kind of person I am!" Allen and Olivia laughed: I always wrapped the pictures in old copies of *The Whoville Journal*.

"Gayle," I continued, "I wasn't sure of the spelling, so I tried to cover every contingency!" The front of her package had scrawled across it *Gail Gayle Gale*.

"You, there, in the green!" I said to a teenager I didn't know who was wearing a green sweatshirt, "Hand this to the blonde lady, would you, please?" The package for the blonde lady – a volunteer who'd been coming for close to a year but whose name I still hadn't bothered to learn – had written on it *blonde lady!* That drew a laugh!

Olivia passed out her handmade presents, then. She'd done some very small paintings on very small pieces of wood – detailed stuff that really showcased her talent. I had no doubt that Olivia would make her living as an artist one day. Apparently, Wendy had the same thought, for she gave Olivia a carry-all on wheels, to hold her art supplies. Olivia was very pleased to have it.

Once all the gifts were distributed – Gayle's gift to me were some much-needed hand- and foot-warmers – we all stood around enjoying the food and the camaraderie. While we may have been very different in our lives outside the barn, we all had horses in common, a love of them, and an understanding of just why everyone else in that room was equally committed to them. It was the merriest party I would attend that Christmas, although I felt a distinct pang when I realized that Allen would be leaving for college in a couple of weeks. At least Lydia was still in the area, even if she didn't make it to the barn regularly anymore. Allen would be two hours away.

"Are you *sure* you don't just want to stay here and make the barn your career?" I asked him in desperation. He had taken over the stall cleaning duty full time when the usual girl quit. But his interests lay in horticulture, and he shook his head good-naturedly in response.

"Dammit!" I exclaimed in frustration, "there's all these new people here now! It took me *forever* just to get used to you guys!" He and Olivia laughed.

"I know!" he said, "and it took you even longer to like us!" I had to laugh, then, myself. The kids knew me well, and weren't afraid to tell it like it was. I would miss these people, and our relationships. Hell, I already did, and they weren't even gone, yet!

Making Do

While the early winter temperatures remained at record highs, there was apparently enough difference between the warmth of fall and the cool of December that Bit's EPM symptoms came to the fore. This had happened the year before, as well, but I completely forgot that fact until I found myself discussing Bit's behavior with Wendy. While he was always bitey at girth-tightening time, Bit was now throwing in some pretty emphatic bucks, too. This was not only dangerous, but it also indicated some sort of physical issue that needed to be addressed. So I stopped by the barn on a rather balmy late December Saturday morning to see what Wendy's thoughts were.

I'd been taking Bit for walks up and down Middlebridge Creek Road. It hadn't gone unnoticed: more than one barn boarder congratulated me on how well Bit was coming along; they all knew what a flighty boy he'd been for so many years. I myself was particularly pleased with his progress: we were walking farther and farther away from Wendy's property, and he remained impressively cool and collected when confronted with passing traffic. But it was not to last. Wendy – who worried about the "what if's" (What if Bit went down into a ditch? What if he ran out in front of a car?) – ultimately concluded that she didn't want me taking him out on the roads at all.

"If something happened, and he jumped in front of a car and people got hurt, I'd lose everything," she told me. I was dejected but I could see her point. This edict brought us back to Square One, though, leaving us with just the trail rides across the neighbor's acreage. Then it struck me:

"Can we ride in the back pasture?" I countered. Bit and I had spent a lot of time there, too, before she put it off-limits. She wanted to use that back pasture for extra grazing. The horses used to enjoy the spaciousness of two pastures, but somewhere along the way, the front pasture got re-fenced with electric wire while the back pasture did not. The back pasture was still fenced with something else, but hadn't been used in quite some time by anyone but Bit and I. Then, out of nowhere, Wendy announced that it would be opened up for the horses again. Now, with the surrounding roads being placed off-limits, I thought that maybe we could get that pasture back again to incorporate into our trail rides.

Wendy nodded her assent. "As long as it's not snowy," she replied. That was one problem solved. Then, as I stood watching her watch Tom the farrier working away at Charlie Horse's hooves, she mentioned Bit's abscess.

"Bit has an abscess?" I frowned. This was news to me. "Why didn't you call me?"

Wendy shrugged. "What could you have done?"

"I could've come out and spoiled him, if nothing else!" I answered. And while this was a sudden turn of events for *me*, I learned from someone else that Wendy had found Bit's abscess on Christmas Eve. That was days ago! I didn't press the matter, but privately, I was a little annoyed: Bit was my boy and Wendy knew that. If she had called me on Christmas Eve, I would've gone out there and seen to him. At the very least, I would've known there was a problem. By the time I spoke to her, though, the abscess had pretty much healed up, and we were moving on to a different problem: swelling in his near front leg. I went home assuming that the two issues were related, but Ron thought otherwise, and told me so when I called him a few days later.

I had gone to the barn to groom Bit. It was all I could do until the swelling issue was resolved, and I wanted to spend some quality time with him. When I walked into the barn, though, something was clearly amiss: off near a set of cross ties lay the remains of a bale of hay. Handsome Harry the donkey and Baby Jack – both of whom enjoyed the freedom to walk around the aisles unrestricted because if they went out with the horses they got picked on – had clearly struck gold, and stood among the piles of hay, munching to their heart's contentment. This was not the way things were done at The Harmony Barn! I called Ron.

"Hey, there's what used to be a bale of hay lying around, and Jack and Harry are making quite a meal of it. Did you guys leave the hay for them? Do you want me to clean it up, or what?"

Ron had no idea what was going on. "No, I'll take care of it. Just put them in stalls for me, would you?" It was then I asked about Bit and his hoof, and was told in response that the swelling seemed to be unrelated to the abscess.

"I know you had him out on the roads. Did he maybe slip or something?" he asked.

"No, he was perfect. There was no slipping, no jumping, no spooking, no nothing."

Ron thought about that. "He might've sprained it running around the mud lot."

"O.k." I replied. "So we wait until the swelling goes down before doing any groundwork?"

"Yeah," he answered, "Wendy's been putting cold packs on it at night. We'll keep an eye on it. He should be fine in a few days."

"O.k." I repeated, "thanks!"

When he came through the barn a half-hour later and had a look around, he said, "Wow, they really *did* get into the hay!"

"Total carnage!" I agreed. "How on earth did they get the bale to begin with?"

"The guys delivered hay today. It probably fell from the loft," he answered

I laughed. "A horse's idea of heaven!"

In the days that followed, the weather grew increasingly winter-like, and I started wearing my long johns out to the barn to groom. The sessions didn't take very long, but it was time spent together, and afterward, as I walked Bit back out to the arena, I'd drill him briefly in stopping and backing up. Horseman Carson James maintains that part of getting your horse to respect you as the boss is getting him to back up out of your space when you ask him to, so I'd gotten into the habit of standing right in front of Bit and asking him to back up. Initially, I had to tug on the lead rope before he'd do it. Now, though, I only had to ask and he'd take two very satisfying steps back from me.

Even if I couldn't currently ride him, I could still teach, and when I remembered all the downtime we'd had the previous winter for the very same reason – a flare-up of his EPM symptoms – I started giving some thought to what sort of things I might spent this winter teaching him. After watching boarder Sally working with Big William, the answer was obvious: work on the things that made Sally and William such a formidable team.

Sally was a major proponent of natural horsemanship, and every possible permutation thereof. William not only enjoyed top-notch traditional care (he was also an EPM horse), but numerous non-traditional treatments as well. He underwent regular massages, had his spine adjusted by an equine chiropractor, experienced aromatherapy, and, on top of all that, carried Sally around on a custom-built saddle that Sally paid through the nose to have made just for his back. But that wasn't all.

Sally had been attending Equine Affaire for years. As much as she enjoyed perusing the tack and other horse-related items for sale (and had purchased a number of pricey items), she spent several days at the Affaire each year watching as many of the demonstrations as possible. She'd even seen Stacy Westfall give a demo once! In addition, she'd arranged for one of the experts to come to The Harmony Barn and give a clinic. I didn't participate because I wasn't leasing Bit at the time. Now, I was sorry I hadn't audited the class; I would've learned plenty just by watching.

These days, I took to watching Sally work with William every chance I got, and I was fascinated. The level of communication between them truly awed me: if Sally *tsked*, William knew exactly what she meant by it. *I* had no idea what she was telling him to do, but somehow, he knew when she wanted him to move forward, and when she wanted him to back up, all with one simple noise. I was pea green with envy, and I wanted that same level of teamwork that they had. This year, I was determined that I would not let Dud's short attention span get in the way of my learning a few things. This year, I would do the Equine Affaire alone, while Dud spent the time visiting his oldest daughter. I couldn't wait!

A Change of Mind

Apart from the exceptional cold on the day of the barn Christmas party, the unseasonably warm weather lasted through the end of December. In early January, things took a turn for the sudden, and rather drastic, worst: one day it was 51 degrees outside, and the next, it had plunged to 28, with a windchill that would freeze your eyeballs if you weren't careful. I spent that particularly cold evening huddled under a blanket, watching the evening news. President Obama had been visiting the parents of the murdered Newtown, Connecticut school children, and he stood at the podium, giving a press briefing on the subject of gun control. A tear trickled down his cheek as he spoke.

It was as he talked that I realized that Dud and I had never gotten around to buying that raccoon-killing gun we'd talked about so many times. I glanced out the sliding glass door, chewing thoughtfully on my lip. Since it was dark outside, Penny and Daffy were floating around in their pond. It was how they spent every evening before being shut into their pen for the night. And ever since that terrified night when they had run right into the house, we'd been locking them in that pen.

They knew the routine by heart now: around 8:00 p.m., I would head out to the pond, remarking as I did, "Time to go in the pen, girls!" They knew exactly what was expected of them, but they fought me in their own silly way every time, by climbing out of the pond, bobbing their heads at me and giving me a full measure of trash-talk.

"I don't think it's time yet, do you, Penny?" Daffy would say.

"It's *definitely* not time yet, Daffy!" Penny would reply.

And then, together, in a deafening duck chorus: *"Not time yet, Kelly! Definitely not time yet! No, not time yet at all!"* And even though their argument came to nothing, they still offered it every single night!

In spite of their objections, I usually managed to herd them into the pen in two minutes or less. The key was in using both arms to help keep them moving toward the pen, as they often had a tendency to veer back toward the pond, or overshoot the pen door. It was if they were testing me every night, to see if I really meant to put them in the pen. Once they were in, I'd put a bucket of fresh water in, close the door, lock it, tell them I loved them, and then go back in the house.

In the morning, without exception, they were more than ready to be released, and, in fact, during the warmer months when we had the windows open, I would often lie in bed, hearing them making an assortment of impatient squeaky noises. It was their way of asking when the hell I was going to get up and let them out. Invariably, as I opened the pen door, they would march down the ramp, bobbing their heads and trash-talking their way out into the yard:

"What on earth took you so long?! We've been stuck in there for *days*! Honestly, can't you get out here earlier – we've missed all the good worms by now!"

I can tell you from firsthand experience: you haven't been trash-talked until a duck has done it!

Since they were spending every single night in that pen, buying a gun didn't feel anywhere near as necessary as it had before. I continued to turn the matter over in my head, though, for several days. There would always be raccoons, and other assorted backyard threats. But the pen was super-strong, and as long as we used it, having a gun no longer felt like a pressing issue. I decided I could live without it. More importantly, I decided that the ducks could safely live without it, too

Groundwork

Between the cold weather and Bit's EPM flare-up, I had to get creative if I was going to get us through the winter without riding. Bit was far too intelligent to be left unchallenged for months at a stretch. Our training happened in a hit-or-miss kind of way, though, doing one thing until I thought of a way to change it up, make it different, and require him to think instead of grabbing impatiently at the lead rope.

"I've *done this* already!" he would say, "Why do I have to do it *again?!*"

"O.k.," I'd reply, "Let's do it differently now!" That always threw him; he expected to be finished altogether if he'd already done the task. Instead, I'd have him do something new and unusual, making him work until *I* said we were done. If I let *Bit* say when we were done, we'd never do anything for more than 30 seconds! And being done required him to do the task correctly. Then and only then did I pull out the Red Delicious apple I always brought with me and let him enjoy it.

The most recent task came to me out of nowhere, when I realized that there were a finite amount of times that we could walk across the tarp, step over the plastic pipe jump, then cross the wooden bridge. When Bit started protesting – which he always did when he felt he'd done the task enough times – the thought struck me to make him do parts of it backward. Horses don't like to back up, but it's an essential part of training, and probably doesn't get done nearly enough. So once he'd gotten all four feet on the wooden bridge, I brought him to a halt, then had him slowly back up and down off the bridge. Suddenly, he was too busy thinking to protest!

Interestingly, the very next day, as I was reading a jolly useful book called The Horse Behavior Problem Solver, by Jessica Jahiel, I came across a chapter that dealt with loading horses onto trailers. Evidently, some horses really resist loading, and Jahiel stresses how invaluable it is to train your horse to load properly: whether you want to transport him to a show, a trail head, or the vet for what might be a life-saving treatment, it's important to train him *before* you actually need to load him. That way, when the time comes, he'll be comfortable walking in without a fuss. In terms of my own training with Bit, more often than not, things were done piecemeal, with no thought as to how learning this particular skill would lead to being able to do that particular skill. Which made reading about loading horses into trailers especially timely, given that we'd just done an hour of work backing down off a bridge. Happily, I realized that I was on the right track. Now, all I needed was to come up with more challenges to keep Bit mentally fit through the long slog of winter that lay ahead.

That might sound like an easy task, but it definitely wasn't. We were extremely limited by circumstances: when there was snow or ice on the ground, we couldn't work outside where he might slip and injure himself. That left us with half an arena. Half, because if it was too cold and/or wet for the horses to be in the mud lot, then we all had to share the arena. Wendy would rope off half of it for whichever herd members were out there (the others would be in their stalls), and Bit and I would get the other half. Our half filled up pretty quickly when I had the tarp, plastic pipe jump, and the bridge all spread out.

One of the other things I thought up was to walk Bit through the obstacle course one step at a time. *Literally* one step at a time. As in, "Step. Good! Step. Good job! Step." Happily, this also turned out to be something that Jahiel suggested as a valuable training aid. In her opinion, if your horse couldn't see what was behind him as he backed out of the trailer, he might become anxious about doing it. But if you were standing there walking him through it, and telling him exactly what to expect ("Back. Back. Down. Back."), then the process was much more likely to go smoothly. It made sense to me, although clearly Bit was a little puzzled: all this taking one step at a time, when you could just reach your destination a whole lot quicker if you ramped up the pace!

Apart from being an aid to easier loading, I began to see how it might help with the mounting block, as well. Bit hadn't quite mastered the art of stopping in just the right place next to it, and I frequently needed him to take just one or two steps forward in order to line him up properly. More often than not, though, if I asked for one step, he'd give me five, which then required another lap around the mounting block until he was lined up in the right position again. Bit learning to take one step on request and then stopping would be a big help at mounting block time, so I resolved to make it a regular feature of our winter training. Other than that, though, I was drawing a blank as to how to keep Bit occupied. It was time to see what Sally and Big William were up to!

Almost Like The Old Days

"Your blanket arrived today. It's in the tack room," came the text from Wendy. Dud would've had a fit if he'd known I spent almost $100 for a new winter turnout blanket for Bit, so I had it shipped directly to The Harmony Barn. I texted Wendy back, saying I'd be out on Saturday. Around the same time, I got a text from Lydia offering to help me with Bit's bomb-proofing any day I needed her. I asked her if Saturday would work, since I'd be there anyway, but she replied that she was bringing her new boyfriend out for the first time and didn't want to leave him high and dry while we worked.

When I pulled into the barn driveway, it was filled with cars, and there were any number of people there that I didn't know. I almost walked right into Lydia, though, as I stepped through the barn door.

"Hey!," I greeted her before telling her that if she wanted, I would drive her around Fordway in search of a cheap apartment. Lydia was in dire need of her own place, and I wasn't altogether sure she'd find one on her own. Fordway, I knew, had a number of complexes that looked like they might be affordable for a young person. She took me up on the offer, and I promised to check my calender and get back to her. When I turned around, there was Allen, home from college.

"Dude! Big man on campus! How's it going?"

"Good," he chuckled in response. We talked about school for a bit before he revealed that the college was in redneck country.

"*Really?* Try to stay out of trouble, will ya?"

"Yeah," he remarked dryly, "Look what happened when Casey went off to college!"

"That would be bad!" I observed. "Think of it like this: if you start doing meth down there at school, we'll have one of the horses give you a swift kick in the ass when you come back! Let's see, now...," I mused, "who would do the kicking? Galaxy's a good candidate, she's been known to kick." Allen laughed at this; Galaxy was known to kick, but she was a very small horse, and the damage would no doubt be negligible.

"Or there's Keeper – he's a cranky old fellow!"

"Keeper likes me, though, he'd never kick!" Allen was fairly confident on that point.

"*I* know: Charlie Horse! He's a *definite* kicker!"

"Oh, yeah! That'll keep me on the straight and narrow!" he answered

"Then it's settled. If the hillbillies offer you meth, just tell them you can't because you'll get your ass kicked by Charlie Horse!"

Allen grinned. "Will do!" he said.

When I finally got around to retrieving Bit's new blanket from the tack room, I found to my dismay that the company had sent me not the navy blue I'd requested, but a black blanket instead. Peeved, I pulled it from its plastic wrapper and saw immediately that it was a very good quality blanket.

I'd ordered the heavyweight thickness, and was pleased to see that it was, indeed, a good thick blanket that would keep him warm during the coldest turnouts. It had a nice-sized tail flap, gussets for ease of movement in his shoulders, leg straps, and adjustable buckles in the front as well as Velcro closures. It was a turnout blanket fit for a king.

"It's *good* to be the king!" I announced to Wendy when she came to inspect it.

She grinned. "It fits him perfectly!"

"I got an 80," I remarked. 80 was the size of the blanket. "When spring comes, I'm going to have something embroidered on the front." At first I planned to put Bit's name on it, but when I thought about it, I decided it would be much cooler to have a big blue ribbon and the words 'Best Horse Ever' instead. I also decided to keep the black blanket, rather than send it back in exchange for blue. The black looked just as good, and cold weather was coming: although there had been a cold blast of air after the holidays, this particular Saturday at the end of January was actually a balmy 50 degrees. And while that warm trend was to continue into the following week, by week's end, the temperature was set to drop by a good 30 degrees, rendering the new blanket a near-future necessity.

"I'll put it in the tack room so that when the cold hits, it'll be here for you to put back on him," I told Wendy.

"O.k.," she replied, "Put it on top of Connie's tack box so I know where to look." Having done so, I promised Lydia that we would do some ground work soon, gave Bit a crunchy apple, and said my good-byes.

"Stay out of trouble!" I reminded Allen as I walked toward my car, "Join a fraternity or something!"

"Do I look like fraternity material?" he asked comically. He had a point

"O.k., forget I said that!" As I drove away, I noticed I had that contented feeling that I hardly ever experienced with other people. Nodding to myself, I reflected that seeing the old barn gang was good medicine. *Maybe,* I thought, *I should start going back out on Saturday mornings.*

My Favorite Doctor

"Hi, Sweetie! How *are* you?!" The cheerful greeting came from my dermatologist, Dr. Ana. Owing to an immoderate amount of suntanning in my youth, I've spent my middle years attempting to mitigate any potentially cancerous moles with bi-annual visits to the skin doctor. Every six months, she gives me a thorough going-over, grilling me for updates on my animals all the while. She'd read both my books, though when I tried to give her copies for free, she insisted on paying, writing checks for more than they were actually selling for on Amazon. She was my favorite doctor.

"How are the animals?," she inquired as she inspected my scalp.

"We lost two ducks last summer," I answered.

"Aww!" She was genuinely disappointed. "How many do you have left?"

"Two, now." I replied.

"Are you going to get more?" she wanted to know.

No, but I'm thinking about getting a pet rat!"

She was checking a couple of moles on my back as she exclaimed, "Hey! My brother had a pet rat! He loved it, it crawled all over him! What about Dudley – will he be o.k. with a rat?"

"God, no!" I chuckled, "his response would be 'we already have *too many animals!*'"

Dr. Ana laughed. "You could talk him into it, though, couldn't you?"

"Well, you know, you have to pick your battles! I'm not sure this one would be a good battle to fight. Besides, I don't know if my cats would respect a rat's need for personal space!"

She nodding in understanding. "We had an unfortunate incident once with a cat and a -"

"*Aaaack!*" I cried, interrupting her. "I don't want to hear bad stories!"

She changed tack then. "You just need a tight-fitting screen on top of the aquarium."

It never failed to amuse me, the fact that Dr. Ana could be so thorough with her skin checks, and yet able to carry on a detailed conversation about my animals at the same time.

"I think we'll take these two moles, just to be safe," she announced as she pointed out two on my left arm. "Is this one new, or has it gotten bigger recently? It's not in my notes."

I always felt sheepish when she asked me questions like this. I mean to say, I have well over one hundred moles on my body. There's no way I could possibly keep track of all of them, so I never bothered with any of them. "I have no idea," was my go-to answer. "Just take whichever ones you want."

"Now," she began as she retrieved a syringe from a cupboard, "are you the one who gets light-headed around needles?"

"No," I answered dryly, "I'm the one who screams loudly and runs from the room!" We both laughed.

"How's the new book coming along?" she asked as she carved chunks of flesh from my arm.

I frowned at the larger chunk in the specimen bottle. "Jeez! Did you *leave me* any skin?"

"A little," she joked in response. She had a terrific sense of humor.

One time, she removed a small mole from one of my toes. I got as far as the parking lot before I glanced down and noticed a troubling amount of blood on my sandal. Turning around, I went back up to the second floor of the building and remarked to the woman at the front desk, "Um...it's bleeding a bit more than I thought it would." The next thing I knew, I was being spirited to a surgical room at a surprisingly brisk pace by three nurses who had appeared out of nowhere. Dr. Ana hurried into the room, glanced at my foot, and without missing a beat said, "I *knew* I should've taken the whole toe!" I just loved her for that!

"O.k., Sweetie, I'll call you in about a week with the results."

"Alright. Hopefully, I'll have Book Three finished by my next visit."

"Awesome! I'm looking forward to it!" And with a squeeze of my hand – she usually hugged me, but I was sitting down at the time – she hustled busily to her next patient.

TO THE RESCUE!

"You!" I exclaimed as I pointed a finger at Barn Urchin Allen. "Just the man I want to see!" I was on two missions that day at The Harmony Barn. One had to do with an injured goose, and the other had to do with the newly-minted Mandy Dickinson. In Mandy's case, I had received the by-now familiar "barn Saturday?" text letting me know that she would be volunteering at the barn that particular day. I hadn't seen her since the wedding in November, and it was now February, so I was keen to stop in and visit. At the same time, I needed to find an extra pair of hands to help rescue an injured goose, and since Allen happened to be walking past the barn door when I opened it, I decided that he would work as well as anyone else.

Wendy's sister Deb had called me earlier in the week. Wendy, Deb, and I had rescued a goose with fishing line wrapped around his leg a few years earlier, and apparently, Deb had kept my phone number. This time, she talked about a goose with an injured wing who'd been hanging around a pond by himself for some time. Other geese came and went, she told me, but this one didn't seem able to fly. I told her I'd look into it.

The pond was located beside the I-490 on-ramp. I could pull the car off the road just fine, but the pond itself was partially blocked by a fence. The only access appeared to be from a business driveway on Route 42. Since I couldn't see any geese at all from my vantage point on the on-ramp, I surmised that the goose had fled. When I checked the area a second time a few days later, I had the same result. I let the matter drop there, but Deb called again that Friday, saying she'd seen the goose, and was available to help catch him on Saturday. Since she lived – handily – right next door to her sister, she suggested that I deputize one of Wendy's volunteers when I was at the barn. I told Deb I'd call her on Saturday morning.

"What are you doing after this?" I asked Allen.

He shrugged. "I dunno. Taking a shower?"

"Is it absolutely *vital* that you shower *immediately* after the barn? Cause I need an extra pair of hands to catch a goose. You up for it?"

"Sure," he answered.

"Awesome! When you're finished here, we'll go, yeah?" He nodded, and with that, I went in search of Mandy.

I followed her, chatting, as she mucked out the last couple of stalls. I made the mistake of telling her that I'd loaded up my clutch purse with all sorts of handy goodies that had been provided in a basket in the Ladies room of her wedding venue. She looked at me, aghast.

"What did you take?" she demanded.

"A little Tide pre-treater thing – very handy, that! A bunch of breath mints." There was more, but I couldn't remember the other stuff. Besides, the tone of her voice told me that she was not amused.

"My mom and I talked about how people took so much of that stuff!" she said with annoyance.

"Well, but...I mean, that's what it was *there for*, right?" I asked with some confusion.

At this point, Wendy wandered by, catching enough of the conversation to shake her head and say, "It's always Kelly, isn't it?"

"Yes, and why do you suppose that is?!" was my retort. Wendy and Mandy both gave me a knowing look then, which I took to mean *because you're always the one getting into trouble!*

"Who do you think provided all that stuff?" Mandy asked me.

"The venue?" I answered.

"No!" she exclaimed, "*We did!* My mom and I put that basket together! You were meant to *use* the stuff and *put it back!* Not *steal* it!"

"Well, I couldn't very well have returned a breath mint, now, could I?" I huffed defensively. "Besides, I thought the venue provided that basket of goodies."

"No!" she repeated irritably, "We did!"

"Did I mention how fabulously you rocked your wedding dress?" I asked in a transparent attempt to mitigate some of her annoyance.

She looked at me through narrowed eyes. "Say more things like that!" As though she'd let me off the hook if I sucked up sufficiently.

"Well, you *did!* And those tiny LED lights on the centerpieces were really pretty! And I *loved* your hair! You wanna help catch an injured goose?" I knew she'd turn me down before I even asked.

After we finished visiting, I called Deb and arranged to meet behind the business that owned the pond. I found Allen and we drove five minutes up the road, pulling up beside the door of the establishment. It appeared to be a business that catered to large truck repair. I knocked on the door, but no one answered, and when I checked the doorknob, I found it was locked. The three of us headed over to the pond, where I immediately spotted the goose in question. He did, indeed, appear to have an injured wing. The pond was small, so I said that I'd walk around the far side, directed Allen and Nancy to fan out on the near side, and suggested we meet in the middle on the other side of the pond. If the goose managed to make it to the pond, I told them, we'd never catch him.

Slowly, I started walking around the pond. When the goose saw all of us moving in his direction, he began to run but couldn't take off. Instead, he fell, and I winced as I watched how he struggled just to get back up on his feet. Something was terribly wrong. Unfortunately, once he regained his footing, he was faster than all three of us, and managed to evade us and get to the pond. Dejected, I watched him swim away. In amazement, I watched as he swam across the pond and *got out* on the other side. The Gods must've wanted us to catch him, giving us, as they did, that second chance to try. Quietly, I called Allen over.

"You're way faster than both of us," I said under my breath; I didn't want to offend Deb. "So I think it's going to be up to you to catch him.' Allen nodded in agreement. We split up, then, the three of us retracing our steps. As luck would have it, the goose appeared to be one dumb bird, because while he tried to evade us by running toward the pond again, he mainly ran parallel to it, giving Allen the opportunity to throw my beach towel over him.

"Cover his head with the towel!" I called as I ran over to him. He'd never caught a goose before, and didn't know that if you cover its head, it will settle down almost immediately.

I saw him struggling to get the towel in place. I caught up and wrapped one end of the towel around the goose's wings. It was then that I was what the problem was: a boney joint in his wing was completely exposed, and the wing swung freely from that joint in a way that told me that Goosey had a serious problem. It made sense that he might've been hit by a car, but I couldn't image how he would have gotten over the pond fence without being able to fly. Allen got the towel over Goosey's head, Goosey relaxed, and I picked him up and placed him in the carrier that Deb had brought along. It was a particularly large carrier, suitable for a German Shepherd-sized dog, and that turned out to work in my favor.

"Well, who wants to drive him to Wild Haven?" I asked, hoping that it wouldn't end up being me. Wild Haven Nursery, with its state rehab license, was the go-to place for injured wildlife. They rehabbed all manner of wild critters, and did a fine job on a 501(c) charity budget. The drawback was that they were located a good 25-odd miles away, and I didn't particularly feel like making the drive. The size of the carrier decided the matter: it was far too big to fit in my little 2-door coupe. Deb agreed to drive Goosey to Wild Haven.

"Let me know what they say about him, would you?" I asked before Deb drove away. She said that she would.

I clapped Allen on the back, congratulating him on his fast moves and telling him, "You're my goose-catching hero, dude!"

An hour or so later, Deb called and told me that Wild Haven said they would take Goosey for an x-ray and let her know what they found. By the end of the day, I received this text:

"Hi Kelly. Wild Haven called me. They checked the goose out further and unfortunately had to put him down. His bones were completely separated and he would never heal right."

I chewed on that for awhile. Something about it bothered me. *Did we do the right thing?* I wondered. I let my mind wander then, and realized that with coyotes in the area – and there were plenty – he wouldn't have survived much longer. Indeed, it was a wonder he lasted as long as he had without being eaten by something. In addition, there wasn't much in the way of food out there; winter had sent the grass into dormancy, and there were no leaves on the various shrubs. And, being a specie that mates for life, he must've been terribly lonely out there all by himself. Euthanasia, I knew, was a much gentler alternative to being attacked and killed. Putting an animal down was always a tough decision, but we *had* done the right thing, I concluded, even if it didn't feel like it.

You win some, you lose some, I mused, but that never made losing them any easier.

The Horsemobile

Step-daughter Lauren had been without a car for some time. Duddy loaned her his, but as the months went by, he became anxious to get it back. Driving around all the time in his gas-guzzling business truck wasn't really a financially sound thing to do when he could be driving a car that used a lot less gas. Finally, the day came when Lauren had saved enough money to start looking. She consulted Craigslist and found a small handful of possibilities. Dud went with her to check them out.

Lauren pooh-poohed the first car she saw. It wasn't in the greatest shape, and she wanted to look at the other cars on her list. The second – a Saab like her father's – met most, if not all, of her needs, and she made the decision to buy it. When Dud came home that day, he gushed over how clean the car was inside and out, and what a good deal Lauren had gotten on it. Indeed, he was so impressed that he started to have car envy. And since Lauren had also found a likely-sounding Saab SUV on Craigslist, Duddy decided that he wanted to see it.

The Horsemobile

The idea of an SUV had been mine. I was more than happy with my zippy little Honda two-door, five-speed manual coupe, but when I started spending more time with Lauren and her three small children, it became readily apparent that two doors were no longer enough: Lauren practically had to climb into the back of the car every time she wanted to secure Stella's car seat, or buckle Liam's belt. Dud began complaining about how inconvenient the two doors were for shopping, and I got to thinking that a bigger car might be a good idea.

I didn't expect to get one quite so soon, though. Duddy had paid off his car loan as one of our Christmas gifts, and it was really nice not to have to shell out a payment every month. But the SUV that Lauren found had piqued his interest, and his keenness on finding a really good car for an exceptionally low price, as she had done, seemed to overrule his sensibilities. Gamely, I went along with his enthusiasm, and rather looked forward to seeing the car myself.

Wondering what to wear for the test drive, and not wanting to look like someone who could comfortably afford the asking price, I had a sudden flash of inspiration and pulled my old barn coat from the back of the closet. This was the Pepto-Bismol-colored coat I'd worn for a number of years before acquiring the one with butt flaps. It had several patches sewn on it, all proclaiming my alliance with The Harmony Barn.

When we pulled up alongside the Washington's trailer, I saw immediately the horse-silhouette stickers on the side windows, and the one on the back announcing in large letters "JUMPER," and I knew that someone in the Washington's house was a horse person. My choice of coat suddenly seemed amusingly appropriate. The bobble-headed horse stuck to the dashboard topped off the equine theme.

I had had a Honda CRV in mind, or possibly a Toyota Rav4. Both were smaller-sized SUV's, which was what I preferred. So I was very surprised to find that the Washington's car was a virtual monolith of a sport utility vehicle. It was *way* bigger than the sort of thing I'd been thinking about. Since it was to be my car, Dud stood back and let me give it a test drive. It was so luxurious, I hardly knew what to think.

While only one of my previous cars had been a clunker, my usual style was low-key, low-maintenance, low-frills. A five-speed manual transmission was as exotic as it got. But *this* thing, with its heated leather seats, fancy features, and just about every extra one could want, was in another league altogether. I felt a little like Cinderella dancing with the handsome prince. Dud was equally enthralled.

The Washingtons hadn't bothered to clean the car out, and with two small children, it was in a fairly messy state. I didn't hold this against them, though, figuring a shop-vac would take care of most of the problem. Dud started crunching numbers with them, and it was agreed that we would take the car to our mechanic in two days' time to find out why the headlights didn't work. On the drive home, I urged Duddy to consider getting a used-car inspection at the same time. He didn't want to do it.

"It's fifty bucks well spent," I argued. "I've passed up buying more than one car after having it inspected. This isn't a dealership, you don't know what you're getting from a private buyer." Dud, ever the cheapskate – I mean frugal – didn't want to shell out for it. Overnight, though, he changed his mind.

"I'm rethinking the inspection," he announced the next day.

"Do you want me to call Fred and have him put it on the schedule?" I asked. He did, I did, and Fred did. I was very relieved because, as it turned out, Fred found a number of things wrong with the SUV, and more than one of them made the Washington's asking price more negotiable. Dud returned to the bargaining table.

I let Dud do the talking. During his back-and-forth with the Washingtons, I glanced around the trailer, taking in the horse prints on the walls, the horseshoe decorations, the horse sculptures, and the old-fashioned wooden muck rake hanging in their hallway. I already knew that the JUMPER was Sarah, who told us that they had used the SUV to haul the horse she used to own to competitions. She'd sold him to her farrier, she said with regret, but with baby Jenny on the floor and four-year old Bobby sitting beside me on the couch, it was clear that she had neither the time, nor the money, to pursue riding anymore. I was cheering Bobby on as he played a game on his Tablet - "Yay, Bobby! You squashed the squid! Way to go, dude!" - when my preoccupation was pierced by a question that Sarah had just asked Dud.

"Wait! What?" I asked with some confusion. "Do we want *what*?"

"Do you want me to take the horse stickers off the car?" she wanted to know.

"Heck, no!" I answered with a grin, "I'll be able to find her in a crowded parking lot!"

"What about the bobble horse?"

"You can leave that, too!" I replied heartily.

"Good," she said, "I'm not sure I could get it off anyway. I glued it on pretty good!"

And with that, the details had been ironed out and the price agreed on. We arranged to pick up the car the next afternoon. And while Dud dealt with a brief bout of buyer's remorse ("What have we done? Did we *really* need to buy a car *right now?!*"), I viewed the Horsemobile, as I dubbed my new wheels, as a good omen. It was strong enough to pull a horse trailer, and had all the necessary hitches and brake light wiring in place. If Sally every *did* get around to buying the trailer she wanted, we could pull Bit and Big William in my Horsemobile. In the meantime, there were so many features in the car that I'd never had before, I actually read the owner's manual from front to back. I wanted to enjoy every single bit of luxury my new used car offered!

BIG BLUE

Sometime in late January, a huge horse by the name of Big Blue took up residence at The Harmony Barn. He had a gentle, inquisitive nature, and the first time I saw him canter, it looked like he was gliding on air. I wondered how well he would assimilate into the herd, knowing that only time would answer that question.

Because Barn Urchin Allen had gone off to a college that required a long commute, he remained on campus during the week, returning home only on weekends. Since he was no longer available to clean Wendy's barn full time, Lydia took over, squeezing the gig in between working her night-shift job and sleeping. I'm not sure she actually *did* get much rest, but it didn't seem to bother her. She was still working one frigid February day when I stopped by.

I had come with the express purpose of giving Bit an apple and a handful of horse cookies. It had been too cold to do any ground work at all for almost a week and I didn't want him to think I'd forgotten him. The apple and horse cookies would have to serve as quality time until it warmed up enough that my fingers wouldn't freeze when I groomed him. I called out to him as I walked toward the arena. He saw me, but he didn't seem particularly willing to approach the wire like he usually did. It was soon clear that the presence of Big Blue had something to do with it.

Blue had been standing at the wire – electric fencing that separated the arena from the stalls – quietly interested in the fact that another human (me) had come into the barn. He remained where he was, and I watched as Bit walked to within ten feet of us and stopped. Blue waved his head at Bit in a mildly-threatening way, and Bit immediately walked away. I called him again, and he tried to return, but was clearly unwilling to get too close to Blue.

This was not good. I ducked under the wire, walked over to where he was, and proffered the apple. After he'd eaten, he moved away again. I ducked back under the wire and chatted with Lydia, who remarked that all of the horses were behaving oddly that day, though she didn't know why. I turned back to Bit just in time to see something I never thought I would see: Big Blue lunged at Bit, his ears pinned, and his teeth bared. Then he immediately spun his hind end around, threatening to kick if Bit didn't clear off. Bit cleared off.

I had literally *just* finished reading a book about horse behavior, an old tome from 1988 called *Horsewatching*, by Desmond Morris. In it, Morris describes the fight for dominance, in which two horses display just the sort of behavior Blue was exhibiting toward Bit. According to Morris, horses will continue these displays, ratcheting up the emphasis as needed, until one horse backs down. The remaining horse is established as the dominant one. Since Bit had backed down, I was deeply troubled by the turn of events, and sought out Ron for answers. I headed up to his office above the viewing room.

"O.k., so I have questions," I announced, describing to him what I had just witnessed. "If Bit's the alpha horse, why did he back down?"

Ron answered in that slow way he has of speaking, not that he's slow by any means, but just that he tends to not rush his words. "Bit and Blue had been playing with each other over the wire [that divided to two halves of the arena] for awhile, now. I *just,* a couple of hours ago, put everyone together for the first time. So this kind of thing is going to happen."

"Yeah, but if Bit backed down, does that mean he's not the alpha horse anymore?" I couldn't imagine how Bit would feel if he lost his Very Important Horse status.

"Not necessarily," Ron replied, "it'll probably be a few weeks before the alpha status is figured out. Bit hasn't given up his girls, yet, so he hasn't backed down entirely."

"Do you think he's likely to?" I wondered.

Ron shrugged. "I dunno. Blue is a *big* horse – 18hh – and that's probably pretty intimidating! And, he's got a laid-back personality, but he doesn't back down, so there's that."

I asked the main question that had been in my mind. "Would it be bad for Bit if Blue became the alpha?" I was thinking in terms of self-esteem, and I hated the idea that Bit might find himself at the bottom of the pecking order.

Ron thought about that. "Well, for one, if Bit's not head of the herd anymore, his stomach would probably settle down because he wouldn't have to worry about all the other horses anymore." I liked the sound of that.

He continued, "And second, he wouldn't be at the bottom of the totem pole. He'd probably be somewhere near the top." I liked the sound of that, too: Bit could be more like a right-hand man, but without all the headaches. How many times had he made his weird huffing sound as we walked away from the barn? It was a call to his herd, no doubt asking if everyone was alright. Not having to worry about the safety of 19 other horses might come as a huge relief to him. Then again, giving up your position as CEO, with all the perks and benefits that that implies, is rarely easy.

Ron had answered my questions, but of course, the answer to the most important question – who would win the fight for dominance – would remain to be seen for however long it took them to decide. Anxiously, I went home, determined to give my First Place Blue Ribbon Champion Horse some extra attention during that trying time. No matter what happened, though, he would always be my best pal.

A Visit With Mandy

"How do you like the horsemobile?" The question was directed at Mandy. I had invited her out for dinner and a symphony concert, and this was her first time in my new used car. She eyed the dashboard suspiciously.

"That horse is kinda creepin' me out!" she replied.

"The *bobble horse?*" I asked in surprise. "It's a *bobble horse!* What's not to like?"

"Hmmm," she answered non-noncommittally.

I knew that she and the new husband were working different hours, and I knew that she wasn't particularly happy to be alone so much of the time. So when I got wind of the annual Whoville Symphony Pro-Am concert, I issued an invitation.

The Pro-Am concert was held once a year. Duddy and I had gone a couple of times and really enjoyed it. The concert involved the professional Whoville Symphony musicians, and any amateurs who cared to participate. Due to conflicting schedules, they only got to practice together a handful of times, but they'd been terrific every time nonetheless. The big plus for the event was that the concert only lasted an hour, so if Mandy didn't enjoy herself, she wouldn't feel that a lot of time had been wasted.

The concert was being held at the Whoville Museum of Art Peristyle. It looked like a Roman amphitheater, only indoors. There were huge columns circling the seating area, and special lighting made it appear as if you were in some ancient Roman ruins at sundown. It really added a lot to the ambiance. We'd decided on a seafood restaurant for dinner, and we headed there beforehand.

Mandy spent the ride telling me about her job as a Speech Language Pathologist. Now that she had earned her Master's degree, she had a lot of important-sounding letters after her name: Mandy Dickinson MA, CF-SLP. And while I had no idea what the letters stood for, it was clear that she had finally graduated from being Shrimp Girl[3] to Career Woman, and that her job involved more than just dealing with old folks. I grilled her on the details.

Apparently, she was being sent to several schools in the area, working with affected children. I had assumed that she would spend all her time at nursing homes, giving swallow tests and helping stroke victims. The business about the school kids was a new twist. Having briefly assisted a gymnastics coach with a bunch of knuckle-headed eighth-graders, I didn't envy Mandy; junior high kids could be a real handful. Indeed, it sounded as though a lot of what she was doing was the sort of thing English teachers used to teach: reading comprehension, vocabulary, and sentence structure. She had a lot on her plate.

I was interested in what she had to say, but I also wanted to broach my favorite subject as well. I summed up the

---

[3] One of Mandy's part-time after-school jobs had been offering seafood nibbles to shoppers at a local grocery store, earning her the nickname "Shrimp Girl."

details of her job duties with, "Riveting!" before steering the conversation toward the topic of when she might come out to the barn and ride with me. I wanted someone to do off-property trail rides with her, and I asked when she thought she might be available.

"Well, it wouldn't be on Charlie Horse!" she remarked dryly. It took me a minute to figure out why, and then I remembered. A year or so previously, we decided to ride Bit and Charlie out in the pasture. The horses spent a considerable amount of time grazing out there so it was familiar territory. But for reasons we'll never know, Charlie decided that he wanted nothing to do with this sort of thing, and almost bucked Mandy right off his back. Wendy saw him buck and immediately called a halt to the proceedings. Clearly, trail riding with Charlie was out of the question. Unfortunately, the other likely candidate, an amiable gelding named Traveller, was also out the question because someone had just started leasing him. That made him off-limits to everyone but the lease holder.

"There's always Galaxy!" I chuckled. Galaxy was one of five rescued Paso Finos who had come to the barn a number of years ago. The other four had been adopted – one by a diminutive policewoman who knew that if she had to get off a standard-sized horse to deal with an issue on the ground, she'd never be able to get back on. The small size of the Paso was a good choice for her. That left Galaxy as the only Paso remaining at the barn.

The joke that had me chuckling was the fact that Galaxy – an ill-mannered little shit who thought nothing of rearing up right in front of you if she didn't want to do as she was told – was at best about 13hh, while Mandy was a towering 5'11". If she sat on Galaxy's back, it was very likely that her feet would drag on the ground! Mandy gave me that look she saves for when I'm being ridiculous.

"Yeah. *Not!*" was the sum total of her response.

"Well, we'll figure something out!" I replied optimistically. In truth, though, there really weren't any other candidates for a trail ride. Either the other horses belonged to private owners, or they were medically unsuitable for riding. Our only hope was that the girl who was leasing Traveller might get tired of him, although this was a slim hope at best: who on earth could get tired of horses?!

CATS!

It wasn't until I was two-thirds of the way through writing this manuscript that I realized there was a glaring omission: not once had I mentioned my four cats. I had written about them in a fair amount of detail in NBM, though, and I didn't really have any updates to add to *Sorry Honey*. So I spent some time turning the matter over in my head, a little dismayed by my lack of fresh material.

The first thing that came to mind, as I chewed on the subject one night while waiting for sleep to overtake me, was the fact that all four cats were now firmly in the double digits: Buddy, the oldest, is 14, Spanky is 13, Junebug is 11, and Gracie Ellen is 10. And, in my experience, all four have reached the age where things will inevitably start going wrong.

I've made a point, since Miss Muffin died in NBM, of spending a little quality time with each cat individually on a daily basis. Buddy, while technically an old man, is still pretty peppy, and can be found racing around the Critter Shack for no apparent reason at least once a day. Otherwise, he spends much of his time sleeping on my bed. Any time I go into the bedroom on a clothes-related errand, I stop to pet him, and maybe snuggle for a minute or two – Bud was never one for lengthy displays of affection – before returning to whatever it is I'm doing.

While Buddy has always had a mainly hands-off policy, it's worth noting that he considers himself the man of the house, and in that capacity, he clearly feels it's his duty to check up on things several times a day. This includes poking his nose into any activity that's going on, making the rounds of the house at least twice each day (thus ensuring that absolutely nothing has changed since his last inspection), and snuggling with me on the bed at night. Happily for all concerned, Bud hasn't had a health-related problem for many years. And in spite of his hands-off policy, I find it interesting that when either Dud or I spend that brief amount of time petting him, Buddy purrs happily every single time.

Spanky, who I described in both of my last two books as a miserable wretch with poor self-esteem, still suffers daily bouts of angst in which he stares at me as he wails unhappily. And while I may well chat with critters on a regular basis, I confess that I have absolutely no idea what it is that makes Spanky so deeply unhappy. Attention from Duddy gives him a temporary reprieve from the worst of his misery, but inevitably, he always ends up mooning around the dining room, announcing his latest bout of despair for all to hear. Apart from the occasional urinary tract infection, Spanky has been in very good health his entire life.

Junebug is as fat now as she was in NBM. She still has a kibble hobby, which explains her Rubenesque figure. Every night, as we watch t.v., Junebug will wander into the kitchen and, no matter how much kibble is still in the bowl, she will sit near it making squeaky noises until one of us gives in and puts more food in it. It isn't just *more* kibble that she wants, it's *fresh* kibble, the kind that doesn't have any other cat's slobber on it.

The most loyal of my four cats, Junebug joins me on the bed at some point every single night. Usually, she sleeps next to my pillow, and her happy purr sends me off to sleep quite peacefully. In spite of her girth, Junebug has been equally fortunate, health-wise.

Three-legged Gracie Ellen Tripod is our friendliest cat. She'll usually approach visitors with a view to being petted, and she diplomatically divides her attention between Duddy and I by spending part of the evening snuggled on his lap, then coming over to the couch to snuggle with me. Once on the couch, she'll roll over onto her back, relax her three legs, tuck her head into her shoulder, and fall asleep. Her underside is completely exposed the entire time, telling me that she has placed all her trust in me. She's always been the most cheerful of our brood, and apart from the broken leg that required amputating, back when she was a kitten, she, too, had enjoyed excellent health. Until she started barfing.

All four cats throw up fairly regularly. Hairballs, mostly, but sometimes undigested food as well (which I believe is hairball-related). The thing about Gracie that caught my attention was that she *kept* barfing over a 24-hour period, until there was nothing left in her to throw up. Concerned, I opened a can of wet food that I had put in a cupboard and forgotten – I only give the cats wet food on Christmas Day – and offered her the can, hoping to tempt her taste buds. When she growled at me to go away instead, I called the vet's office. They managed to get us in that same day.

The vet was stumped when the x-ray and blood work came back normal. So was I. I assumed it was something she'd eaten. Even though she's spent her entire life with me, save for the first six months in which her leg got broken, Gracie has still retained a street cat mentality in which she's never quite sure where her next meal will come from. The fact that I've fed her every single day for ten years doesn't seem to count for anything, which was why I thought she might've gotten into something she shouldn't have. But the x-ray showed no blockage of any kind. The vet gave her an anti-nausea shot and told me to keep an eye on her to see if anything changed.

By the next day, it was clear that something was very wrong. Gracie moved from spot to spot around the house, trying to find a quiet place to get comfortable. Except she obviously felt crummy enough that she wasn't going to get comfortable anywhere. I called the vet's again, and again, they got us in that day. I explained to a different vet what had transpired the day before. This doctor (I was starting at a new veterinary practice. While I hadn't learned the names of all the vets yet, the new place was considerably closer to where I lived) suggested they do a series of barium x-rays. They would shoot some barium into her mouth, and take an x-ray every hour for a period of time to see how it traveled through her system. I wasn't surprised by the idea – yesterday's vet had mentioned it as a possibility as well. It meant that Gracie had to spend the day there, but since there were no other options on the table, I agreed, gave her a hug and a kiss, and said I'd come back to visit later.

Now I was worried. No matter how many times I had been through this before, I never learned from it: some things just aren't fixable. I would take the critter to the vet, reassured by the assumption that they could fix whatever the issue was. Too many times, there *was* no fix. I feared that that would be the case now with Gracie.

I went home and told Duddy what had transpired. In spite of the previous days' x-ray that cost $285, and the barium series that would cost $330, his only comment was, "It's getting expensive, isn't it?" I said yes, and left it at that. To his credit, my frugal husband said no more. It would've been pointless in any case: while I *do* have a line that I won't cross, animal-health-wise, it has nothing at all to do with cost, and everything to do with quality of life.

I once had a beloved cat euthanized when she was diagnosed with diabetes at the age of 14, not because it would've cost money to treat her, but because I knew that her temperament would not tolerate the treatment required. That didn't make my decision any easier, but I knew then as I know now that it was the right thing to do for that particular cat.

Later the same day, I went back to visit Gracie. I don't want any of my critters thinking that I've dumped them in a horrible place and that I'm not coming back. She looked so miserable that I didn't pick her up as I normally would have. Instead, I stuffed the upper half of my body into her cage and spoke to her quietly as I gave her some reassuring pets. After a time, a third vet came in. This one turned out to be Dr. Carrolton, the large-animal vet who treated The Harmony Barn horses. I'd heard a lot about him, but had never met him until now. He called me over to a computer where he sat, pulling up Gracie's barium x-rays. Very nicely, and very competently, he told me what he thought the problem was.

"See this small area here? The area where the stomach meets the intestines looks like it's been squished?" he asked. Looking at what his finger was pointing to on the screen, I nodded. "I'm 85% sure that this is the problem, that this area has spasmed, making it hard for the contents of her stomach to pass through to her intestines. I'm not sure whether the spasm caused her vomiting, or her vomiting caused the spasm – it's a chicken-and-egg thing – but you can see how much barium is still in her stomach; it all should have passed through by now." His calm manner gave me some confidence, but the million dollar question had yet to be asked.

"*Please* tell me this is fixable," I said quietly.

He nodded. "There's a pill. You'll give it to her every day for a week or so, and it will relax the spasm." That was a relief! It was decided that she would stay at the hospital overnight, and, barring any complications, I would be able to take her home the next day.

"You're welcome to go back and sit with her some more," Dr. Carrolton said, but I shook my head.

"She wasn't all that thrilled about the visit. It was kinda like, *It's nice to see you, now go away!* She definitely doesn't feel very good."

Dr. Carrolton nodded. "We'll get her started on the pills, and give her some easily-digestible wet food. She should start feeling better soon." I thanked him for his time, then headed home.

I can't say that I felt much better. As I had told numerous critters over the years, "It's my job to worry about you!" And worry was what I did the rest of that day, and overnight. I'd been lucky, all those years the cats had enjoyed their collective good health. But something serious like this always serves as a reminder that their days are numbered. They always have been; it was a decade without serious problems that had lulled me into a false sense of security. And while Junebug had always been my favorite cat, the crisis with Gracie showed me how much I took her cheerful presence for granted. I was not prepared to say good-bye just yet, but fortunately, I wouldn't have to: by the next morning, her condition had improved, Dr. Carrolton was pleased with her progress, and he gave me the green light to take her home.

After a week in which I crushed up chunks of pills and hid them in her wet food, Gracie seemed back to her old self, although I, with my wake-up call, stopped taking her so much for granted, and determined to cherish those evening snuggles for as long as we were able to enjoy them. There's nothing quite like a crisis to put things into perspective, is there?

Rats!

It took a month or two to work up the courage to broach with Dud the subject of a pet rat. I'd given the matter a lot of thought, and had come to the conclusion that it might be fun to have one. I'd read that rats are very smart, very clean animals, and I had enjoyed the hamsters of my youth. So one night, out of nowhere, as we watched t.v. I threw the question out for consideration.

"What do you think about having a pet rat?"
"No," came the immediate reply.
"But they're supposed to be really smart animals!"
"No," he repeated.
"And very clean animals, too!"
"No!"
So much for that idea!

The Good Dog

Pete Mitchell was dying. And while no one but me was actually using the "d" word just yet, the gravity of his situation became clear during a phone conversation with his wife, Pat, in which she asked me, "You want some ducks?" It was then that I knew that things were pretty dire.

It was Pete's third go-around with cancer. The first time, it was in his lung. Later, it was colon cancer. Now, it was in his prostate, and the prognosis was not good. He was scheduled to do chemo, but Pat's expectation was that it would make him as sick as all the other chemo sessions had in previous years, and she was certain that he would end up in the hospital yet again, suffering the ill effects that chemo is famous for. She didn't know if he could survive them. I couldn't get a handle on whether she actually wanted him to do the chemo or not, but it was clear that she thought his time was coming, and that Pete thought so, too. I told her that, of course, I would take the ducks.

You may remember Pat and Pete from CCL. They had fed the abandoned McKinnon's Pond ducks for some years. Pat got to know all of the domestics, to the extent that if one became injured, she would call me and describe in perfect detail the duck with the problem. When Black Swede Ducky became lame due to a fishing line injury, it was Pat who offered to take him in. That was 8-odd years ago. In the time since, they had taken in five or six other domestics who had been injured at the pond, and Pat had felt sufficiently moved by all the adoptions that she made a sign on an old piece of wood that read *Lame Duck Dude Ranch*. The sign hung from a tree in their front yard.

The number of rescued ducks in residence at the dude ranch dropped, though, over the years, as age and ill health took their toll. Now, there were only the original Ducky, and a Rouen I had named Handsome. Pat told me that with all the health issues on their plates, neither she nor Pete had the time or energy to devote to the ducks anymore. Indeed, their pond was so stinky and dirty, she reported, that the ducks refused to go in it. I reassured her that the boys would be fine with us and our two Pekins, and although Pete didn't want to let them go – I suspect he viewed giving them away as the first nail in his coffin – Pat was firm in her wish to hand them off to me.

She was having a bad time of it in ways other than Pete's cancer. Her favorite cat had died just a week before, she told me, and Lady, the dog she had rescued from a neglectful neighbor, was reaching the end of her life. Lady's back end suddenly didn't work anymore. Pat and Pete would put her on a stretcher and carry her out into the front yard. They would leave her there for the day, lying on a soft pile of straw, food and water nearby. At night, they would carry her into the garage where much the same set-up took her through until morning. Pat knew that Lady wouldn't be around much longer, but I think she was too overwhelmed to know what to do about it. We made arrangements for me to pick up the ducks in two days' time. That gave me at least a day or so to figure out how to get Dud on board with two more ducks. I decided to let the decision seem like his.

When you're a long-term spouse (and while we haven't been married long, we've certainly known each other for a few decades), if you have any sense, you learn how to finesse things. It's no good just making pronouncements as though you're a dictator. Much as Dud and I both like doing that, we also both know that it isn't effective. So that night, over dinner, I told Dud about the phone call with Pat, taking care to mention that it was obvious that Pete wouldn't be around much longer.

"Pat wondered whether we could take the ducks," I finished, bypassing entirely the part where I had already told her that we'd do it. Then I put some meatloaf in my mouth and chewed, biding my time.

"What ducks?" he wanted to know. Dud had a vague knowledge of Pat, Pete, and their rescue ducks, but he had never met any of them.

"Two drakes that developed leg injuries. They limped so bad that they never would've survived the winter at the pond. Ducky's the first one they adopted, and Handsome was the second or third. In any case, neither she nor Pete are up to taking care of them anymore. Those ducks are old, though; they won't last a whole lot longer."

"*How* old?" he asked.

"At least as old as Ethel, and she was eleven or twelve when she died."

Dud digested that information, spread some butter on a piece of bread, and said, "Well, it would be the right thing to do." I waited to see if there was any more, but that appeared to be the extent of his thoughts.

"I'll tell Pat that we'll take them, then," I answered quietly.

And that's how you finesse a husband!

When Saturday came, I loaded two critter carriers in the car and headed to the Mitchell's. As I pulled into the driveway, I saw immediately what Pat had told me about Lady: there she was, a big, shaggy dog of indeterminate breeding, lying on a pile of straw. She had never been a particularly friendly dog with strangers, but she had taken to me the first time I met her.

"Careful," Pat had warned all those years ago, "she doesn't always like humans."

So I stood just on the other side of the chain link fence and said, "Hi, pretty girl!" At which point she wagged her tail and approached me. Pat looked on in amazement.

"She's never done *that*!" she said in surprise.

I shrugged. "Well, I *am* the Critter Lady! Sometimes, it seems like animals know that." Apparently, Lady had been one of those who did.

Lady had originally belonged to a fellow in the neighborhood who was always gone. While he was away, Lady spent hours chained up outside. Pat was mystified by the fact that no matter how long the man left Lady alone, the dog was always happy to see him when he came home. Still, it was no life for a dog, and the situation weighed heavily on Pat's mind. Eventually, she offered to walk the dog, and the fellow agreed to let her. After a time, Pat did a little finessing of her own, and Lady came to live permanently with her and Pete.

They would take Lady along when they went to feed the ducks. She was already old and stiffly arthritic by then, but she would jump out of the old station wagon and wander around, sniffing things and generally enjoying being part of a pack. To her credit, she never once chased the ducks. Pat loved her dearly – I'm sure Pete did, too – and they gave her the kind of life that a good dog deserves to have. I always admired Pat her determination to treat animals well, even if they *did* belong to someone else! And now, all these years later, it was clear that Lady had reached the end. It was only what the Mitchells would do about it that remained a question.

Once we'd caught the ducks – and for two gimpy old geezers, they were surprisingly agile – and I loaded the carriers into the car, I went back to Lady and sat down on the ground next to her. I knew that I probably wouldn't be seeing her again, so I made a point of fussing over her. It was as I did that I noticed her sides heaving, in exactly the same way as Miss Muffin's had done in NBM. I had taken Muff to the vet, expecting them to fix the problem, only to be told that it was fluid around her heart, there was no fix for it, and the kindest thing to do would be to put her down. Now, here I was looking at exactly the same thing with Lady. I looked up at Pete, who had been standing nearby.

"You see her sides heaving like that?" I asked him. He nodded.

"But her mouth isn't panting. What this is, is fluid around her heart. It presses on her heart and makes it hard for her to breathe. Is she on any medications?" Pete nodded again.

"She's got a heart pill, a couple of different things," he said vaguely. "I haven't given them to her lately." He probably didn't see the point in giving her pills when she was so obviously near the end of her life.

"One was a water pill," he added as an afterthought.

"The water pill is for this," I gestured toward Lady's heaving belly, "You might want to start giving her those again." Pete said that he would.

It's important not to judge, here. If I thought one of my critters was close to the end, I don't know that I would bother with medicines that weren't going to change the situation, either. Mostly, I was trying to plant a seed; neither Pete nor Pat seemed to know what to do about Lady. Perhaps if they knew more specifics, like the fluid around her heart, they might start thinking about The End, and how to facilitate it. I knew they were perfectly capable of choosing euthanasia for an animal in need; I just didn't know if they knew *when* it should be done. When I called Pat the next day, though, to give her an update on the relocated ducks, she told me through her tears that they had a 2:00 appointment to have Lady euthanized.

"She has these open bed sores on her that we didn't know about," Pat went on, "*big* sores, and she's in pain. We didn't know that, either. She's been so good, such a sweetheart, that when she growled at me, I knew she was telling me it was time." I agreed, and offered to go with them to the vet's, but she declined. We arranged to go for a walk on Tuesday – Pat had been looking for a new walking buddy and I had volunteered – and I assumed that she would tell me about things in her own time, if she wanted to. In the meantime, all I could do was give her the usual condolences.

"Pat, you guys gave her *such* a good life! And she loved you for that! You guys took great care of her, and I always admired the fact that you didn't let her spend her lifetime being lonely at that guy's house. I only wish I had some magic words to say now, but I don't." Pat thanked me for my kindness, and rang off. I spent the rest of the day feeling rather subdued. I had liked Lady very much. She was a sweetheart of a dog who ended up with much more than she'd started out with. She'd had a good life with the Mitchells. Even if she had lived a much longer life, though, it would still have been just as hard to say good-bye and let her go. Such is the nature of love.

Introducing Ducky
and Gimpy

Would you be surprised to learn that I made the exact same mistake when bringing Pat's two drakes home that I made when I brought Ethel and Boyfriend home? Of all the mistakes that I *have* learned from in my time, protecting my ducks a little too overzealously has not been among them. It was only when I saw the abject terror in their eyes, that third night I herded them into the shed, then picked them up and dropped each rather unceremoniously into a carrier, that I flashed back to the first days with Ethel and Boyfriend and realized I was making the same mistake again.

I suppose the drakes would've learned to live with spending their nights in the shed if I hadn't added the frightening element of picking them up (they didn't want to be handled) and putting them in separate carriers (they didn't want to be segregated), but after giving the matter some thought, I couldn't reassure myself that raccoons couldn't break into the shed if they had a mind to. So I frightened them to the

Nth degree by doing both of the aforementioned, rather than just herding them in and letting them be.

The girls had not been happy about the new additions. In the first place, I don't know that they felt like their 2-duck flock needed increasing, and in the second place, the boys acted as though they hadn't seen females up close for years – which, technically, happened to be true. The boys made a beeline from their carriers right to the girls, and chased them around the yard with a fervor I didn't know they possessed at their time of life. The girls looked at me like *what have you done?* And I couldn't answer them. At least, there was no answer that they were going to like. Putting the boys in the shed at night seemed, therefore, like a good opportunity for the girls to have some quiet time to themselves. It didn't last long, though.

On the fourth night, when I herded the girls into their pen, Ducky and the newly-renamed Gimpy followed them. There was no quibbling, no fear, no nothing; they simply followed the girls into the pen and settled in the straw. Since the girls didn't seem to mind, I bid them all good night and shut the door. That was easy! From then on, the four shared the pen, although not without the occasional display of dominance from one drake or the other. Even so, a certain parity was reached, and the ducks paired off quite quickly – Penny with Gimpy (both of a rather dominant mien), and Daffy with Ducky (both of whom displayed more passive personalities).

Initially, it didn't occur to me that with four ducks pooping in the pen every night, we'd be going through a lot more straw. Happily, Pat offered to let us take what they'd been using all this time, which amounted to a considerable number of bales. When Dud and I went to pick up the straw, we saw for the first time the ingenious home she and Pete had fixed in the garage.

It was the ducks' nighttime quarters, the place in the garage that the drakes had walked into voluntarily every night for eight years, and what it was was an igloo made from bales of straw. It was constructed in such a way that there was a u-shaped tunnel within that the ducks could walk into and, on particularly cold winter nights, sleep in as well. When we had all the bales loaded into Dud's truck, there were sixteen of them!

As Dud secured the load, I pulled Pat aside and said quietly, "If you ever feel up to parting with the Lame Duck Dude Ranch sign, I'd love to have it as a legacy! But no rush!"

"Let me think about it," she replied. I knew from experience that Pat and change are not always on friendly terms – especially in this instance, where a large part of her and Pete's lives had altered considerably with the loss of so many animals in a short span of time. I nodded my understanding and repeated, "No rush!" A day or two later, though, she offered to let me have it, and I gratefully accepted. That *Dude Ranch* sign was, for me, one of the last tangible reminders of how Pat and I had both cared for a gang of abandoned animals that no one else wanted.

Equine Affaire!

If I had any sense at all, I would've poked around on the internet, trying to get a clue as to where Eric Clapton's Columbus house is *before* I actually left for Columbus. Unfortunately, as is typically the case with me, it didn't occur to me to do that until *after* we left Columbus and headed home. I suppose it was just as well: when I finally did get around to looking into the matter, I found that opinions on the subject varied so widely that it was impossible to narrow it down to any one area. Some thought he'd bought property in Dublin, Ohio (north of Columbus), and some thought they'd seen him hanging around in German Village (south of Columbus). In the end, the only thing I knew for sure was where I would choose to live, if *I* were a British rock star with a wife who was a Columbus native, and that was Delaware County; specifically, that portion that runs parallel to the Olentangy River.

Also known as State Route 315, the Olentangy River Road features a number of housing developments which favor the sort of McMansions that most can only lust after.

The downside of these developments, though, is that while the houses are huge, the lots are not. And if I paid that much money for a house, I would want at least five acres of property between myself and my nearest neighbor. Why the *nouveau riche* settle for such small plots of land is beyond me. Happily, though, the Olentangy River Road is also home to any number of stunningly beautiful older houses on considerably larger lots.

Those houses are incredibly beautiful. Well-maintained, with multiple-acre lots, and the sort of landscaping that costs at least $10,000, they sit snugly atop gently rolling hills, commanding expansive views of the river and beyond. Most copied some period in time – Colonial, Tudor, etc. – in a tasteful manner that, unlike McMansions, didn't feel the need to show off how much money had been spent building them. They're all exceedingly fetching, and if I ever won the lottery and decided to move away from Whoville, Olentangy River Road is where I'd go. Naturally, there's no way of knowing exactly *where* Eric Clapton's Columbus home is, and it seems unlikely that I'll ever find out unless he decides to email me and let me know. Eric, you can reach me at K7lly@yahoo.com. I promise I won't tell anyone where you live.

Getting back to reality, I told Duddy that I wanted to spend more time at this year's Equine Affaire than we had the year before. Even so, I had no idea exactly how big the Affaire was until I got a look at the complimentary brochure the parking lot attendants were handing out, and I didn't do that until after we were back in Whoville. The brochure ran to 78 pages, imparting a wide variety of information on the week's activities. Indeed, there were so many things going on, it would be impossible to see everything in one or two days.

Looking over the brochure, I counted 7 buildings in use on the Ohio Expo Center grounds, four of which offered, among other things, trade shows with over 450 of the nation's leading equine-related retailers, manufacturers, and organizations. In addition, there were more than 200 clinics, seminars, and demonstrations on a wide variety of equestrian sports and horse training, management, health, and business topics. This was no small event! We parked the car and wandered in, making a mental note of where the cotton candy could be found. It's never a full day for me at this sort of thing until I've located the cotton candy vendor.

It didn't really matter which building we started in, the mission was the same regardless. Last year, the mission had been to find a really good-quality bareback pad, and we accomplished that in the first building we entered. This year's mission, though, would prove considerably harder, and, in fact, we perused several hundred vendors in two different buildings before I found the sort of bitless bridle I'd had in mind for Bit.

We found Wendy, Connie, and their Hilton Herbs booth in the Celeste Center. They had arrived on Wednesday and would be there until Sunday. No doubt they'd be exhausted and ready to get home by the time they left, but while we visited, they were still fresh and cheery. Wendy loaded us up with a free Harmony Barn tote bag full of Hilton Herb samples, various lotions and potions intended for your horse's well being, and – my personal favorite – a giant pen with the Harmony Barn logo on it. With that, we bade them well and began wandering.

When we came to a round pen set up in a corner of the building, and found that a talk on trail riding safety was scheduled for an hour's time hence, we decided to take our time perusing the other vendors in the building and kill an hour in the process. Of all the tack vendors we talked to, not one offered a bitless rope bridle. Halters, yes. Bridles, no.

As it happened, I was looking for the sort of thing that Sally used on Big William. She had explained to me that she liked the rope version, called a *bosal,* rather than a leather one, because it was lightweight, and offered gentle pressure on various area's of William's face. It had made sense at the time, and I was pretty sure she'd bought it somewhere at the Affaire. But with over 450 vendors, and none in the Celeste Center who carried a rope bosal, it became clear fairly quickly that we would have our work cut out for us. Surprisingly, I managed to find Sally among the throng of humanity milling about, which seemed like a stroke of good luck. When I asked her where she thought we might find a rope bosal, though, she couldn't say exactly where. Back to Square One.

It was Sally who got me interested in thinking outside the usual equine box. As it happened, we turned out to be of like minds on the subjects of tack and training, although she knew much more about both than I did. I always made a point of asking her questions when I saw her at the barn, and I usually stuck around to watch if she was riding that day. When she explained the bosal to me, I was intrigued.

I had never liked the idea of putting a bit in a horse's mouth. I would much rather the horse respond to my commands by choice, rather than because I was causing discomfort in his mouth. I had never used a bitless bridle before, but once Sally put me onto them, I knew it was my next must-have equine item.

Dud and I settled on the bleachers for the trail riding safety clinic. The clinician made a lot of very good points, some of which I actually managed to remember. The ones that stayed with me had to do with keeping emergency equipment on your person, rather than in a saddle bag – indeed, her first piece of advice was to *have* a saddle bag. If your horse bucked you off and ran away, though, your cell phone wasn't going to do you any good if you had put it in the bag. Likewise if you were allergic to something (bee stings were mentioned) but had put your Epi pen in the bag rather than in your jacket pocket.

Other helpful hints included keeping your horse's nose out of the butt of the horse in front of you – it's a good way for your horse to get kicked, and not letting the person behind you get whacked by the same branch that smacked your face. Always check and tighten your girth several times, keep your horse under control by not letting him run back to the barn when you're done on the trail, and always keep Banamine in your saddle bag in case of injuries. The clinician also suggested having sunscreen and a first aid kit in your bag as well.

It was all very practical, and immensely helpful because, while I already do wear the "hunter's orange" vest that she suggested, many of the other ideas hadn't occurred to me. Once she'd finished the clinic, we headed to the Bricker Building.

We stopped short of going in. There were a number of food vendors in the area, and we'd worked up an appetite wandering all those vendor booths in the Celeste Center. I enjoyed a side of German potato salad from local Columbus eatery Schmidts, who are well known for their German cuisine. Dud settled for the sort of heavily processed, calorie-ridden, double-decker hamburger that would no doubt shave a couple of years off his life, but he seemed to enjoy it. Thusly fortified, we entered the Bricker Building.

If the Celeste Center with 140-odd vendors had been the appetizer of all things equine, the Bricker Building, with over 400 vendors, was the main course. There were so many vendors, we never got anywhere near to seeing them all. It wasn't all just tack, either; the offerings varied to such horse-related items as stalls, barn roofs, clothing and decorative items, jewelry, horse insurance, and – my favorite, two years' running – the motorized poop sifter.

The poop sifter was invented by a fellow who had more than one patent under his belt. Searching for a way to make mucking out stalls easier and less labor-intensive, he conceived of an open-weave metal barrel that rotates via a small motor, sifting out the stall bedding while spitting the poops into a waiting bucket. You still had to pick the poops, but you no longer had to shake the bedding off your pitchfork. It was actually a great –though at $1600, somewhat pricey – idea.

Somewhere near one-third of the way through the Bricker vendor booths, we came upon a modest setup that had bridles neatly lining a wall, and a large (fake) horse head on a pillar nearby. As with every other purveyor of tack, I stopped and asked the by-now rather hopeless question, "Do you have any rope bridles?"

Her "No, and I'll tell you why," answer gave me a lot to think about.

In the first place, she told me, no horse should have to endure a bit in his mouth, no matter how "gentle" or "humane" it claimed to be. I agreed wholeheartedly with her: imagine having a piece of metal forced into your mouth by someone who might not be gentle with the reins attached to it.

In the second place, she went on, rope bridles have knots in them that put pressure on sensitive areas of a horse's face, and she felt that was uncomfortable, too. I saw her point. Sally had mentioned "pressure points" in our discussion of Big William's bosal. This woman was expanding on the idea. She made a lot of sense.

What she offered, she said, was a bridle system that didn't press on sensitive areas, but indicated your desired commands in a much gentler, more comfortable way. She took one of the bridles off the wall and showed me how to put it on her demonstration horse (so *that's* what that fake horse head was for!), explaining as she did how the system worked, telling the horse exactly what you wanted him to do, but without the discomfort of other types of tack. She had these bitless bridles in leather (which I was hoping to avoid, because it tends to be stiff and unyielding), and in another material that was very lightweight, and required no more attention that a little hosing off if your horse had been sweating on it. I chose the lightweight one, and a pair of matching reins, as well. This was just the sort of thing I'd had in mind to advance Bit to the next level of training.

But, boy, did it cost an arm and a leg!

To be fair to Dud, who'd made every attempt to be patient but was starting to get a little cranky about all the money we were spending (we'd stopped at a candy booth, as well, and bought $22-worth of things like homemade fudge and those yummy cinnamon almonds you usually find at county fairs), I – quite magnanimously, if I do said it myself – offered to be finished shopping.

"We have what I came for," I told him, and I'm pretty sure he heaved a sigh of relief. We *had* bought more than just tack and candy, though. The grandchildren had to be considered, and we found a few interesting things to give them next Christmas. Unfortunately for Dud, just when he thought we'd make a clean get-away, we happened on a vendor selling horse-related books. Uh-oh.

I *love* books. I really love *horse* books! And I found one rather quickly that I felt would be a good investment, a book called *The Rider's Problem Solver,* by Jessica Jahiel, the woman who also wrote the very helpful book I mentioned in an earlier chapter called *The Horse Behavior Problem Solver.* Having read the latter, I knew that the former would also be a good read, chock-full of useful information. Jahiel, as it turns out, is an award-winning writer, as well as a renowned lecturer and clinician, which may explain why her advice is so spot-on.

I paid for the book, pointing out to Dud at the same time the fact that the book seller was using a device called a "Square" to handle my debit card. The Square attached to her phone, which had an app on it, and made accepting plastic card payments incredibly easy. While Dud – who's thinking about getting a Square of his own for his roofing and remodeling business – asked her several questions, I happened upon another book I knew I couldn't pass up: *Over Under Through – Obstacle Training for Horses (50 effective exercises for every rider)*.

"I *must* have this book!" I announced as I handed it to Dud. He gave me that look he gets when his patience is nearing its end.

"You *must* have it?" he asked in annoyance, reaching for his wallet in resignation.

"Yes!" I answered, "It's perfect for Bit!" I couldn't wait to start reading it!

At that point, we both agreed that it was time to get out of there and go visit Dud's eldest daughter, Sarah. I didn't even want to think about how much money we'd spent, but, you know? You do these things once a year, and it's a chance to get out and see what's new and interesting in the horse world. Dud begrudged my cavalier spending attitude, but he had known going in that his wallet was going to take a beating. Usually, he tried to be philosophical about it, but he didn't always succeed.

We found Sarah waiting for us at North Market. We decided to go see what the workers were doing with her kitchen in the Short North before heading out to dinner. Sarah and her partner had bought a house at the tail-end of the housing slump, getting it for the sort of price you'd never find a house in that neighborhood for now. It was a two story, two bed, one bath affair, with exposed brick fireplaces in the living and dining rooms, and both bedrooms. It definitely needed fixing-upping, but it had a lot of potential, and they'd decided to start with the kitchen. The outfit doing the job was hard at work when we got there.

The kitchen was undergoing quite a transformation, and it was easy to imagine what it would look like when it was finished. In addition to re-arranging the location of the fridge, and adding extra cabinets and an island, the workers were also installing hardwood floors throughout the first story. It was going to be a very pretty house in a beautiful, recently-gentrified neighborhood. Much of it – and German Village lurked somewhere up the road, similarly-gentrified – did, indeed, look like the sort of place an Englishman might feel at home.

Having been to London numerous times, where the narrow brick homes line up shoulder to shoulder throughout the city, I saw a definite resemblance in the style of architecture, and the way the houses all stood tall and slender. Because real estate was at such a premium in London as well as the Short North, people tended to build up instead of out. In some of the nicest neighborhoods in England's capital (Chelsea springs readily to mind), you'll find extremely narrow 3- and 4-story houses. Apparently, the same is true in many other European countries, and Columbus, Ohio, as well.

We made our way to a new restaurant called The Avenue. Sarah told us that it had opened a short time earlier, and had gotten good reviews. Like any good steak house, Dud and I were keen to see how it compared with those in Whoville. The place proved so popular, though, that we couldn't get a table. It would be an hour wait, said the hostess.

Dud and I had been through this sort of thing before, and had wasted enough time driving to other restaurants only to find that they had similar wait times, that we knew by now we'd have to suck it up and wait it out. We headed to the bar for beverages, and killed time standing around waiting for people to leave. Some seats opened up at the bar well before our hour was up, and we elected to eat there instead of continuing to wait for a table.

The menu looked promising, and we all ordered steak. This was Sarah's first time having a steak oscar – steak topped with crab meat and Bearnaise (or Hollandaise, depending on the restaurant) sauce. It's a wonderful combination, and I almost ordered it myself, but decided against. Sarah was quite taken with the concept and ate the whole meal, complaining afterward of the sort of uncomfortable fullness that God invented doggy bags for. We all passed on dessert, having bought a monolith of a chocolate cake "bomb" filled with whipped cream, from a shop in North Market, but ended up not eating it; there simply wasn't any room left in our bellies. We spent some time visiting with Sarah before Dud took her home and I put my jammies on. I turned out the lights in our fourth floor hotel room, pulled back the curtains and sat on the arm of a chair, looking over downtown Columbus.

According to Sarah, Columbus is the only city of its size in Ohio that hasn't suffered from serious shrinkage over the years, and, looking at all the buildings clearly occupied with conducting various business transactions, I have no reason to doubt her. In fact, it's a booming town with a booming economy, and nowhere is that more evident than in the new housing construction you see everywhere you go. Columbus didn't look like much to me – compared to big cities like Chicago, or Atlanta, say – but it was a tidy little place, seemingly free from the ubiquitous meth-heads one expects to see wandering the streets. I'm sure they're around *somewhere*, but the downtown area itself was clean and bustling with purpose. That night, as I watched out the window, I saw numerous people walking their dogs to a small green space near the hotel, and they looked as though they felt completely safe walking around after dark.

I like cities. I like the energy, and the possibilities they offer. I like the hustle and bustle, and the way they all seem to differ slightly from one another (although, as writer Bill Bryson observed about the UK, there's a Boots the chemist on every high street in every city you visit, and a similar truth about a Walgreen's on every corner exists in the US). I entertained briefly the idea of living in Columbus or its environs, until I realized that even Sarah's property on a corner lot wouldn't be big enough for four ducks. So much for that idea!

The next morning, we took Sarah to breakfast in a hole in the wall in German Village. It was so tiny, there was a line out the door, waiting for a table. When the hostess offered us seats at the counter (the place had a counter!), we happily accepted.

The hole in the wall restaurant was a step back in time. The counter alone was reminiscent of the early '70's, which is the last time I can remember Whoville having one. The friendliness of the other patrons, as well as the staff, was equally reminiscent of a time when people still valued a sense of community. Indeed, I enjoyed a lovely chat with the woman sitting next to me, who gave me the lowdown on what, on the menu, to order, as well as what she liked about living in German Village. Neighborliness, she said, was what she valued most.

Directly in front of us was the cook and his grill. A narrow aisle ran the length of the counter, and was so narrow that the waitresses had to squeeze past the cook to get by. There was so little space for the cook to put the plates of food that there was a constantly-rotating series of waitstaff squeezing in to grab them. All the while the hostess – who didn't have much to do at this point, given that all tables were full – kept up a running commentary with me (complete with occasional arm-touching as you do when you're emphasizing a point) about the Equine Affaire, and the fact that her 14-year old daughter had taken up riding at the age of three. It was quintessential small town chatter, and, having spent the vast majority of my life in a small town, I fell easily into the pleasant pace of it.

We dropped Sarah off at her workplace, and then hit the road. It would be a 2 ½-hour drive home. I mentioned to Dud a candy shop I'd seen on the northbound side of the highway, and expressed a wish to stop in: candy is my life, and I'm always keen to restock my supply. I couldn't remember any more about its' location, though, beyond the fact that it was "north of the sausage place."

The sausage place was an outpost on the northbound side of SR 23. Out in the boondocks, it was the last place you'd expect to find anything other than cattle farms, but there it was: Mom Wilson's Sausage Mart, est. 1959. It sold, naturally enough, sausage and various other pork-related products. Out of sheer curiosity, when we were returning from the previous year's Equine Affaire, we stopped in at the Mart to check things out.

Mom Wilson had died some time ago. Her recipes live on, though, and we purchased several items at the Mart, and enjoyed them over the subsequent months. We did not, however, feel a compelling need to stop in again. So we drove past Mom's Mart, and kept our eyes peeled for candy.

I couldn't remember the name of the candy place. The only thing that stuck in my mind was a rectangular red building. When we had driven far enough that I was about to give up hope of finding it, a billboard hove into view, assuring us that Coon's Candy was just up the road. Goody! Dud pulled in and I hopped out of the car expectantly. When I walked into the store, I saw that half of it contained what appeared to be gift items, and half of it contained candy. I made a beeline for the candy.

There were so many jars full of so many candies, it made my head spin. Mentally reviewing all the junk food we'd bought at the Affaire, as well as North Market, I decided to be prudent and ended up putting several things back on the shelves. But when I caught sight of the fudge, it was every man for himself, and damn the consequences!

According to their claims, Coon's makes some of the world's finest fudge, and I was keen to find out whether that was true or not. I perused the flavors, a little disappointed that they didn't seem to have what I wanted most, until my eyes fell upon the one flavor that I would quite possibly kill for: vanilla praline fudge. I had to have some!

"Forget everything else!" I told Dud, "I want the fudge!" Actually, we bought the fudge, some old-fashioned licorice, *and* a lollipop that had an actual worm in it, that I planned to dare one of the grandsons to eat. Suffice to say, in my later experiment to find out whether it actually *was* the world's finest fudge, I concluded that it was definitely up there in the top 2. It was damn good fudge!

When we got home, and I unpacked all the bags of goodies that we'd acquired, I thought about when I might get to the barn and try out Bit's new equipment. I could've sworn that the forecast for the weekend promised spring-like weather, but when I caught the news that evening, the meteorologist was talking about who was getting snow that night, how much, and when. Wait....*what???*

In the first place, it was April, for cripe's sake, and in the second place, I didn't actually *want* 3-5 inches of snow. Sighing heavily in resignation, I put the bag with Bit's new bridle in it on one of the dining room chairs, where it would have to wait until better weather came our way. We got 5 inches of snow that night.

Munster Man

While I knew that Dud had had dogs before in his life, I didn't know he wanted another one until he had brought the subject up several times over a period of weeks. Wistfully, he talked about Buckwheat, the German Shepherd he owned back when he was married to his first wife. I, of course, remembered the dog of his youth, a Norwegian Elkhound named Bippy. Bippy was an amiable old girl, overweight when I knew her, and stiff with arthritis. She was a sweet dog and everyone loved her.

Since Dud had fallen in so easily with my gang of cats, it never occurred to me that he might feel something was missing. I like dogs, I just never wanted the responsibility required with them – the frequent potty breaks, the poop scooping, the exercise. Cats were always so much easier for me to care for: in the midst of some of my worst depressive episodes, all I needed to do was make sure there was food, water, and a reasonably clean litter box.

I gave a great deal of thought to the matter of adding another critter to the household. It would be no small undertaking, trying to mix a dog with four cats who had never had to deal with anything more aggravating than each other. I knew I didn't have the energy to train a puppy, and, when I turned the idea over in my head, I came to the conclusion that if we were going to commit to a dog, it should be an older one, the kind that rarely get adopted because they're considered too old to be worthy pets. I broached the subject with Dud one night.

"I've been thinking about a dog. I don't have the energy for a puppy, so if we're going to do this, I would want to get an older dog." Communication is a funny thing, though. What constitutes "old" to one person means something else entirely to another.

"I guess we could do that. A two- or three-year old dog would be o.k."

"No, I mean an *old* dog, someone who deserves a good end of life. Like ten or eleven."

"No way!" he said vehemently, "Forget I ever brought it up!"

"*Seriously?!* What's wrong with an older dog? They're already broken in, laid back and all that."

"Forget it," he said again, "I'm not adopting a dog that old!"

Sadly, I shook my head. "You're a cold-hearted man, Dud," I said quietly. And that's where the conversation ended. But it didn't stop me from thinking about things.

So I pulled up the Whoville Humane Society's website on the computer when Dud wasn't looking. There were a number of pit bulls available, and I'm sure they would've made lovely pets, but the dog that caught my eye was a German Shepherd mix named Sissy. She was 11 years old.

I let the matter simmer on the back burner of my brain for a few days, knowing that I could not – and would not – bring home a dog that hadn't also been vetted by Duddy, but wondering nonetheless whether she might be a viable candidate. If I was going to go to bat for her, I'd need to meet her first, and see whether she'd even be suitable for our household. A few days later, I checked the website to make sure she was still there, and decided that I would go visit her without telling Dud.

The Humane Society put me in one of their "bonding rooms," and brought Sissy in. They brought another dog, too, some sort of terrier mix named Jax. I was told that, having come from the same home, they needed to be adopted together, although that could change in a matter of days if no one wanted the pair. The WHS tried hard to keep bonded animals together, but had neither the room nor the resources to keep them indefinitely. If two weeks passed without interest, they would then adopt them out separately.

As it happened, the terrier was far more personable than Sissy, but Dud wanted a big dog, and so did I, so I passed on Sissy – who didn't measure up in the personality department, and Jax – who did measure up but was a much smaller dog than we wanted. I left the facility wondering whether I should drop the matter altogether.

I spent the next several days thinking about dog ownership while I continued to check the Humane Society website. I realized that I was taken more with the *idea* of a dog (and all the fun things that came with dog ownership, like taking them swimming, going on vacation with them, etc.) rather than the dog itself. This was not good! Then I saw a new listing at the shelter that changed everything.

He was a Shepherd mix named Munster. His mug shot was adorable: he had the sort of smiley face that you couldn't help but immediately fall in love with. And he was five years-old. I hightailed it back to the shelter for a look.

Munster was as likeable as you would want a dog to be. Cheerful, interested in his surroundings, and happy to play with me (he chose a ball from a box of toys), I was instantly taken by him. I liked his happy demeanor, I liked that he knew how to sit, and I liked the fact that he consistently allowed me to take the ball from his mouth without biting or growling. This was a dog Dud needed to meet.

The Humane Society had a handy policy in which, for a $20 donation (which came off the price of adoption, should you decide to do that), they would put your animal on hold, which meant that for the next 24 hours, no one else could look at him or consider him for themselves. You had that long to think it over and decide whether you wanted to take him home. Two families had already placed Munster on hold, and both families had, for whatever reasons, changed their minds.

The hold idea put me in a lather of indecision – twenty bucks is twenty bucks, after all, and if Dud didn't want him, the HS would keep our money. I decided to take a gamble that Munster would still be there in a few hours time, and I rushed home to find Duddy.

"I need you to take a ride to Mansing with me, and no questions asked," I told Dud. Naturally, he wanted to know why.

"No questions," I repeated, "Just have a little faith and a sense of adventure." That got him: more than a few times, I'd accused Dud of lacking a sense of adventure, and he hadn't liked it. He agreed to go for a ride.

I had a speech planned out in my head that I was going to say on the way to the shelter, but Dud was on the phone the entire time. It was only as I pulled into the WHS parking lot that he hung up and turned his attention to me.

"I've given this a lot of thought," I told him, "and haven't settled my mind to it one way or another, so if your answer is 'no,' that's fine and I won't fuss." Dud had his own accusations with me, and one of the main ones was that if he didn't agree to something I wanted, I would pester him until he gave in and said yes. Technically, that accusation was 100% correct, but in the matter of dog ownership, I meant what I said; his decision would be final no matter what it was.

We approached the reception desk and I announced to the man behind it, "We'd like to visit with Munster." A volunteer directed us to one of the bonding rooms and went to get the dog in question. Dud had no idea who – or *what* – Munster was, but he went along with things quietly enough. As we waited for them to bring the dog in, I gave Dud an overview. "He's a Shepherd mix, he's five years-old, and he'll let you take the ball out of his mouth."

Dud frowned. "How do you know all this?" he asked.

"I met him earlier today," I replied. When they brought Munster in, Dud fell immediately under his spell.

"Munster *Man!*," he cooed. Munster ran right up to him and smiled that winning smile. It didn't take long for Dud to realize that I had not only given my consent to getting a dog, but that I'd picked the right one in the bargain. We spent 15-odd minutes with Munster, and then decided to put him on hold. "We have things to talk about," Dud explained to the volunteer.

The thing was, though, that we never actually talked about it much; it just kind of became a done deal. We agreed that the cats would be deeply unhappy.

"What do we do about that?" Dud wanted to know.

"We install a baby gate between the front room and the dining room. The cats get the west side of the house, and Munster gets the east side."

"What about the ducks?" he asked.

"We keep Munster on a short leash, of course!"

"This would be *so* unfair to the cats!" he exclaimed.

I shrugged. "Do you really want to pass on this great dog and wait til all the cats die?"

Having decided to take the plunge, we paid the adoption fee (discounted to half-price since he'd already been at the shelter awhile), then went to Maytag's and bought a crap-ton of dog paraphernalia. We ultimately spent over $500.

First came the dog crate, the baby gate, the bed, the bowls, the collar and leash. Later, we'd go back for a rubber-backed mat because he slopped so much water outside of his bowl; the treats; the stake and cable so that he could hang out in the yard with us; and the Frontline because he seemed to be a tick magnet. And, once we'd taken him to our vet for his complimentary wellness check, we dropped another $100 on heartworm medicine. He tested negative for heartworm, but the cure is also the prevention, so we loaded up on a year's-worth of it.

Munster was a dream from the moment we took him home. Well-behaved, he rarely barked, never had an accident, and, apart from a keen interest in the things he couldn't have (cats and ducks), he was content to be a follower and let us do the leading. That would turn out to be the thorn in my side, as Dud preferred to be Mr. Nice Guy, rather than Mr. Boundary Setter. Fortunately for me, I'd spent four years training a thousand pound horse, so working with Munster came surprisingly easy.

He had clearly been taken care of by someone. Why they would surrender such a nice dog was beyond me. He knew how to behave on a leash, and only ever pulled when a squirrel caught his attention. I decided that our first lessons would be learning the meaning of the words *"leave it!"* Happily, he picked up on it pretty quickly, making our 2-mile walks at the park much easier.

The cats were, indeed, very upset about the new resident. They retreated to the bedroom and stayed there for quite some time. Their food station was now in our bathroom, and their bathroom was now in our front room. I tried to spend as much time with them as I possibly could, but nothing would make up for them no longer spending the evenings with us on the couch. There was no telling when – or if – they would ever come around. They would ultimately decide that in their own good time.

Ducky the Dickhead

When the new ducks started the mating season with a fervor I hadn't expected, Dud expressed dismay at how the drakes kept chasing Penny and Daffy around the yard, harassing them all day long and constantly trying to mount them. Penny, in particular, looked exhausted and bedraggled, and a considerable number of feathers were missing from her neck. While some feather loss was to be expected, things were getting way out of hand.

The initial reassurances I gave Dud ("They'll cool off in a few weeks or so.") proved incorrect. If anything, mating season brought out the worst in both drakes, and Ducky went from being the docile duck I'd thought he was to an aggressive bully that neither one of us particularly liked. Not only did he bother both girls, but he continually tried to chase Gimpy off his turf, as well.

"Ducky! Get off her!" we'd yell at him. He'd ignore us and pin Penny's head to the ground, requiring one of us to go out and chase him away. Once we went back in the house, though, he'd be back to his usual tricks almost immediately.

If he wasn't all over Penny, he was biting Daffy and pulling out mouthfuls of her wing feathers. He became extremely unlikeable.

"I don't like him!" Dud announced. "I wouldn't mind getting rid of him!"

"What do you have in mind?" I asked, eyeing him warily.

"We could have him put to sleep," he replied.

That seemed unfair. Technically, there was nothing wrong with Ducky except that he had a limp and was a complete dickhead. I sighed. Even with my patience and good intentions, *I* was tired of Ducky's behavior, too.

"What about that woman in Bowling Green, the one we took Girlfriend Duck to a couple of years ago?" Dud wanted to know.

I shook my head, "I heard she was trying to get rid of the animals she already had. I doubt she'd want another." Thinking back, she had never had the best set-up for ducks anyway.

The woman in question, Sharie, had agreed to take in six Pekins that Animal Control Officer Dave and I had rescued from the lesser pond near McKinnon's in NBM. When I asked where Dave was taking them, he replied rather mysteriously that he wasn't allowed to tell me, and then he drove off with the cage full of ducks. Several years later, when I needed a home for another duck, Dave gave Sharie my phone number, and when I explained to her that Girlfriend needed a home, she agreed to take her. Dud and I drove the Pekin out into the countryside.

Sharie lived on a farm with her father. There was a small pond around which ten-odd ducks ranged. There was no proper shelter for them, a safe place they could go to avoid predators. When Sharie gave us a tour of the property, we saw a horse, a donkey, and enough chickens to suggest that Sharie wanted to rescue animals, but didn't know when (or possibly *how*) to say 'no.' Even so, we left Girlfriend in her care and didn't give either of them another thought until Dud asked his question. Thankfully, when I turned the matter over in my head, I remembered another possibility, a fellow up in Michigan named Mark.

Officer Dave had given me Mark's phone number after he and I had rescued four Pekins who had been dumped at McKinnon's Pond. They hadn't gone into the water yet, which made them much easier to catch. Dave and I – with a little help from step-daughter Lauren – had corralled them near the men's bathroom and gotten them into a large cage pretty easily. What to do with them next, though, turned out to be a contentious matter.

Dave wanted me to take them home – he had called Mark and we'd arranged for Dud and I to drive the hour up into Michigan to hand off the ducks the next day – and I wanted Dave to take them to his animal facility for the night. Dave didn't want his facility getting all pooped up but I held firm, telling him we'd be by in the morning. Sighing, he reluctantly took the them to the new critter holding area of the Whoville Police Department.

Dud and I drove the ducks well into the Michigan countryside the next day. We had some trouble finding Mark's house because from the road, you saw nothing but part of a driveway. The rest of the drive, and the house itself, were far enough down a hill that they couldn't be seen from the road. Once we turned into the driveway, we were stopped by a sturdy gate, the kind you could open and close remotely. I had to call Mark and let him know we'd arrived. Then the gate opened and we drove toward his house.

The house itself suggested that a person of some means owned it: sizable but unpretentious, it was considerably larger than any other house in the area. The property was well over five acres, and featured a substantial pond with several islands in it. Milling about were more domestic ducks and geese than I could count.

Why Mark had agreed to take on four more ducks was beyond me, unless he was from the Sharie school of rescue and had difficulty saying no. Still, he seemed to take good care of his charges: a couple of gimpy ducks who couldn't walk were sequestered in a pen where they could enjoy the sun without being bullied by the other ducks. If nothing else, I knew that he would give our four rescued Pekins a good home. We chatted with him for a few minutes, then headed back to Ohio.

I filed his number away in my cell phone contacts under Mark Ducks, and I remember sending Dave a text saying, *I think we could use this guy again!* but I forgot all about him until Dud mentioned euthanizing Ducky the Dickhead. It was worth a shot, so I called and left a message, explaining that we had one male duck with a limp that we couldn't find a home for. He called back and told us to bring Ducky up on Sunday. While we waited for the day to come, we said all manner of snotty things to Ducky:

"Enjoy it all now, you little bastard, because your days here are numbered!" was my comment.

"Say good-bye, Ducky, you dickhead!" was Dud's.

"Do you think Daffy will be o.k. without him?" Dud asked worriedly on the drive up to Mark's. His concern was touching, but I reassured him that I thought both Daffy and Penny would be thrilled to have one less drake pestering them.

"I don't think they were particularly happy when the boys joined them, anyway," I remarked. I could still see Penny's accusatory *what have you done?* look in my mind's eye, and I knew we were doing the right thing.

"Ducky will have plenty of other ducks to pick on, and plenty of girls to bother, up at Mark's," I said, "and our three will get on just fine without him!" Dud nodded in agreement.

"What's the story on this one?" Mark asked when he met us at the gate. I had already told Dud that this was one of those rare exceptions when lying was acceptable, and I'd added, "Leave the talking to me!" If Dud talked, he'd spill the beans about Ducky being a dickhead, rather than a rescue, and I worried that Mark wouldn't take him if he knew it was strictly a matter of behavior.

"Could've been a school project," I answered Mark, "he looks too old be be an Easter duck, but we have some schools in the area who raise a duckling as a science project and then dump them when they're finished with them. That might've been the case here."

Mark nodded. "It's a shame they still do that! But I think you're right, he's not a young duck."

Dud piped up then about us not having enough room for Ducky, even though we have a few ducks of our own. I would have kicked him, but Mark would've seen me do it. Instead, I steered the conversation away from anything to do with Penny, Daffy, and Gimpy.

"Have you lost some critters, Mark? It looks like you have less than the last time we were here."

"I actually have *more*," he said, chuckling, "the geese had babies."

"How about those islands in the pond? They still there?"

He shook his head. "Originally, I had seven. Now, with erosion and all the dabbling they do, I'm down to three!"

I nodded. It was the middle of May, but a cold front had dropped the weekend highs into the 40's, and sufficient wind blew to create a wind chill in the 30's. We'd made enough polite chatter, and gifted Mark with twenty bucks in the bargain, so I thanked him again, expressing my heartfelt appreciation before we hopped back in the car and cranked the heat. Driving away, we both heaved a sigh of relief. Once the mating fervor calmed down – molting season was due to start fairly soon – the three remaining ducks would enjoy a nice, peaceful existence, and so would Dud and I.

Again With The Rabbits!

I found neighbor Russell on the doorstep as I brought Munster back from a walk. "Did you need Dud?" I asked. Russell said no, that he was actually there to talk to me. I gave him one of my stern looks.

"Is this a rabbit issue, Russell? Have you mowed another one?"

He looked sheepish. "No. I was mowing around a nest, though, and one of the bunnies ran out. He's not moving."

"Russell, Russell, Russell!" I sighed. "Why is it *always* you?!" We headed to his back yard. I instantly saw the large ball of rabbit hair on the grass, and peered down into the hole beside it for a look. Pulling back another fluff of hair, I saw several baby bunnies huddled together. Russell pointed out where the one had run to, a foot or so away. He was hunkered down in the grass, clearly hoping we wouldn't see him.

When baby bunnies didn't move, Russell always assumed that they were dead. He didn't know that not moving was pretty much their sole means of defense. I reached down and gently closed my hands around the bunny, picked him up, and tucked him back into the nest. I covered the top with the errant ball of hair and stood up.

"Baby bunnies leave the nest really young," I told Russell. "Once they leave, they don't come back. I don't think this one left because he was ready, though. I think he left because he was scared. Even so, I would guess that this bunch are just about ready to take off; it may be a few more days. Can you just mow around them in the meantime? Can you wait?"

He nodded. "I stopped mowing anyway and started draining the pool." Russell had bought a new above-ground pool to replace the old one that leaked. When I looked around, I saw puddles of standing water in his yard.

"There was another nest around here somewhere," he said, gesturing toward an area that was now flooded. We both started looking for the nest but couldn't find it.

"Jesus, Russell! Did you *drown* them?"

"I don't think so," he replied, but he sounded a little vague about it.

I gave him another stern look. "Hmmm!" I growled as I walked away, "if you *did*, I don't want to know about it!"

The First Horse

"Bit cut his leg pretty good kicking the stall. When you come out please put bath soak on it. No riding for awhile. Lots of walking. It will heal. Watch out he doesn't kick. Baby is down so we are letting her rest." That's the unexpected text I got from Wendy. With the exception of a brief visit in which I gave Bit an apple and a pat on the neck, I hadn't been out to the barn for a couple of weeks. The weather had been so cold and crummy that I didn't have the heart to be out in it for any length of time. The day I got Wendy's text, I'd actually planned to take Bit for a ride because the weather had finally turned decent. And now this. *No riding for awhile,* she said. *Poop!* I thought. I decided to go anyway, to get a look at his injured leg.

The bit about Baby didn't come as a surprise. A boarder horse, Baby was an arthritic mare whose owner lived in North Dakota. Baby was such a decrepit old horse that going down was routine. Indeed, Ron and Wendy had retrieval down to an art form: because Baby couldn't get back up on her own, they would get a couple of stout straps around her, connect the straps to the tractor, and let the tractor do the heavy lifting. I'd watched them do it once, and while it sounds simple enough, it rarely was. Still, Baby deserved the same good, watchful care that all the other boarder horses received, and she got it: no matter how long it took to get her back on her feet, Ron and Wendy kept at it until they'd succeeded.

The owner, Carlene, used to have a psychiatric practice in Whoville, and my shrink of 18 years had worked there. Carlene had a notice in the lobby of that practice offering EAP – Equine Assisted Psychotherapy. I'd never heard of such a thing, so I began asking questions, and the answers piqued my interest.

EAP was a relatively new thing at that time – at least, it was new in our neck of the mid-western woods. How Carlene explained it was that the client, the therapist (Carlene was the one who was trained), the horse, and a horse expert all got together at a barn and did exercises with the horse. There was no riding; it was strictly ground work. The best part about it: my insurance would cover it! I signed up and arranged to meet Carlene at the Post and Harness Stable.

The exercises did not go particularly well. There were two reasons for this: 1) I had no previous horse experience, and no previous assertiveness experience. Both are helpful – if not necessary – elements to possess if you want to succeed at the tasks. 2) It must be said that Carlene wasn't the best therapist I'd ever come across. I don't want to sound like I'm blaming her for my lack of success, but I do think she could've been more helpful in teaching me what I needed to know.

In any case, after a couple of sessions at the Post and Harness, Carlene moved her horses to The Harmony Barn. She had several: there was Baby, the EAP horse, who wasn't actually a baby at all, but closer to middle-age; there was Princess, a small pony that Carlene had rescued and was trying to rehab; and there was Old Reg, a retired champion who was a sway-backed geezer even then. We continued our sessions at The Harmony Barn until I dumped Carlene for being an ineffective teacher, and signed on for some riding lessons with Wendy's daughter Connie. It was the beginning of my association with the barn, and of my time as a horsewoman.

Old Reg died after a year or so at the barn, leaving Baby and Princess to move along with Carlene when she relocated to North Dakota. For reasons I'll probably never know, she later brought the two horses back to the barn, and they've resided there since. Carlene came back every now and again to visit, but otherwise entrusted their care to Wendy. Wendy put Princess out with the herd, but often let Baby roam the aisles. Baby didn't particularly like when the other horses came sniffing around; apart from Princess's company, she preferred to be alone. As she aged, going down became a regular habit.

It may have been exhaustion, it may have been the arthritis, it may have been something that no one knew about, but for whatever reason, Baby would lie down on the ground – no matter whether it was mud, snow, rain, or some other unpleasant condition – and wouldn't be able to get back on her feet. So when Wendy mentioned Baby being down in her text, it came as no surprise. What *did* come as a surprise was what happened after I got to the barn to inspect Bit's leg.

Apparently, Bit and Big Blue had been playing enough halter tag across the electric fence that some optimistic soul – Wendy, no doubt – decided to put them in stalls next to each other to see what would happen. Obviously, she was hoping that they would make peace and get along, but sometimes, Wendy's optimism backfires.

I'm guessing that Blue did (or said) something deeply offensive that Bit took exception to, and kicked the wall between them in response. It must've been one hell of a kick because an entire board was missing. And Bit's leg – which had a great deal of the skin scraped off from his hock down to his pastern – must've dragged across the jagged wooden divide in the process. I remembered the *watch out he doesn't kick* part of Wendy's text but I needn't have worried: when I sprayed him, he actually held the injured leg out as though he wanted to make sure I got good coverage with the bath soak.

It was odd that Wendy was at the barn in the middle of the weekday, until I asked about Baby. Wendy pulled out her cell phone and showed me a picture she had taken of Baby when the horse went down the day before in a quagmire of mud. It must've been very unpleasant for the old girl to lay like that, wet from the mud but unable to get up. When Wendy and Ron got her back on her feet, though, she went down again in one of the portable pens, and that was where she was now.

"The vet's on his way," she told me.

I chewed on that for a minute. "He's coming to....?" and made a small cutting movement across my throat. We were always careful not to say upsetting words like 'euthanize' out loud. You never know how much English the horses understand and we didn't want to freak any of them out.

Wendy nodded in answer to my question. Evidently, it was "time." Wendy had already spoken to Carlene, and, as it turned out, had already called several other people, too. Sally – owner of Big William, Lydia, and volunteer Gayle had all been notified. In fact, when I walked out to the pen, Gayle was just leaving, tears streaming down her face. While I finished grooming Bit, I decided to stick around for The End. I put Bit back out in the mud lot, then turned my attention to Baby. She was lying quietly in a stall.

The portable pen she was in was made up of separate pieces of sturdy metal fencing, which connected at the corners to form a square pen (or, if you had more than four sections, a round pen). It was desirable to have "down" horses in such pens because once they'd passed, all Ron had to do was take the stall apart in order to get the tractor in place to haul the body out back. Indeed, I noticed that once they'd gotten her up, this last time, they'd left the straps in place; they must've known the end was near.

Sally just happened to have an hour free from her job as a massage therapist – a timely hour, as it turned out – and she quickly changed into her barn clothes, then took up a position by Baby's head. Lydia knelt nearby, and I hunkered down between them. Both women were crying. Initially, I didn't feel particularly sad, but once Sally started whispering in Baby's ear about having seen an eagle flying overhead on the way to the barn, and telling Baby that the eagle would show her the way home, my eyes started welling up.

The vet came. Dr. Carrolton, who had taken care of Gracie the cat when she was ill, was also the barn's vet. He had struck me during Gracie's illness as a caring, compassionate, decent man, and watching him gently explain to Lydia how the proceedings would go only served to confirm my initial impression. He told Lydia exactly what to expect, and then went about the business of euthanizing Baby.

Wendy didn't stay. She needed to get back to her nursing job at a doctor's office. Before she left, though, I watched as she bent over Baby, gently placed her hand on the side of Baby's head, and said quietly, "It's o.k., girlfriend. You can go. It's all right." She didn't want the old mare thinking that she had to stick around for Wendy's sake.

Dr. Carrolton gave Baby two injections, then stood back with Ron while we three women – and Barn Urchin Allen, who had come to clean stalls but decided to kneel down with the rest of us first – all watched as slowly, gently, quietly, life left Baby. There was no trauma, no thrashing about, no struggle. She simple went.

Sally went back to whispering in Baby's ear, sobbing as she reminded her which horses would be waiting to greet her – Newt the mule, her friend Old Reg, Mikey the geriatric gelding – and I lost it again, this time because I only just then remembered that Baby had been the very first horse in my life. Baby had been the start of all things equine, from my lessons on Crazy, then Ruckus, and then Bit, to leasing and training my boy, to attending Equine Affaire, and everything in between. It had been a much longer road than I had realized, and I had never given Baby her proper due. My only consolation now was that she had died so peacefully, surrounded by people who had loved her. May we all go as calmly as that.

As often happens, in my experiences of death, after the crying was done and the good-byes had been said, came the relief of laughter. Allen, Lydia, and I had wandered over to the electric fence so that I could give Bit an apple. We got to joking, then, about how, the last time I had worked with Bit, I'd done some refresher work with the mounting block. I'd been teaching him to stand still, then take a step or two on command in order to get into a good mounting position. After he'd done it right a couple of times, I decided to hop on him bareback, just to take the lesson up a notch. The minute I got on his back, though, Bit tried to buck me off. Twice. I almost fell off but managed to catch myself just in time.

"And now you're rewarding him with an apple," Allen remarked dryly.

He was good at that. Allen always had a good line ready, and it was a relief to be able to laugh a little after having shared such a sad moment with them. We three – and all the other long-term volunteers – had already learned the hard way that when you open your heart to love, animals will break it every time. It never gets easier to deal with, but I doubt that it ever occurred to any of us to stop loving them because of it.

Virtually every long-term barn volunteer that I knew over the years had some dysfunction going on in their lives. I've chosen not to reveal details here because it's not my place to do so. Suffice to say, though, that for whatever personal reasons there were, the horses became our balm. Our medicine. Our sanity. They were there for us when no one else was. They accepted us, returned our affection, made us laugh, kept us company. The least we could give them in return was a peaceful passing. And no matter how many times we had to do it, we knew that, as long as we were able, we would continue to be there for them at the end. No horses anywhere could have a finer, more loving funeral cortege than those of The Harmony Barn.

A Very Close Call

The James Taylor concert turned out to be much more than we expected. In the first place, we had damn good seats, and in the second place, the man was a consummate entertainer. Indeed, during a 30-minute break in the middle of the show, he never actually left the stage. Instead, he sat down at the stage's edge and spent the entire half hour signing autographs. In addition, he smiled throughout the entire show. Given that he was 68-years old at the time, and that a number of his contemporaries – David Bowie, and The Eagles' Glenn Frey among them – had passed away quite suddenly in 2016, we counted ourselves very lucky. We got home late, and found ourselves still jazzed at a time when we would normally be snoring away.

We decided to stay up and watch an episode of our latest craze, a British whodunit called *Broadchurch*. We were only a few minutes into it when we both heard a frantic scrabbling of claws on the kitchen floor. Dud leapt out of his chair, and I was a half-second behind him. We found Munster near the baby gate, with white cat Buddy clinging to his face.

Evidently, Buddy had squeezed through the gate, but hadn't figured out how to get back on the other side of it before being confronted by Munster.

I couldn't tell whether Munster had a mouthful of Buddy or not, but I knew immediately that Dud's admonishment, *"Munster! Leave him alone!"* would be completely useless. I stepped into the fray, then, grabbed Munster's mouth and, with one hand on his lower jaw and one on his upper, prized it apart. Buddy took off running and ended up behind the t.v. console. Disgusted with our new dog, I could only manage a growled, *"Get in there!"* while waving my arm toward his kennel. I locked him in, then turned away.

Decades ago, as a child in single digits, I took my pet hamster out to play in the grass. I didn't see the neighbor kids or their dog until it was too late. Suffice to say, my hamster didn't survive the attack, and it was this bad acid flashback that came to mind as I doubled over in emotional agony, certain that Buddy was either dead or dying. Whatever the case, I couldn't face it.

I remember Dud telling me to pull myself together, to go check on Buddy.

"I *can't!*" I wailed helplessly.

"You *have* to," he answered.

"*No!No!No!No!Noooooooo! I can't do it!*" I moaned.

At that point, Dud went over to the console and looked for himself.

"I don't see any blood on him," he told me.

Slowly, fearfully, I tiptoed over to the console and peeked behind it. It was as Dud said: Buddy was curled up behind the console, but there didn't appear to be any blood, or indeed, any wounds at all. I knelt down in front of him and began a whispered chant:

"I'm so sorry, Buddy! I'm so sorry! It will never happen again! I promise you, it will never happen again!" Dud broke into my chant, asking what I wanted to do next. I assessed the situation with a fairly measured response, given my state of mind.

"Get my critter carrier out of the car and bring it to me." He went as requested and came back with not just the carrier, but a towel, as well. Apparently, I was bleeding. When I looked to where he pointed, I saw several wounds on my right wrist, and blood dripping off my middle finger. I didn't think my injuries warranted attention, though; Buddy was all that mattered. I gave a cursory swipe to my hand with the towel, then gently placed it over Buddy. Only his head was showing. Next, I opened the carrier door, and put the thing right where I had been kneeling.

I instructed Dud to come over and take my place. His job would be to keep Buddy from jumping over the carrier and running off to some unreachable part of the house. Meanwhile, I went to the other end of the console, pushed it away from the wall, and knelt down behind Buddy. Gently, I pushed him toward, and then into, the carrier. Quickly closing the carrier door, I raced toward the bedroom and put it on the nightstand. Behind me, I heard Dud tell Munster, "You totally blew it, dog!" He already knew that I would take Munster back to the Humane Society the next day.

Keeping Buddy in the carrier, I ran my hands carefully over his body. I found no puncture wounds, but wasn't content to leave it at that: he might've had internal injuries I didn't know about, and my fear now was that he would die in the night while I slept. To that end, I took up a mantra as I lay in the dark, trying not to sleep but knowing that it would eventually overtake me.

"Please, God, don't let him die! Please let him live! Please don't let him die tonight!"

Hours later, a meow woke me. Not just any meow, but a Buddy meow. He wanted out of the carrier. Fumbling in the dark, I opened the door. Buddy leapt onto the bed, climbed over my pillow and Dud's, and jumped down to the floor. He spent the next two days under the bed.

In the morning, completely exhausted, I sat on the couch while Dud shared with me his belief that while Munster *could've* killed Buddy, he *didn't* because he wasn't (in Dud's opinion) being malicious, but rather, playful. Clearly, he didn't want me returning Munster, but with every point he made, I stated flatly, "It's not fair to Buddy."

"But I think they might all end up getting along, if we're patient," Dud said earnestly.

"It's not fair to Buddy," I repeated dully. I couldn't think beyond that, and I frankly didn't care what Dud had to say. As far as I was concerned, it was a *fait accompli,* a done deal. Dud sighed in resignation.

"O.k. but in my life, I've never given a dog back. If they weren't on the way to be euthanized for being sick or injured, I didn't give them back. If you need to, I understand, but I'm not going to do it. You'll have to return him yourself."

I nodded. "Yes," I answered. No problem!

I was so tired, I couldn't set my mind to anything. I surfed the channels, but found nothing to hold my attention. Sighing, I turned off the t.v. and laid down on the couch for a nap. It was when I woke up that things took a different turn.

I laid on the couch thinking about the reasoning I'd initially used with Duddy, that we weren't likely to find another dog with Munster's temperament and cheerful nature. I thought about Munster himself, and how horribly confusing and frightening it must've been for him when he was dropped off at the Whoville Pound. Then, when no one wanted him, he was taken in by the Whoville Humane Society, where two families tried to adopt him without success. *Then,* his adoption price was lowered because he'd been at the Humane Society for "too long."

After all that, two strange people take him to a strange place where he has no idea what the rules are, and what his place in the pack is. I remembered how he'd get up and follow us around, even if we were only going ten steps away: he wanted to make sure he could keep us in sight. The first few nights in his pen, we'd lie in bed listening to him whimper softly. And now I was thinking about taking him back to the shelter where the confusion and fear would start all over again. I didn't particularly want to live with that in my head.

"I'm willing to consider letting him stay, with conditions," I announced to Dud.

"O.k. What are the conditions?" he asked.

"We reinforce the baby gate, we put him in the kennel every time we're not here. And he's always on a tight leash out in the yard."

""O.k., I can put a bi-fold door here instead of the gate," he suggested, "it would look nicer than the gate." It was a good idea and I told him so. He installed it the next day. I wasn't as quick to forgive Munster, though. For a number of days after the attack, I gave him the cold shoulder, speaking in clipped tones, and withholding my friendship. I knew that couldn't last forever, though. I held out for a short while, but after a week, he was back in my good graces. Provisionally. Now that I knew what he was capable of, I took nothing for granted: if he saw an opportunity, he would chase cats and ducks, and if he caught them, they might well die. For the rest of Munster's life, it would be my job to make sure that didn't happen.

Another Dickhead Duck

If I had thought that the absence of Ducky would improve the state of affairs among the remaining ducks, I was woefully mistaken. To my considerable surprise, Gimpy picked up where Ducky left off, bullying Daffy to such a degree that her neck remained devoid of feathers. Every time Duddy or I looked out the window, there he was, chasing after her, climbing on top of her, and tugging ferociously at her neck. If Dud or I intervened, Daffy – who we assumed would take the opportunity to run in a different direction than Gimpy – would run right after him, as though a bullying drake was better than a rescuing Duddy. It got so bad that I was at my wit's end.

"I wouldn't mind if he went, too!" I remarked to Dud irritably.

Dud shook his head. "You agreed to take them," he answered. Fat lot of help he was!

I thought about waiting until the summer molt started, and seeing whether that dampened down his ardor, but that seemed unfair: Daffy was being bullied *now*, so now seemed the time to do something. What that something was, though, I had no idea.

I did chuck him in the carrier one night. As I herded them toward the pen, Gimpy kept turning around and trying to nip Daffy, as though he didn't want her in the pen with him and Penny. He did this several times until I'd had enough. I got the girls safely in the pen, then turned my attention to Gimpy, who was looking more than a little confused at the turn of events.

"That's *it*, you little bastard! I've had enough!" I fetched the carrier, set it up where he couldn't see it, then proceeded to chase him around the yard. For a lame duck, he sure was a fast one! Eventually, I caught him and walked him over to the carrier. As I did, he flapped his wings in an attempt to get away. I held on tight and raised my arms, which gave him the sensation of flight that that flightless duck would never have experienced on his own. Apart from his terror at being caught by the evil Kelly, he seemed to enjoy his brief time in the air.

I plopped him unceremoniously into the carrier, then set it next to the pen window, where he and the girls could see each other. In less than five minutes, though, I realized that any wily raccoon could figure out how to open the carrier, so I picked it up and settled it in a corner of the pen. Now, all three ducks could be together, though without Ducky being able to pick on Daffy in a confined space.

Around the same time, I started holding Gimpy in the pen in the mornings when I let the girls out. I used the pond skimmer to keep him at the back of the pen as the girls made a mad dash for the door. They had no idea why I was picking on Gimpy, of course, but they didn't seem to mind having the yard to themselves for the few hours they got before Gimpy was finally released. In spite of the tough new measures, Gimpy seemed every bit as aggravating as always.

"You're expendable, Gimpy! Don't forget that!" I'd tell him as I'd shake a threatening finger at him. I didn't tell Dud what I was thinking, which was that I was genuinely sorry that I'd agreed to take Pat's ducks. It had upset the balance in the yard, and neither girl seemed the least bit happy about it. Neither was I.

I gave some thought to what my options might be. They came down to two things: I could farm him off to Mark Ducks, or I could have him euthanized. I leaned toward the latter, but decided to continue my wait-and-see approach. Even so, time was running out and my patience was running thin. I would not wait and see much longer.

Blue Ribbons

If you recall the last chapter of NBM, I mentioned buying blue ribbons for Bit. It was my way of showing him how far he'd come in our time together. And, it gave me a laugh: the older the ribbons, the better I liked it, and I'd frequently buy ribbons from the 1950's on Etsy. Indeed, one person sold me a lot of ten old First Place ribbons for a very reasonable price.

By this time, I had commissioned Dud to make me a plaque out of wood to put a batch of those ribbons on. He rounded the corners of the rectangular plaque as per my instructions, and drilled two holes so that I could pass twine through them and tie the thing to the hook on Bit's stall door. It was large enough to hold five First Place and Best of Show rosettes. I kept the extra ribbons in a box in my car, along with a stapler. When any of the ribbons lost its' rosette, I'd pull it off and replace it with a fresh one. None of the ribbons dated later than 1959.

Wendy mentioned the barn visitors who had come to have a look around. I think they were considering whether to board their horse there. Given that Bit's stall was the only one in the barn that had anything on the door, the visitors were drawn to his plaque. Wendy said that they read the wording on the ribbons, then turned to her in some confusion. "How old *is* this horse?" they asked.

The Urchins took in all in stride, of course. They knew me well after all those years. Allen would tease me about having the oldest First Place champion horse in history, while Wendy would ask where I put all the trophies. She could laugh all she wanted, though: I had bagged two totally awesome trophies on Ebay, old ones made of real metal instead of cheap plastic. One dated from 1948. I displayed them proudly on a shelf in our front room. If Dud knew how much I'd paid for them, he would probably divorce me!

Whenever I went out to the barn to work with Bit, I'd walk him over to his stall and point to all the ribbons hanging on the door. "First Place blue ribbon champion horse!" I'd tell him. Sometimes, he'd lead *me* to the door, as though he wanted to make sure the ribbons were still there. We'd stand and look at them for a moment, and I'd announce, "You're the championest horse in the whole barn, Bubby!"

Given that we'd never win ribbons any other way, finding the old ones (which were of much better quality than anything made nowadays) was a fun way of affirming how far we had come together. In four years, I'd taken him from a frightened-by-his-own-shadow meatball to a fairly confident horse who spooked so infrequently that it was now a surprise when he actually did.

It had been hard-won confidence, though. I'd literally had to do every task myself before he would be willing to do it. Every mud puddle had to be walked through by me before he'd set foot in it. Once he saw that I wasn't drowning, or being eaten by a Lock Ness Puddle Monster, then he'd screw up his courage and walk through himself. It was kind of like Bit throwing me to the wolves and seeing whether I'd survive, but I didn't take it personally. On the hotter summer hot days, those puddles actually felt pretty good!

There were other challenges besides puddles. In our fourth year of leasing, Ron decided to dig a trench from the pond in the back pasture through the front pasture. I had no idea what he was doing, but it appeared as though he was looking for a way to drain the pond that overflowed regularly and impeded the poop-filled tractor's trips to the poop pile at the back of the property. It must be said, though, that Ron's usual work speed was on par with a snail's pace, which meant that the trench project remained at a standstill for quite some time. Since the trench obstructed the only access I had to the back pasture, I decided it was time to get Bit to cross it.

Crossing over a two-foot wide trench sounds easy enough, until you know that horses have rather skewed vision. What looks to the human eye like a two-foot wide trench looks to the horse like a gaping chasm of death. I stood on the far side of it, holding tight to Bit's lead rope while he debated how serious I was about having him cross it. Sometimes, he thinks that if he holds out long enough, I'll change my mind. I have no idea why, I haven't changed my mind about a task once in four years. Still, Bit likes to hope!

I changed position several times, standing first on the far side of the trench, then standing on the near side of the trench, and then straddling the trench in a weird sort of compromise position. Bit was impressed by none of them, but I held firm. When all else failed, I pulled out the prize: a Red Delicious apple. Bit never refused an apple, and this day would be no different.

I held the apple under his nose, letting him get a good sniff. Then, when he opened his mouth to take a bite, I pulled it back, and held the thing out over the trench. He knew exactly what I meant by it: if you cross the trench, you get the apple. In a surprisingly short span of time, given all the procrastinating he'd just done, Bit took a few tentative steps toward the edge of the trench, then stepped over it as though he'd been crossing trenches all his life.

I never had a problem getting him to cross that trench again.

Boarder Sally didn't approve of bribery. When she'd see me do it, she'd open her mouth to say something, and then bite her tongue. You could tell that she was *dying* to tell me that that was not the way to train a horse, but she had it easy: Big William was a gentle giant with an amenable temperament, and Sally could afford to bring in the sort of trainers that no one else at the barn had the money for, including me.

She once had a woman in to do a weekend workshop, but the price was steeper than I was willing to pay. Sally learned a great deal from her, though, as she did from all the clinics she attended at Equine Affaire every year. Sally didn't have to resort to Red Delicious apples because William picked up on the clinics' teachings very easily. Training Bit, on the other hand, was like teaching a foreign language to an unwilling pupil. Something about that challenge, though, made the successes all the more satisfying: while we may not have won those ribbons in traditional competitions, we certainly *earned* them through all our hard work.

The End of Things

Exactly one week to the day of Munster's attack on Buddy, it happened again. Because Munster was always on a leash when he was outside, I had taken to putting the ducks in their pen early in the evening while it was still light out, then letting Munster out into the yard unfettered by restraints for a little ball-chasing. He seemed to enjoy retrieving the tennis balls that Dud and I would throw for him, and he almost always brought them back and let us take them from his mouth. We were in the midst of a game of toss when neighbor Russell said something to Dud over the fence. Russell was tearing down his old above-ground pool and installing a new one, and he wanted Dud's opinion on some aspect of it. Dud went over to where he could see Russell over the fence, and I joined him.

Every minute or so, I'd look back toward our yard, keeping tabs on what Munster might be doing. A baby bunny had taken up residence, and even though I would shoo him under the fence before letting Munster out, I worried that he might come back in at the wrong time. The second or third time I looked around, I saw a black blur running across the far end of the yard. Munster saw it, too.

I took off running, hollering at Munster the whole time, but he beat me to the thing and caught it. I made a grab for his choke chain, and it somehow slipped Munster's head and came off in my hand. Munster lunged into the shrubs, ignoring my screams to "leave it," and I drew a complete blank: how was I supposed to catch him when I now had nothing to grab? I did the only thing I *could* do, I beat him with the collar.

This was no small thing for me. I don't hit animals. Period. But I had no other options, and the black thing, which turned out to be a cat, was looking up at me in terror; Munster had it in his mouth and was no doubt biting down hard. At the last second, my brain made my hand move, so that I hit Munster on the neck rather than the head. I heard Dud in the background, yelling, "You can't do that!"

"Oh, yes, I can," I snarled in response as I hit Munster again. That second hit worked. Dropping the cat, he backed up, his posture letting me know that he knew he was in big trouble.

"Get over there," I growled at him, gesturing with my hand, directing him to move away from where he was. He moved. Dud was still yelling at me, telling me that it was Munster's yard and he was allowed to do what he thought right in his own yard.

"*Wrong!*" I shouted back, "It's *my* yard, and *my* rules!"

"How's he supposed to know which cat he's not allowed to chase?" Dud retorted.

"*He's not allowed to chase any of them!*" I screamed at the top of my lungs. I was so rattled, my hands were shaking. Dud reiterated the bit about it being Munster's yard.

"I guess the cat didn't see the *No Trespassing* sign!" My voice was dripping with sarcasm. I happened to turn around, then, as an afterthought. I saw that the black cat was peering at me from behind a shrub. Seeing its' opportunity, it dashed up a nearby tree, wobbling a little as it ran across a branch that reached over into the empty lot next door. I was still shaking as I walked back into the house. That the cat was still alive was lucky happenstance.

"That's *it,*" I said to Dud, "he's going back." And this time, there would be no reprieve.

As it happened, Dud left early Monday morning for an out-of-town job. He wouldn't be back until Friday, which was a good thing: it gave me plenty of time to think.

"Don't be mad at me," he said as he kissed me goodbye. He didn't understand that it was Munster I was mad at.

The shelter was closed on Monday. I spent the day in such agonized debate that I couldn't bring myself to call them on Tuesday. By Wednesday, although I was still in a lather of indecision, I did call. They told me that I could bring him in the following Tuesday.

"Sorry?" I questioned the staffer, "what's wrong with today?"

"We don't have room for him today," she answered.

"Then how do you know you'll have room next Tuesday?"

"We assume that there will be a few adoptions by then, which will clear enough room that we can take Munster back." I sighed. I had assumed that I could return him before Dud came back from his job. Now, I would have to hear him pleading for me to reconsider all weekend. And while I knew in my heart that sending Munster back was the right thing to do, I didn't really *want* to. So I kept the Tuesday appointment with the shelter, but decided to do a little research online in the meantime.

There was a local outfit called *Sit Stay Down*, that had a decent reputation, so I checked out their website. They offered all sorts of dog training, and gave an extensive list of issues that they would break your dog from doing, like chasing animals, eating poop, that sort of thing. It seemed promising, so I gave them a call. The fellow I talked to scheduled a home visit with me for Friday morning. I looked forward to hearing what he had to say, but I took care not to get my hopes up.

When Orlando sat down with me at the end of the week, he gave me a sheet of paper listing the various types of training they offered. There were one, three, and seven day board-and-train options, where Munster would board at Orlando's house. Orlando would train him, then bring him home and teach me what I would need to know. There were group lessons, which were cheaper than one-on-one lessons. There were options for Orlando to come and train at our house for varying numbers of days. It all sounded good until he handed me another sheet of paper, this time with the prices for all the options.

The cheapest turned out to be a one day lesson at my house for $649. That was the *cheapest*. The option I really wanted – but knew that I'd never be able to talk frugal Dud into – was three days of board-and-train. That one cost over $1700. I couldn't imagine him ever agreeing to it. Still, I told Orlando that I would discuss it all with Dud. He arrived home a few hours later.

He had a gig that night. Dud plays guitar in an acoustic duo, and they have gigs a few times a month. He was keen to take a shower and get ready to go, so he hurriedly kissed me as I watered plants around the yard, then he went inside. I got to thinking, then, about all the things that Orlando and I had discussed, and how and when to bring it all up with Dud.

All the while, something at the back of my brain kept knocking on the door at the front of my brain. It took a few minutes to realize what the something was. I had moved around the back yard, watering various plants and shrubs, and had unwittingly ended up near the fence that divided us from the empty lot next door. The closer I got to the fence, the more insistent was the knock on that cranial door until I finally tore my brain away from the issue of dog training long enough to give some conscious thought to what my brain was trying to tell me: it was a smell. A foul smell. A dead animal smell. *A dead animal smell.* My heart sank.

I went around to the other side of the fence. It didn't take long to find the black cat lying dead next to the fence. Judging by the advanced rate of decomposition, the thing – which appeared to be no older than five months – must've died shortly after the attack. I was left with no doubt about Munster's future. I went into the house and waited for Dud to finish his shower. When he dressed, I took him out and showed him the dead kitten.

"He must've fallen out of the tree and died," Dud said. *Sure,* I thought, *he fell out of the tree because he was mortally wounded, and died where he landed. Or he died in the tree and fell off the branch.* Dud's attempt at alleviating Munster's guilt was transparent. I should've expected that, but I hadn't because I assumed that he would be as horrified by this turn of events as I was. He wasn't. He didn't really care about what happened to a stray cat. In his view, it never should have come on the property to begin with. It probably never even occurred to him that this was exactly what could have happened to Buddy.

"We're going to have to give him a decent burial," I announced. I said it on purpose: I wasn't about to let Dud shrug off this poor kitten's death without making him brutally aware of it first. Before he left for his gig, I made him dig a proper hole, then I picked up the corpse and gingerly tried to arrange it with some respect in the hole. When we went back inside, he asked about the dog training. I showed him the list of options, and told him that I didn't have the heart to keep Munster, let alone train with him.

"All I'm hearing is *you, you, you!*" he said angrily. "It's all about what *you* want! What about Munster?"

I shrugged. "Munster blew his last chance when he killed the kitten." I said simply. Dud went off to his gig with little else to say.

I spent the weekend being extra nice to Munster. We took some good walks, I gave him lots of snack treats, and I spent time snuggling with him. He liked climbing up onto Dud's recliner and draping himself across my lap. I did all these things with him because I saw no reason to treat him badly. I imagine that it gave Dud some false hope that I had changed my mind, but that was not the case. I just wanted Munster to feel loved, not hated, before I took him back to the shelter.

On Tuesday, I took Munster for our regular 2 mile walk at River View park. My appointment at the shelter wasn't until 3:00, so later in the morning, I took him for a last walk on the farm property behind our house.

There are over 100 acres of crop land back there, accessible by a drive that bisects the empty lot next door. At the end of the drive, there are several acres of meadow, and then vast acreage that some unknown soul farms every year. Munster and I followed faint tractor tires through the meadow. Munster would hurdle the tall grass, lunging this way and that, smiling happily as he ran. He always seemed to know just how far he could go before the 15-foot retractable leash stopped his forward progress. He would slow to a trot at the last minute, then walk until I caught up. Then he'd repeat his grass-hopping foray all over again.

My heart melted when I thought about what would happen in a few hours. How could I give up that goofy mug? That broad smile? That cheerful personality? My mind raced from one thought to another: had I missed something? Was there some possible way he could stay on with us? I had never had to make such a heartbreaking decision before, and I vacillated between what I wanted, and what I knew I had to do. I desperately wanted to find a way to keep Munster, but I had four cats to think about, and there was simply no other choice than to send the cat killer back.

I had gathered up all his things into a large bag. The shelter had told me that I could bring anything of his that I wanted, so I made sure to pack his Kong, and his snack treats, and the last bit of the rawhide bone that he'd been chewing on the day before. I put the bag in my car, then went back in and snapped the leash on his collar. I looked at Dud, who was standing in the kitchen with a numb expression on his face.

"Do you want to say good-bye?" I asked him. He nodded.

"C'mon, Munster!" he said as he walked into the family room and sat down on the couch. He patted his lap but Munster was focused solely on me. I kept trying to turn Munster around so that he would see Dud, but being on the leash, he knew we were going somewhere and that was all he could think about. I should've taken him off the leash; I see that now. I didn't see it then. Dud gave up after a minute or two.

"Just go," he muttered as he walked away. I loaded Munster in the car and drove off.

If Dud thought that returning Munster would be easy for me – and later, as the resentful chip on his shoulder grew in size, I suspect that he did – I can assure you that it was *not*. I cried the entire drive to the shelter, and the entire drive home. In between, while we waited for a shelter staffer to attend to us, I sat on the floor and fed Munster some of his Kong snacks. I talked to him cheerfully, telling him what a good dog he was, and how much I loved him. I didn't want him knowing how utterly shattered I was that things hadn't worked out. But he didn't seem to notice that anything was wrong. Indeed, when I let him out of the car, and he recognized the shelter, he started whining to go *in*.

He seemed happy to be back in a place he recognized, and once we were inside the building, he whined some more, wagging his tail and sniffing all around the room. He clearly wanted to go to where he heard the dogs barking.

It was not the first time I'd seen such behavior: every time we walked our two miles at River View park, if he saw another dog – or even just another human – on the trail, he would whine and try to approach them. He *really* wanted to meet them, and I had to hold him carefully back in case they didn't want to meet him. Still, it registered in my mind, and as I sat on the shelter floor and reflected on those walks and that behavior, I got the sense, as I did every other time it happened, that he was searching for his people, and that we – Dud and I – were not them.

Don't get me wrong, Munster enjoyed us well enough. He cared whether I was mad at him, and when I used a sharp voice, he would shuffle over to where I stood, sit down right in front of me, wag his tail and give me a look that said *please don't be mad at me!* Looking down at that goofy smile, I could never stay angry for long.

But there always seemed to be something missing for him, and every time we walked anywhere near people or dogs, he always whined and tried to go to where they were, as though Dud and I weren't enough for him. Indeed, when the shelter staffer took hold of his leash and began to lead him away, he never looked back. He just wagged his tail happily and went with her.

Through my tears on the drive home, my mind continued to search for alternatives. Surely there was some idea that I hadn't yet thought of? There had to be *something*! But there wasn't. There was just cold hard reality: I had owned four cats for over ten years, and they were my first responsibility. If Munster hadn't killed the black kitten, we could've come to some workable solution involving *Sit Stay Down* training. But with the cat's death, I knew that I would never be able to fully trust Munster again, and I didn't want to live with that on a daily basis; it would simply be too much stress.

Dud was no help. He had done things like let Munster off the leash, out back on the farm land, just to see what happened. Then he'd come home and say matter-of-factly, "I think he'll be fine off the leash." I would tighten my lips, holding back from saying the thing inside my head, which was *right, he'll be fine off the leash until he spots a squirrel or a rabbit, and then you'll never get him back!* Or he would have Munster out in the yard on his stake and tether while he worked, and announce that night over dinner, "The ducks walked right by him and he ignored them. I think they'll be fine together!" I resisted pointing out how far removed from reality Dud's claims actually were.

The fact of the matter was that I was the one who took Munster for all his long walks; Dud's walks involved little more than pooping and peeing. I was the one who saw how he behaved around squirrels and bunnies. I was the one who had any authority with the dog, and any respect from him; Dud was just a fun playmate. One night, as Dud let him out for some ball chasing, I looked out the door just in time to see Munster chasing a rabbit. Dud's "Munster! No!" fell on deaf ears as I knew it would, and Munster did indeed ignore him. But the minute I hollered, *"Munster!"* he stopped running and turned away from the rabbit. It was a small thing, and I suspected that the day would come when he would ignore me, too, but for the most part, I laid down the law, and I enforced the rules.

Dud's claims of Munster's good behavior were fantasy at best, and dangerous assumptions at worst. I could easily imagine having to spend the rest of Munster's life keeping strict tabs on whatever Dud was up to with him, and I didn't want to do that. If I wasn't going to have adequate back-up with a dog capable of killing animals, then I didn't want to have a dog that was capable of killing animals.

The shelter wanted me to fill out a three-page questionnaire before I left. It asked a number of questions about why I was returning Munster, and I was very careful with my answers. The questionnaire offered several answers to choose from, ranging from "growls at animals" to "bares teeth" to "bites" to "attacks." There was no way I was going to sign Munster's death warrant by telling the shelter that he attacked, let alone killed, so I marked the "growls" box. Where they asked me to write a few words about Munster, I wrote *He'd be great with a 10-year old boy and a cat-free house! He's happy and cheerful and loves to be with his pack.* I wasn't lying. It was all true. I just didn't mention killing cats, and the fact that he always seemed to be searching for someone or something other than what he had.

I told Dud nothing about any of this. I knew he was sad, and I knew he was angry. More than once, he'd asked me why I'd "talked him into getting a dog" in the first place. Aside from the fact that the point was moot, I always replied that I had told him up front that if he didn't want to have a dog, we didn't have to get one. It would do him no good now to hear my disconcerting thoughts about Munster's incessant search for someone else, and I doubted that he would care how much crying I'd done in the process of returning him.

To make matters worse, the day after I returned Munster was our wedding anniversary. We managed to have a nice time staying at our usual out-of-town bed and breakfast, and wandering the village shops as we did every year, but there was an unhappy undertone. Dud addressed it in the card he gave me, writing that *yesterday wasn't easy for me, and it will take a little time to let go.* That was putting things mildly. In fact, the more time that passed since Munster's return to the shelter, the bigger the chip on Dud's shoulder seemed to get: while Buddy refused to go back out into the eastern half of the house, it only took Gracie a couple of days to decide that she wanted to be where we were. She tried to spend a whole afternoon on Dud's chair with him, but after a few hours, he got impatient.

"Gracie, you've been up here long enough! Go lie on the couch!" he told her.

I chided him with, "She loves you!"

He answered me with, "So did Munster!"

I let that hang in the air for a moment, then said quietly, "You can hold it against me for now. But not forever." He made no reply.

Nothing Works Like
An Apple

Having decided that Bit and I had pretty much conquered all the challenges that the barn property had to offer, I decided that it was time to take Bit off the property, put him in a trailer and go somewhere else to ride. When I presented the idea to Wendy, though, she looked doubtful.

"There's a lot more to it than just riding," she told me.

"Like what?" I asked naively.

Wendy shrugged. "Loading him into the trailer, for one." I began to see her point. There were logistical aspects that I would have to learn, and teach Bit, before we could even think about leaving the property. Clearly, my new mission would be to teach Bit how to get into, and out of, the trailer.

We were headed for just that mission one Saturday when I saw to my dismay that Wendy's niece, Sandy, was already trying to load her horse Rudy into the trailer. I stood a few feet away, letting Bit graze while I watched Sandy and Rudy. She was getting nowhere with him; he simply refused to go in. This went on for a good ten minutes. Sandy would walk Rudy in a circle, then lead him up to the trailer. She would walk in, and he would balk. After a time, she gave up altogether.

It was as I watched them that I remembered the lesson I'd learned from barn co-owner Ron. Ron was the recognized head of the herd. Even so, the horses didn't always do as they were told, and I watched once, years ago, as he tried to load a horse into the trailer and it refused to go. Multiple times, he walked it up to the trailer, and multiple times, the horse refused to get in.

"At what point do you give up?" I asked him.

"You don't," he answered. Giving up would mean the horse would learn that if he just held out long enough, you would quit asking him to do the thing, and that's not a lesson you want your horse to learn. So Ron stuck to it, and ultimately, the horse got in the trailer.

I was thinking about that as I watched Sandy and Rudy walk away. I realized then that training Bit to go in the trailer would be a big investment of time, because if Bit didn't want to, he wasn't going to, and it might take all afternoon to change his mind. I thought about that as I lined him up in front of the trailer. I walked in, and to my considerable surprise, before I even turned around to ask Bit, he'd already walked in, too.

But of course, Bit had no intention of making things easy, and, indeed, the very next training session, he refused to even consider the idea of loading into the trailer.

"You just did it yesterday, Bit!" I said, exasperated.

Wasn't me!

"Yes it was!"

Nope!

"Bit! I was here! I saw you get in!"

Did not!

"Did, too!"

Wasn't me!

"It was, too, you big meatball!" And out came the apple. They work every time, even if it does take 30 minutes just to get his two front feet in.

Thus far, I've met with limited success in this latest endeavor. Limited because it never seems to get any easier to get him in the trailer. It's usually two feet in, then two feet out. Repeat for 25 minutes, and then consider myself lucky when he finally decides to walk all the way in. At this rate, we might actually go on our first off-site trail ride by the next millennium. If I'm lucky.

THE RIGHT THING татаTO DO

My heart ached, in the time after I returned Munster. I had trouble sleeping. I would lie awake nights and beg the Gods to please find him a good, loving home. The days passed slowly, without the purpose required when Munster was there. Now, instead of peeing, pooping, and taking long walks, I had more time on my hands than I knew what to do with.

I tried to counter my sorrow by reminding myself of all pluses a Munster-less household held: no more having to schedule my days around peeing, pooping, and talking long walks. No more dividing the house into two factions. No more cats being confined to half a home. But every time I tried to shake off the canine ghost who lurked within, I saw that dopey grin of his, smiling eagerly whenever I said, "Let's go this way!" I saw the big shaggy beast who loved to jump up on the recliner and mash himself against the armrests, happy to have been invited to lie across my lap. I saw a dog who was perfect, but for one fatal flaw.

I told none of this to Duddy. We didn't talk about Munster at all. Even so, I was mind-reader enough to know that he was holding a grudge, and that the chip on his shoulder continued to get bigger every day. I knew that we would have to talk about it at some point, but knowing the venom that Dud was likely to spew at me, I was in no hurry. In the meantime, our marriage seemed at a standstill: I slept in the bed, and Dud slept on the couch. We didn't say much to each other, and an uneasy silence reigned most of the time.

About a week after Munster went back, the dam broke, and accusations were hurled at me like bullets from a gun. Dud wasn't just angry that I'd sent Munster back, he was also angry that I hadn't consulted him.

"You didn't even talk to me about it!" he said angrily.

"That's because you were busy defending a dog who had just killed a cat!" I retorted.

"It was a stray, *probably feral* cat!" he argued, as though it being a stray made it somehow exempt from consideration.

"That doesn't mean he didn't have a right to live!" I replied as I shook my head sadly.

The argument faded off from there, both of us feeling as though the other didn't understand us at all. *How could he not know that this is my life?* I wondered. What did he think that Critter Lady thing was all about?

To my surprise, he left a note for me on the kitchen table a day later. In it, he said that he wanted to move forward and let go of his anger, fearing that it would drive a bigger wedge between us. *I know the right decision was made about Munster,* he wrote, *and I'd like to think that I would have come to the same decision with you.*

I wrote my own note back. *Caring for animals is not just a fun hobby for me. It's a calling, a passion, and a commitment that I take very seriously. It's who I am.*

We had both said our piece, and while that should've put paid to the Munster part of our lives, it didn't. I continued to toss and turn every night, tortured by my decision to return him to the shelter. I forced myself to stay off the Whoville Humane Society website; I was curious to know whether he had been adopted or not, but it seemed best not to open the can of worms again. So I stayed off the site. For a time.

Almost two weeks after Munster had been returned, I could take it no more; I went to the WHS website and had a look. Munster was still there. As I walked through the house, a thought struck me so suddenly that I had to stop and consider it. Dud walked in, then, and I asked him to sit down with me in the family room.

"This doesn't necessarily mean anything," I began, "but I checked the website just now, and Munster's still at the shelter. He hasn't been adopted." Dud looked at me, puzzled. I went on.

"Ever since he's been gone, I've prayed every night for God to find him a good, loving family. It just occurred to me today: what if *we're* the good, loving family?" I looked back at him, impassive. I didn't know whether we should try to get him back or not – or if it was even possible – but I knew this much, and I said it to Dud, "My heart hurts. It's been hurting since I took him back. What do you think? Do you want him back?"

Dud paused only briefly before he answered, "Yes!"

"Today?" I asked.

He nodded. "Today. Let's go."

"They're not open yet," I replied. "I'll call them at noon and make sure he's available." And so I did. The person on the other end of the line assured me that Munster was still available, and not on a hold. Dud and I got in the car and headed across town.

As I drove, I thought about all the things we had bought for Munster the first time around. I had given the shelter a good many of them: the bowls, the expensive dietary supplement, the collar and leash, the pad he slept on in his cage, the bag of food. We would have to buy these things all over again, and quickly. To my considerable surprise, frugal Dud didn't complain at all as the shopping list grew longer and longer.

We spoke with the shelter director, explaining that we missed Munster so much that we made some changes in our home to accommodate both him and the cats, and we were hoping that we could have him back. We said nothing about the dead kitten for fear that she would turn us down. I wondered whether this sort of thing had been done before. Did people lose their ability to adopt from the shelter if they sent an animal back? Would we have to pay the adoption fee again?

I needn't have worried. The woman smiled happily, said, "He's a great dog, isn't he?" and personally went through the shelter's inventory to try to find any of the items I had left there before. She only managed to find collars and leashes, and let us choose whichever ones we wanted. She told us that she had taken Munster off the books, which meant, apparently, that not only could we have him back, but that we didn't have to pay another fee to do so. Then she brought him into one of the bonding rooms.

Dud had asked me pensively if I thought he would remember us.

"Of course he will!" I had answered. And of course he did. He raced into the room, jumped all over us, wagged his tail happily, then set off on an inspection of the room. He peed against a wall, nosed around a basket looking for snacks, then ran back over to us again. As I tried to fasten the collar around his neck, he sat down and put both front paws on my knees in a gesture that seemed unmistakeably to say, "I'm glad you're here!" Two weeks to the day he was returned to the shelter, we were walking him out the door again. I felt much more certain, this time around, that bringing him home was the right thing to do.

When we got home, I immediately went online and did two things. First, I found some reasonably-priced training lessons and signed Munster and myself up for them. It was called a "good manners" class that taught the usual sit, stay, down, and come, and the fellow on the phone sounded like he knew what he was talking about. Second, I researched area doggy daycare outfits, finding one on the other side of town that looked promising. I told Dud that I wanted to drop Munster off once or twice a week so that he could spend a few hours socializing with other dogs. He didn't object. Taking control of Munster's training, and his play time, made me feel much more positive about having him back again: if I could train him properly, perhaps I could put a stop to his habit of chasing animals.

Later that day, Dud stuck his head out the back door and inquired, "Hey! You wanna...?" and gestured toward the bedroom. Apparently, getting Munster back had put him in a frisky frame of mind. But I had things to do: the duck chores needed doing, the dog needed walking, and I really needed to get out to the barn and work with Bit.

I grinned as I answered, "Sorry, honey, but the critters come first!"

Epilogue

One of the most tedious parts of writing a book is the proof-reading. Because I self-publish, and because self-publishing costs money, I try to find as many mistakes as possible before I submit the manuscript for publication. Being a stickler for detail, I've learned the hard way that proof-reading over and over is the only way to ensure that the book comes out exactly as I want it to. One of the problems with that, of course, is that I end up having to read the damned thing eight or nine times. By then, I'm so tired of it that I don't want to read it ever again!

Another problem is that as I read through the pages, I found a few inconsistencies. I'm sure you found them, too:

Why didn't I put the ducks in their pen every night, instead of waiting until Boyfriend Duck had been killed?

Why was I o.k. with relegating my four cats to one side of the house for the rest of their lives?

Why did I bring Munster home again when I already knew he would kill small animals if given half a chance?

All three are good questions, with not-so-easy answers. I had frightened Ethel and Boyfriend so badly with all that chasing them around the yard every night that I simply didn't have the heart to continue. And, unfortunately, herding them into the pen was not even on the radar then; the fact that I herd the others now is happenstance: they all walked into the pen one night of their own accord, and, with a little encouragement from me, they've done it ever since.

Sequestering the cats on one side of the house was not the ideal solution to the killer dog problem. The ideal solution, obviously, would have been to not get a dog until all four cats had passed. But we fell in love with Munster, and wanted to have our cake and eat it, too, which causes me a fair amount of guilt over the cats' new living arrangement. These days, I spend as much time as I can with each individual cat, and they spend the better part of 20 hours a day sleeping. It's not a perfect situation, but it works for the most part.

As for Munster, I've given his two reprieves a great deal of thought and have come to no logical conclusions. The fact of the matter is simply that the heart wants what it wants, and as most of us have experienced in life, folks generally lead with the heart, and not the head.

Dud and I both had reservations about getting Munster back. While the doggy daycare and the Good Manners class went a long way toward feeling like I had a modicum of control over him – I knew that I would never have *complete* control – it was very disconcerting when the class trainer told me that Munster appeared to have some Husky in him, and that Huskies were notorious cat-killers.

"What've they got against cats?" I asked, aghast.

The fellow shrugged. "Small animals," he replied, meaning that Huskies had something in their DNA that compelled them to chase, and kill, small animals. And here I thought they were just sled dogs.

That new information took some of the shine off my affection for Munster. I had hoped that we might train some of that aggression out of him, but you can't change centuries of DNA. At best, I might be able to provide him with more acceptable distractions.

I lost some weight, taking Munster for all those walks. Since my Reese's peanut butter cup addiction had caused a considerable weight gain, losing weight was a good thing. And, as we got farther into our Good Manners class, he behaved much better on those walks.

The classes themselves were a mixed bag: on the one hand, bringing to class a hungry dog who had been deprived of his breakfast practically guaranteed that he'd pay attention. On the other hand, his attention seemed to wane after about 45 minutes. Still, we kept at it, and we practiced at home, and slowly but surely, a new and improved Munster began to show. I would never be able to trust him completely, but as long as Dud and I maintained an understanding about what our dog was capable of, we all got along much better.

It should be noted that in spite of Munster's animal-killing DNA, Dud loves him more than I can say. I had no idea just how much Dud wanted a dog until Munster came home with us. Ever since, Duddy's taken charge of most of Munster's poop-and-pee walks (especially the early morning and late night shifts), studied up on feeding him a raw meat diet, shops for the raw diet ingredients, and gives the dog massive doses of fun and love. While I'm sure that the cats would strongly disagree, I have to say that I think getting a dog for Dud was one of my better decisions.

I continue to debate the issue of whether to euthanize Gimpy the duck. He's still a dickhead, and the longer his behavior goes on, the more I learn toward humanely ending his life. As of this writing, though, I haven't made a decision one way or the other; you'll have to tune in to Book Four to find out!

Animal Control Officer Dave – who I haven't actually seen much of since Aimee Van Staten rescued the ducks off McKinnon's Pond – studied to get his real estate license, with a view to making it his second career, once he retires from the Whoville Police Department. I hope that when the time comes, he'll make sure his replacement is properly trained: the ACO gig is not just about trapping pesky raccoons and returning lost dogs to their rightful owners. Indeed, a great deal of Dave's job requires kindness and compassion, as well as a love of animals. Dave has all three of those qualities in abundance.

As for me, life at the Critter Shack continues to revolve around animals. I wouldn't have it any other way!

Until next time, please be kind to all the critters!

Kelly Meister-Yetter is a writer, photographer, blogger, and author of *Crazy Critter Lady*, and *No Better Medicine*. She shares her life with a dog, three ducks, four cats, a barn full of ornery horses, and one increasingly beleaguered husband. Based on her years of experience rescuing animals in need, Kelly also acts as an advocate for their care and humane treatment, donating her time and resources to numerous animal welfare organizations. When she's not volunteering at a horse rescue facility, Kelly enjoys training her horse, and waiting on her cats hand and foot. Kelly, the critters, and her husband live in Northwest Ohio.

You can find Kelly at www.crazycritterlady.com

Made in United States
Cleveland, OH
31 January 2025